Supporting Students, Meeting Standards: Best Practices for Engaged Learning in First, Second, and Third Grades

Gera Jacobs and Kathy Crowley

This book is gratefully dedicated to all those who work with primary grade children around the world and to their students, with our wish that they will develop the skills and dispositions they need to become engaged citizens who care about their world and each other.

Supporting Students, Meeting Standards

Best Practices for Engaged Learning in First, Second, and Third Grades

Gera Jacobs and Kathy Crowley

National Association for the Education of Young Children
Washington, DC

naeyc®

National Association for the
Education of Young Children
1313 L Street NW, Suite 500
Washington, DC 20005-4101
202-232-8777 • 800-424-2460
www.naeyc.org

NAEYC Books

Chief Publishing Officer
Derry Koralek

Editor-in-Chief
Kathy Charner

Director of Creative Services
Edwin C. Malstrom

Managing Editor
Mary Jaffe

Senior Editor
Holly Bohart

Senior Graphic Designer
Malini Dominey

Associate Editor
Elizabeth Wegner

Editorial Assistant
Ryan Smith

Photo Credits

Courtesy of the authors: 3, 10, 11, 23, 25, 27, 32, 40, 44, 61, 68, 69, 80, 81, 88, 90, 104, 105, 107, 120, 133, 156 (both); copyright © Ellen Senisi: cover, 5, 13, 20, 37, 53, 63, 65, 75, 85, 97, 109, 113, 121, 128, 132, 136, 139; Michael J. Rosen/ copyright © NAEYC: v, vii, 17, 78, 118

For the images of their students and faculty, NAEYC and photographer Michael J. Rosen would like to express their appreciation to Indianola Informal K–8 in Columbus, Ohio, and Wickliffe Progressive Elementary in Upper Arlington, Ohio.

Credits

Cover design: Edwin Malstrom

Index: Donna Drialo

Library of Congress Control Number: 2014945037

ISBN: 978-1-938113-12-3

NAEYC Item 358

Contents

Introduction 1

Chapter 1. Scaffolding Children's Learning and Meeting Standards in the Primary Grades 3

Best Practices in the Primary Grades 4

Meeting Standards While Supporting Best Practices 5

Using Resources for Effective Learning and Assessment 6

Brain-Based Learning 7

Creating a Welcoming Environment That Promotes Learning 8

Considering Room Design 8

Try This! 9

Fostering Independence and Learning Through Room Design 10

Wish Lists 10

Establishing a Meeting Area 11

Designing Interest Areas That Invite Learning 12

Differentiating to Meet the Needs of All Students 13

Motivating Students Through a Growth Mindset 14

Promoting Learning—and More—Through High-Quality Teacher–Student Interactions 15

In a Nutshell 17

Chapter 2. Fostering Students' Positive Approaches to Learning and Social and Emotional Development 19

Positive Approaches to Learning 19

Hyson's Framework for Approaches to Learning 20

Developing Positive Approaches to Learning 20

Try This! 21

Steps in Problem Solving 21

Nurturing Students' Social and Emotional Development 21

Developing Social Skills 22

Try This! 22

Try This! 22

Think-Pair-Share 24

Supporting Emotional Development 25

Home<->School Connections 27

In a Nutshell 28

Chapter 3. Meeting the Common Core State Standards for English Language Arts 29

Engaging Young Readers in Literacy-Rich Primary Classrooms 29

Reading in the Primary Classroom 30

Begin the Day With Opportunities for Reading 30

How to Select Appropriate Texts for Students 30

Readers' Workshop 31

Helping Students Select Their Own Just Right Texts ... 31
Integrating Literacy Throughout the Day ... 33
Engaging Learners With Literature and Informational Texts ... 34
Key Ideas and Details ... 34
Four Reciprocal Teaching Strategies ... 36
Craft and Structure ... 37
Integration of Knowledge and Ideas ... 38
Range of Reading and Level of Text Complexity ... 39
Research-Based Strategies Related to Text Complexity ... 40
CCSS Foundational Reading Skills ... 41
Engaging Learners With Print Concepts and Phonological Awareness ... 41
Engaging Learners With Phonics and Word Recognition ... 42
Engaging Learners With Fluency ... 43

Nurturing Young Writers ... 45
Writers' Workshop ... 45
Writers' Workshop Mini-Lessons ... 45
Independent Writing ... 46
Author's Chair ... 48
Celebrating Students' Writing ... 48
Engaging Learners With Writing ... 48
Try This! ... 49
Text Types and Purposes ... 49
Try This! ... 50
Dual Language Learners ... 51
Production and Distribution of Writing ... 51
Research to Build and Present Knowledge ... 54
Try This! ... 55
Range of Writing ... 55

Promoting Effective Communication Skills ... 56
Engaging Learners With Listening and Speaking ... 56
Comprehension and Collaboration ... 56
Presentation of Knowledge and Ideas ... 56
Engaging Learners With Language Development ... 57
Conventions of Standard English ... 57
Knowledge of Language ... 58
Vocabulary Acquisition and Use ... 59
Try This! ... 59
Try This! ... 60
Bloom's Revised Taxonomy by Anderson and Krathwohl ... 61
Try This! ... 62

Creating Engaging Literacy Centers ... 62
Why Use Learning Centers and Stations? ... 62
Examples of Literacy Centers and Stations ... 63
Library Center ... 64
Listening Center ... 64
Writing Center ... 65
Try This! ... 65
Poetry Center ... 65

Comprehension Center 66
Read the Room Center 66
Rhyming/Word Family Center 66
Buddy Reading Center 66
Word Study Center....67
Spelling Center 68
Computer Center....68
Interactive Whiteboard Center 68
Managing Centers 68
Home <-> School Connections....69
Meeting Standards—and More!....71
In a Nutshell....72

Chapter 4. Meeting the Common Core State Standards for Mathematics 73
The Importance of Mathematical Practices....73
Mathematical Practices From the Common Core State Standards....74
Cognitively Guided Instruction 74
Problem-Solving Strategies 74
Manipulatives 75
Math Journals....76
Six-Step CGI Method....76
Math Centers 77
Engaging Activities for Meeting Mathematics Standards....77
Operations and Algebraic Thinking....79
Try This!....80
Solving Word Problems With the C.U.B.E. Method....82
Number and Operations in Base Ten....82
Ideas for Having Fun With 100 83
Number and Operation—Fractions 84
Try This!....85
Measurement and Data....85
Try This!....86
Geometry 87
Try This!....88
Engaging Math Centers....88
Math Bulletin Board Center 89
Menu Math Center 89
Geometry Center....89
Measuring Center....89
Math Game Center....90
Digital Learning Center 90
Authentic Assessments at Centers and Throughout the Math Curriculum 90
Home <-> School Connections....91
Meeting Standards—and More!....92
In a Nutshell....93

Chapter 5. Fostering Involved Citizens Through Social Studies 95
The National Curriculum Standards for Social Studies 95
College, Career, and Civic Life (C3) Framework and Inquiry Arc....96
Using Long-Term Studies and the Inquiry Arc to Meet Standards 97

Conducting a Long-Term Study Following the Inquiry Arc 97
Phases of a Long-Term Study 98
Maps and Globes: A Long-Term Study Example 99
Try This! 100
Integrated Approach 101
Engaging Activities for Meeting Standards in Social Studies 101
Geography and Cultural Understanding 101
Try This! 102
History 104
Economics 105
Civics 106
Try This! 107
Try This! 107
Home<->School Connections 108
Meeting Standards—and More! 109
In a Nutshell 110

Chapter 6. Meeting the Next Generation Science Standards 111
The Next Generation Science Standards 111
Scientific and Engineering Practices 112
Crosscutting Concepts 114
Disciplinary Core Ideas 115
Disciplinary Core Ideas in the Next Generation Science Standards 115
Supporting Learners in Meeting Science Standards 115
Engaging Activities to Explore Science and Integrate the Curriculum 117
Investigations in Physical Sciences 120
Investigations in Life Sciences 122
Try This! 123
Try This! 124
Investigations in Earth and Space Sciences 124
Try This! 125
Investigations in Engineering, Technology, and Applications of Science 125
Try This! 126
Home<->School Connections 126
Meeting Standards—and More! 127
In a Nutshell 129

Chapter 7. Reaching Beyond the Standards 131
Promoting Learning Through the Arts 131
The Visual Arts 132
Try This! 133
Try This! 133
Music 134
Dance 134
Theater 135
Authentic Assessment Through the Arts 135
Gaining Appreciation for Cultures Through the Arts 135
Supporting Children's Physical Well-Being and Health 136
Movement Throughout the Day 136
Try This! 136

Try This! 137
Focus on Health Concepts 137
Home <> School Connections 137
A Call to Action 138
Join the Conversation 138
Engage Students in Meaningful Learning 138
Collaborate 139
Commit to Helping All Students Succeed 139
Using Both the Art and Science of Teaching to Support Students 139

Frequently Asked Questions 141

References 149

Children's Books 154

About the Authors 156

Acknowledgments 157

Index 158

Introduction

This guide was written for teachers and all who work with first-, second-, and third-graders—students in the primary grades—to describe best practices for promoting learning and development while helping students meet standards. The book provides research-based teaching strategies, drawing on the work of the National Association for the Education of Young Children (NAEYC) and research in the field of education as well as in neuroscience on how the developing brain works.

Because teachers are decision makers (Copple & Bredekamp 2009), this book offers assistance for the many decisions you make every day. You will find ideas for creating a warm, welcoming environment that promotes learning; engaging experiences and activities that help students meet standards; and ideas for authentic assessment to document and scaffold student progress and improve instruction.

The standards movement has generated a great deal of discussion, both positive and negative, among educators, legislators, families, and other stakeholders. Some have questioned whether national education standards, including the Common Core State Standards (CCSS), are too rigorous, expecting more of students than is warranted. Some express concern that the standards do not give attention to important domains such as social and emotional development. Others have praised the focus on higher-order thinking, problem solving, and communicating, as well as the higher expectations they believe will serve students well in the future. These higher expectations have resulted in added stress though for many teachers, students, and parents. This book is designed to ease that stress with information, ideas, and suggestions for helping primary students meet standards as part of a curriculum that reflects students' developmental needs.

The book uses the CCSS in the chapters on language and literacy and mathematics; the Next Generation Science Standards (NGSS) in the chapter on science; and the National Council on Social Studies College, Career, and Civic Life C3 Framework for Social Studies State Standards. These national standards emphasize learning in which students are actively involved in solving problems, providing evidence for their answers, and clearly communicating what they have learned in a variety of formats. *Supporting Students, Meeting Standards: Best Practices for Engaged Learning in First, Second, and Third Grades* includes research-based practices that foster this type of learning. The experiences and activities in the book are not limited to these standards, however, and can be used with other sets of standards as well. The book takes a constructivist approach and includes ideas for integrating the curriculum, which will help teachers balance the many demands on their time.

Because standards do not include everything that is important for students to learn, the second chapter of the book discusses the foundational skills of positive approaches to learning and social and emotional development, which are so necessary to students' success. Throughout the book, sections titled "Meeting Standards—and More!" address topics that are not included in most standards but are important for helping students become confident learners who care about their community and their environment. Each chapter in the book also includes ideas for differentiating instruction to meet the needs of all students, including dual language learners, students who require special assistance, and those who are achieving above typical expectations for their age group. Many of the ideas that are suggested for specific groups can be used successfully with all students.

Supporting Students, Meeting Standards provides a variety of suggestions for effective teaching practices. Choose those that fit best with your interests, teaching style, and setting, and the characteristics of the students you teach; adapt them as necessary. Some ideas are very easy to implement; others may not feel possible due to circumstances beyond your control. Adapt the suggestions for your class and individual students; recommended activities that are just right for a first grade class may also work for third-graders who need additional support or intervention. The ideas in this book are designed primarily for teachers of first, second, and third grades, including both experienced and preservice teachers. However, those working with other grades will find concepts they can use as well. We hope this book renews your joy in teaching as you support students in meeting standards and help them become enthusiastic, independent, lifelong learners.

Scaffolding Children's Learning and Meeting Standards in the **Primary Grades**

1

When you walk into Rosa Santiago's primary classroom, you hear a buzz of happy voices from children involved in a variety of literacy activities. Students are reading in pairs on cozy pillows, writing drafts of their stories about birds they've been researching, listening to a new audiobook through headphones, and working on punctuation in a small group with the teacher. All of the students are meeting standards—and enjoying learning!

First, second, and third grades—the primary grades—are a time of incredible potential. Students are eager to learn and build on the academic skills they have acquired. Their brains are rapidly developing, enabling them to tackle increasingly complex cognitive tasks. Although there is great variation in their development, their language and communication skills are maturing, and peer relationships are more influential than at younger ages. Primary grade children are growing in their ability to make mental representations, but they still have difficulty grasping abstract concepts without the aid of real-life references and materials (Tomlinson 2014).

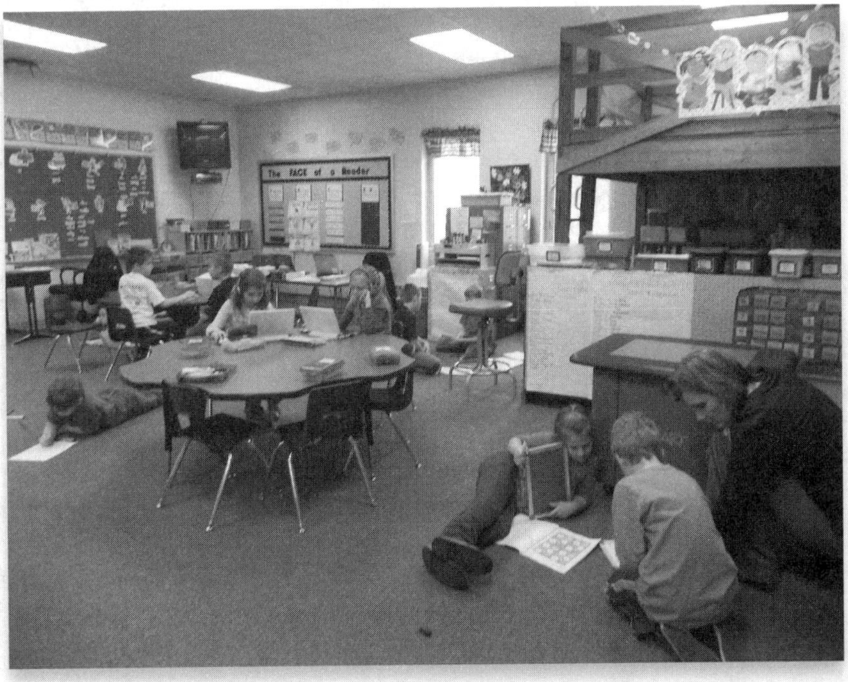

The standards movement, and especially the advent of the Common Core State Standards (CCSS), has elevated the significance of the primary years. The goal of the CCSS is to enable all students to acquire the skills they need to be college and career ready (Common Core State Standards Initiative 2014) by the end of high school. Thus, the standards at all levels focus on such skills as communicating effectively, working independently, possessing strong content knowledge, using evidence to support a point of view, and understanding other perspectives and cultures. To meet the CCSS, students—even from the early grades—need to become problem solvers who persevere until they arrive at a solution. They must make connections between what they are currently learning and what they already know, as well as to their own experiences. They must also use reasoning, draw conclusions, provide rationale and evidence for these conclusions, represent their thoughts, and communicate these thoughts to others.

Research shows that having high-quality teachers who scaffold students' learning is the foundation of an effective education (Reutzel & Cooter 2013).

Best Practices in the Primary Grades

The CCSS require students to acquire content knowledge *and* the skills, such as knowing how to gather information from resources to answer a question, they need to use this content as lifelong learners. However, the standards do not address everything that is important to children's learning. Students also need to become compassionate, contributing members of the community, with good social skills and respect for others. There is no doubt that education is essential to achieving this goal and to addressing many of the problems society faces today. Research shows that having high-quality teachers who scaffold students' learning is the foundation of an effective education (Reutzel & Cooter 2013). Teachers scaffold students by providing the support they need. They work to increase student competence and independence, gradually reducing the amount of assistance students need. Deborah Kenny (2012), founder of the internationally recognized Harlem Village Academies, affirmed this in her quest to create a truly transformational school: "It is now widely understood that talented people—high quality teachers—matter more to a child's education than any other factor" (235).

The National Association for the Education of Young Children (NAEYC) provides guidance for primary grade teachers. In *Developmentally Appropriate Practice: Focus on Children in First, Second, and Third Grades* (2014), Copple and colleagues discuss best practices for working with primary students, including how to create classrooms that are appropriate for their stages of development. They recommend that teachers make decisions based on what they know about child development and learning, what they know about students as individuals, and each student's social and cultural context. This knowledge, coupled with the implementation of standards, enables teachers to set challenging but achievable goals to help students continually make progress and gain a deep sense of pride. Our task as teachers is to intentionally think about what will be best for children (Epstein 2014). The CCSS, the Next Generation Science Standards (NGSS), and other national and state standards outline *what* students need to learn. To the extent possible within district and school policies, educators need to decide *how* they are going to help students learn the skills and knowledge described in the standards. The CCSS document notes, "The Standards define what all students are expected to know and be able to do, not how teachers should teach. For instance, the use of play with young children is not specified by the Standards, but it is welcome as a valuable activity in its own right and as a way to help students meet the expectations in this document" (National Governors Association Center for Best Practices & Council of Chief State School Officers 2010a, 6). Striving to help students meet standards should not cause teachers to abandon what they know about best practices in teaching; the opposite is true. If students are to achieve the goals outlined in the standards, teachers must apply

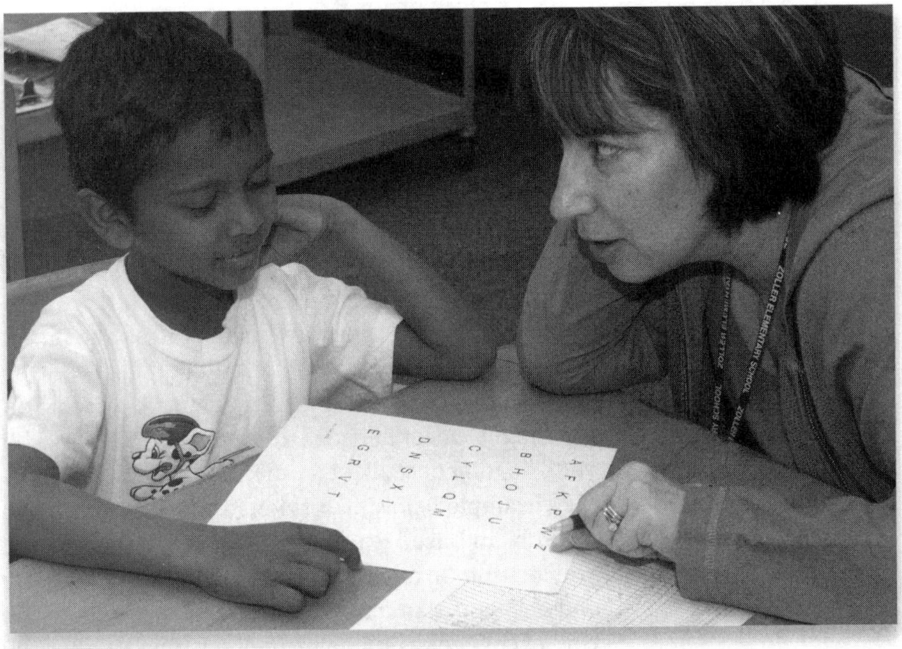

what they know about best practices and child development. This will ensure that children grow in all areas of development, including cognitive, language, physical, social, and emotional.

In *Growing Minds: Building Strong Cognitive Foundations in Early Childhood* (2012), Tomlinson discusses best practices for the primary grades: "No matter what the subject area, teachers should keep learning concrete, relevant to children's everyday lives, and connected to previously learned material. A new concept must have a tangible referent, something real and familiar. Children are more likely to learn about, say, measurement and distance if the task is fun and imaginative yet based in their reality" (30). Meaningful, enjoyable experiences are some of the best ways for students to learn. Hands-on, relevant materials allow children to explore, experiment, and understand concepts. Think back to when you were in school. What made learning most meaningful for you? For many, it is engaging activities and projects that are remembered most, not reading from a textbook or completing yet another worksheet.

Meeting Standards While Supporting Best Practices

Goldstein and Bauml (2012) discuss the challenges of trying to meet standards while following best practices. They recommend that teachers begin by learning about the standards, school policies, and expectations related to curriculum, as well as whether their administrators are flexible in how policies are carried out. Next they suggest that teachers "think of the required materials and content as the small seeds from which you can grow engaging, meaningful lessons expressly for the children in your class" (81). They propose doing this by

- **Supplementing** and **enriching** required lessons with interesting materials and activities, including the arts
- **Cherry-picking** the best activities from the mandated programs
- **Substituting** more meaningful activities that can teach the same concepts for those activities that are less relevant to students' needs
- **Adjusting the pace** by shortening some of the mandated activities while still accomplishing goals

These strategies provide additional time for more engaging activities, such as learning centers and hands-on investigations, which enable students to meet standards in a meaningful context. Goldstein and Bauml also recommend that teachers showcase children's learning to administrators, colleagues, and parents to demonstrate how students are meeting standards through these more meaningful activities. Think about daily activities in your classroom that are most effective in helping students meet standards and how you might enrich them with other meaningful activities.

For teachers to best implement their curriculum and meet standards, Oertwig, Gillanders, and Ritchie (2014) recommend that teachers use what they know about students and adjust their teaching to best meet students' needs and interests. They note,

> Even the most restrictive environment leaves room for teachers to be creative and make decisions about their teaching. Curriculum is malleable, and teachers make decisions every day about what they teach that allows for customization. The difference is that the best teachers make those decisions intentionally by incorporating and adapting aspects of the content to match the specific needs and learning preferences of the children they are currently teaching. (81)

It is easy for teachers to become overwhelmed by standards and other requirements they must meet, but breaking up tasks into smaller parts makes them more manageable. One technique that helps is printing out a list of the standards students are expected to meet in each subject. Store them in a binder or file folder. Throughout the year, document students' work on each standard by adding the dates you addressed it. (See example below.) For science or social studies units, short- or long-term projects, or problem-based learning challenges, indicate which topics the students studied when you focused on a particular standard. The information in these binders or file folders will help you plan for future years. While some standards may require only a short period of concentration, many will become a daily focus of the curriculum.

Standard	√	Date(s) Addressed	Unit/Topic	Activity
CCSSMath2.MDA.3 Estimate lengths using units of inches, feet, centimeters, and meters			Birds	Estimate eagle wingspan from photos on Internet using various units, research to find actual lengths and make model

Using Resources for Effective Learning and Assessment

Distinguished teachers create a culture for learning, with high expectations for students (Danielson 2010). They use a variety of teaching resources, including materials that connect to other disciplines, a wide range of texts, and the Internet and other technology tools. They develop connections in the community, such as with colleges, museums, and libraries, that provide access to additional materials and guest speakers. Using a variety of resources helps students make sense of new information.

Rich experiences provide background knowledge that enhances children's content learning and their reading and writing skills. Some children may have limited experiences. To build children's background knowledge, teachers can use a wide variety of fiction and nonfiction books. Reading a chapter each day can create a shared context and contribute to the sense of connectedness in the classroom. Teachers use community resources, such as materials available from local museums or libraries. They also make use of video clips and other online resources, and physical or virtual field trips (see, for example, Two Way Interactive Connections in Education [TWICE] at www.twice.cc or Center for Interactive Learning and Collaboration [CILC] at www.cilc.org/).

Teaching for understanding and helping students acquire twenty-first century skills, such as critical thinking and problem solving, communication, collaboration, and creativity and innovation, enable students to apply what they have learned to solve problems in all areas (Kay & Greenhill 2013; Partnership for 21st Century Skills 2010). For example, provide real-life tasks for students to practice computation: "How much water does a family drink in a week if there are four people in the family and each person drinks six cups of water a day?" Extend the problem: "How much would the family drink in a month? How much in a year?" Students may enjoy working on a Challenge of the Week math problem individually or in small groups over the course of several days, such as, "Each day this week at 10:00 in the morning, how many feet were in our classroom? How many toes?"

Authentically assessing students through their daily work in meaningful tasks allows teachers to see students' progress toward meeting standards. They use this information to inform their teaching, knowing what children have mastered and where they need more instruction or practice. The information obtained through authentic assessment is used to differentiate the curriculum to meet the needs of all students. Such information is also shared with families as teachers partner with them to support children's development and learning (Copple & Bredekamp 2009).

Brain-Based Learning

Teachers have one of the most challenging jobs in the world. Students come to school with increasing complexities: Some face significant difficulties in their home lives, while others have physical, academic, or behavioral challenges. A growing number of children in the primary grades speak a language other than English at home and are learning English at the same time they are learning academic content. Although teachers have long been held accountable for their students' learning, just as doctors and other professionals are held responsible for their work, there is increased pressure at the state and national levels. The Common Core Standards, Race to the Top competitions, and pressure from the public and lawmakers for higher test scores has intensified the demands. Some teachers have been asked to implement new programs, while increasing the amount of time they put into reading, writing, and mathematics. There are no easy answers or quick fixes to these issues. However, educators have more information than ever before to rely on while providing the best education possible for each student. One source of information is the brain research conducted in recent years that provides relevant information about how children acquire and process knowledge in the early years of development.

Neuroscience research shows that the early years, including the primary grades, are pivotal in all future learning (Kaufeldt 2010). A child's experiences enable nerve cells, or *neurons*, in the brain to connect with each other, forming connections called *synapses*. These synapses form pathways in the brain that carry and transmit information. Because the networks and regions of the brain are interconnected, learning is influenced by many things, including emotions, motivation, memory, and past experiences. When children are happy, excited about learning, and free of stress, their brains process and store information more successfully, allowing more efficient retrieval (Kaufeldt 2010).

Hands-on, sensory-rich activities help students strengthen the skills they are putting into practice and form connections in the brain. Providing activities that involve multiple regions of the brain, such as those responsible for sight, hearing, and reasoning, increases the probability that the information will be stored permanently (Kaufeldt 2010; Rushton, Juola-Rushton & Larkin 2010). Presenting information both verbally and visually helps students focus on, process, and remember the information. In addition to reading about a topic, they can learn with their other senses through touching and manipulating objects, listening to music, watching a video clip, or occasionally smelling or tasting something related to what they are learning.

The brain is constantly searching for meaning and easily dismisses information and facts it finds meaningless, so providing activities that students find meaningful and that relate to the world around them is vital. This promotes the growth of brain cells and the formation of neuron connections, which strengthen learning pathways in the brain (Kaufeldt 2010). Opportunities for movement also increase students' ability to focus and pay attention throughout the day. This may be especially true for boys, many of whom find it difficult to sit still and concentrate for extended periods of time (Crawford et al. 2014).

Connecting information across learning domains helps solidify meaning and therefore promotes long-term memory, storage, and subsequent usage of learned material. The Common Core State Standards for English Language Arts (National Governors Association Center for Best Practices & Council of Chief State School Officers 2010a) recommend using an integrated model of learning, in which students study a topic or theme "for a sustained period" (33) that involves several different subjects. Students read a variety of texts on the topic and expand their writing skills as they write about what they have learned. Such topic studies help students apply their new knowledge and skills, which is part of the higher-order thinking called for in the CCSS. Topic studies are also an effective way to maximize the time teachers spend with students, as students learn about several subject areas at a time. This is especially true if the chosen topics and texts relate to science and social studies concepts addressed in the curriculum.

Creating a Welcoming Environment That Promotes Learning

Effective teachers create an environment that welcomes, supports, and celebrates each student. As children begin a new grade, typically in a new classroom, the teacher has an opportunity to establish or build on each child's excitement and enthusiasm for learning. By intentionally planning an environment that engages students in learning, encourages collaboration, and provides opportunities for practicing skills and making discoveries, teachers foster students' continued interest in learning. Sharing their own passion for learning with children adds a collaborative aspect to the learning journey.

Considering Room Design

Motivation and interest are powerful tools for learning and working toward meeting standards. Primary classrooms should be places where students are so engaged in learning there is nothing else they would rather be doing; ideally, students are focused like an athlete who is in the zone. The arrangement and contents of the classroom environment set the stage for this type of deep pursuit of knowledge and are key to effective teaching and positive learning outcomes. The room might include inspiring posters that teach new concepts, book displays that encourage delving more deeply into topics, and well-stocked areas that invite further exploration of children's interests. Room arrangement conveys to all who enter how learning takes place and what is valued.

When designing a primary classroom, start with what you have and work within the parameters set by the school. For example, if you want to promote collaboration among students and do not have access to tables, consider arranging desks in groups of two or four to encourage group work and discussion. The room arrangement should be flexible, enabling students to work at various times in large and small groups, with partners, and individually.

Third grade teacher Angie Bickett makes her classroom feel more like home by taking a photo with the students in her class and placing it in a frame with the word *Family* engraved on it. The class talks about being a family or community, which means they respect each other and each person's differences, use good listening skills, and support and stand up for each other. You might make a school family or school community photo album and update it throughout the year, highlighting events, classroom visitors, and special projects.

Focused attention is a powerful way to promote brain development (Kaufeldt 2010). Add items to the room that draw students' attention and interest and entice them to learn. This could include a science corner or windowsill with activities that change with the seasons, such as observing bulbs growing in clear containers or charting the growth of a class pet or sweet potato vine throughout the year. Special touches of texture and sparkle attract students' attention and add warmth. For example, polished stones and sparkling gems make inviting math manipulatives that will make meeting math standards more engaging. A pair of soft pillows or cushions invites students to sit and read.

Teachers and students alike enjoy spending time in inviting classrooms, and a well-planned environment can help students learn. For example, on a whiteboard in a prominent place in the classroom, write a question of the day for children to consider. Display posters that take students to unexplored regions with breathtaking geographical features or that inspire and teach with quotations or poetry. Provide books in many different areas of the room to invite children to read whenever possible and explore a variety of genres and topics. To enrich the topics of classroom study, add books to each interest area. In the science area, display books on science topics along with equipment, instructions for experiments, and materials such as pinecones, seashells, and unusual rocks. Place math-related books next to math manipulatives and inspiring books featuring artwork and artists near art supplies. For a study of another country, include foreign currency, an-

Try This!

As you arrange and decorate the room before students arrive at the beginning of the year, save space to include the artwork and writing children will create that reflects their interests, class topics, families, and cultures. Displaying their work helps students develop a sense of ownership and belonging—they are part of a learning community. It also conveys that what they do is valuable and motivates students to do their best. Where possible, showcase student work in inexpensive frames or frames made from construction paper or cardstock.

Stand in the doorway of your classroom and ask yourself, What messages does it convey to the students and families who enter? What would invite children to this space? Consider the characteristics of the students as you thoughtfully add to the room, making sure it reflects the diversity of the children in the class. Include fabrics, materials, books, and posters from families' varied cultures. Use natural and authentic items, such as shells, pinecones, rocks, and driftwood, as much as possible. Live plants add interest and help students learn how to care for living things. You may find a florist, garden store, or family member who would be happy to donate a few plants. Regularly review and update the classroom environment throughout the year to reflect the current needs, abilities, and interests of the children.

tiques, or historical clothing along with books about the country. These additions help to maintain students' interest, attention, and learning.

Classroom materials can be obtained from many sources. Some schools have a variety of math, science, and art materials available, sometimes tucked away in storage closets. Searching the Internet will yield information about reusable resource centers that offer free or low-cost recycled materials to teachers. Educational grants are available for obtaining materials (see, for example, www.edutopia.org/grants-and-resources). Websites such as www.adoptaclassroom.org/, www.supplyyourschools.org, and www.adaymadebetter.com allow teachers to post their classroom and project requests that donors can contribute to. Families and community members are another source of donated classroom items, such as zip-top plastic baggies and buttons.

Step back and review the overall appearance of the room. Is it engaging without being overstimulating? This is especially important for students who have difficulty focusing or have certain learning disabilities or sensory disorders. Both you and the students will be more productive if supplies are neatly organized and labeled—in English and in students' home languages. Providing storage space such as shelves, bins, or other containers for unfinished projects allows in-depth work to be carried over from one day or week to the next. Scheduling time to stay organized is critical to maintaining a supportive learning environment.

Wish Lists

Some primary teachers create a supply list of materials they need for the classroom, such as pencils, scissors, paper, clipboards, tape, and glue. They send this list to families and ask for donations, collect the materials, arrange them in containers, and place them in appropriate locations throughout the classroom. Students can compose thank-you notes for the donations, gaining additional practice to help them meet writing standards. Consider adding clipboards to this list. Students enjoy using clipboards for both indoor and outdoor activities, such as writing, making lists, and tallying and tabulating data. If families are not able to send clipboards, you may be able to requisition enough for your classroom and keep them from year to year.

Fostering Independence and Learning Through Room Design

Arrange materials to maximize students' independence and creativity, ensuring that needed supplies are labeled, organized, and readily available. This frees up time for teaching and empowers students to be responsible for their own learning. Students often relish the opportunity to take on classroom responsibilities such as sharpening pencils or being part of a cleanup crew. Having easy access to needed materials also promotes children's ability to solve problems independently, especially when students are supported by a social atmosphere that views mistakes as an opportunity to learn.

In early childhood programs in Reggio Emilia, Italy, the environment is viewed as another teacher, with the potential to help students learn through the materials and activities that are thoughtfully placed throughout the room. Teachers can follow the example of the educators in Reggio who treat children with deep respect as competent and capable learners, making materials easily accessible to enable them to pursue their ideas and plans (Wien 2008).

Arrange the room so that students can enter, hang up their jackets, put personal items away, sharpen pencils, and independently take care of other daily tasks. They might indicate the type of lunch they are ordering by moving their name to a designated spot on the interactive whiteboard or placing their name cards in the appropriate envelope. As students are taking care of these routines, allow a few minutes for them to settle in and talk with you and their classmates. This helps them transition into the school day and be ready for more focused learning. Students might read a book, write in their journals, or begin solving a problem of the day, while other students finish up routines that might include eating breakfast, depositing assignments in a homework basket, or placing other notes and forms in a classroom mailbox.

Some teachers use family connection journals for students to record daily homework assignments, spelling words, and upcoming events. Families are asked to sign the journal each night to indicate they have seen it and add any comments that would be helpful for the teacher to know. As students are involved in their morning routines, walk around the room, welcome and touch base with each of them, and check their journals for any news from home. This provides an opportunity to foster relationships with all of the students and their families.

Establishing a Meeting Area

A central feature of primary classrooms is a meeting area where the day starts and ends with a whole-class meeting that helps to build a community of learners. A morning meeting provides time to organize the day and share upcoming events (Vance 2014). Closing the day together allows teachers to review key concepts, challenge students with a new word to explore before the next meeting, and share excitement for the coming day. This meeting can end each day or be a special Friday event. A morning meeting also enables the teacher to introduce skip counting by 5s, review the guidelines for using the new tablet computers, and read aloud a chapter from *Sonia Sotomayor: A Judge Grows in the Bronx/La juez que creció en el Bronx*, by Jonah Winter. Discussions about class issues, such as ways the class could keep the interest areas more tidy or how to show care and concern for a classmate who is seriously ill, are also held in this area, with all students encouraged to participate and share their ideas.

The meeting area provides a more intimate setting for learning and discussion and allows for movement as children transition from other areas in the classroom to the meeting space. An area rug or carpet squares add comfort and a homelike feel. Place a basket of materials in the area with items such as markers, self-stick notes, and highlighting tape. If possible, locate the area near an interactive whiteboard, chart, or easel, and provide individual whiteboards, chalkboards, or clipboards for each student to promote engaged participation.

Consider other ways for all students to be engaged while one child is writing an answer on the whiteboard during large or small group activities. For example, try using morning meeting books with multiple sheets that match the class activities. Each day at group time students record the information in their own books as the group discusses it. On one sheet students might make tally marks indicating the number of days they have been in school, and work on place value as they convert that to ones, tens, and hundreds. On other forms they could record information about a current event or graph the number of letters in the names of everyone in the class. One form could be a blank calendar that could be used for a variety of activities, depending on the skills you are emphasizing. Students could fill in the month and add the date each day. This form could also be used to add a word of the day, solve a math problem, or count down the number of days remaining in school (see chart below). Additional sheets requiring more advanced skills can be added throughout the year. Sheets with new songs and poems enhance literacy skills and add interest. Examples of forms can be found on sites such as www.jmeacham.com/calendar/calendar.binder.htm.

MONTH ________________________________

Sunday	Monday	Tuesday	Wednesday	Thursday	Friday	Saturday

Designing Interest Areas That Invite Learning

Interest areas, such as a literacy center, can be integrated with most primary curriculum models. They might be an integral part of the daily routine or one of the many strategies in your teaching toolkit. In this book the term *interest area* describes a space that houses resources for a particular subject area where students can engage in active, meaningful learning individually, in small groups, or in pairs. Storing materials for each

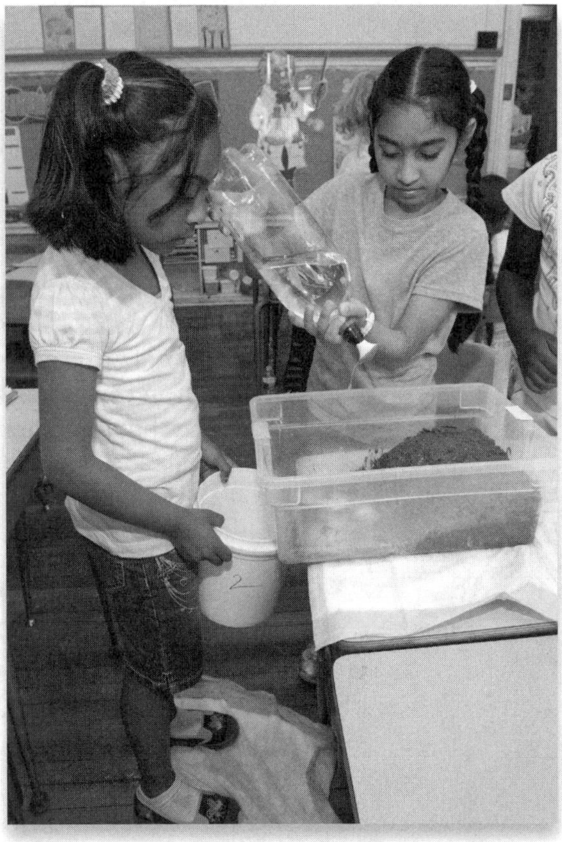

subject area in one place helps with room organization, makes it easier for students to find needed items, and helps students develop concepts and vocabulary. For example, in the science area students learn terms and form mental schemas, or webs of information, about scientific concepts as they associate the items in the interest area with the science topics they are studying.

The hands-on learning that takes place in interest areas helps scaffold students' learning and encourages them to be *minds-on* and mentally engaged as they construct knowledge. Students are more likely to stay focused when they are measuring with cubes or comparing the sides of a balance scale than when they are simply listening to an explanation or watching a demonstration. Learning gained through manipulation, experimentation, and the use of several senses tends to be more permanent than that acquired by simple rote memorization (Danielson 2007). In addition, whereas listening activates only one area of the brain, when students combine listening with movement and talking—for example, by explaining their thinking to a peer or teacher or writing their findings—they activate more areas of the brain and make important connections (Dodge 2009).

Activities in interest areas can address standards and provide opportunities for students to practice newly acquired skills and gain proficiency in reading, writing, math, and other subjects. With inviting spaces and the necessary tools, students actively investigate, discover, and make connections as called for in the CCSS. Centers with choices of engaging activities can promote more focused, self-directed learning. While most of the students are exploring in interest areas, the teacher can work with individuals and small groups.

Interest areas can be set up in a variety of ways—on tables, bookshelves, windowsills, countertops, two or four desks grouped together, or any other available space. Think creatively and make use of bulletin boards, pocket charts, or even individual drawers or cupboard spaces. Create and store portable interest areas in clear plastic boxes, backpacks, tote bags, or other containers. A poster board folded into three sections works for some content areas. The boards are easily stored together and can be used on individual desks or tables (McDonald & Hershman 2010). There is no limit to the types of centers you can create to help students meet standards as they advance their skills in a variety of subject areas and topics. You will find additional ideas for designing interest areas throughout this book.

Differentiating to Meet the Needs of All Students

Effective teachers differentiate practice to meet the needs of every student. Differentiation requires knowledge of each student's skills, abilities, interests, and needs. Building relationships with students and their families facilitates and informs teachers' work with children. James Comer (2004) maintains that no significant learning occurs without significant relationships. This is true for all students, at all ages. Fostering relationships with dual language learners helps them feel more comfortable talking with teachers and peers, which in turn promotes their overall language development and other academic skills. Children on the autism spectrum are more likely to learn and progress if their teachers build a positive, trusting relationship with them. Being calm and consistent and working with them individually strengthens teacher–child connections and helps enhance their ability to pick up on social cues. Interest areas, discussed previously, are very effective for differentiating instruction.

Successful differentiation requires teachers to maintain accurate, up-to-date records and files on children that include information from families, observational notes, assessment results, and work samples, as well as Individualized Education Program (IEP) goals for those who have special needs. Lesson plans should specifically mention strategies that will be used to meet individual needs and ensure that each student grasps the material being covered. For example, when working on math standards related to addition and subtraction, the lesson plan could indicate that you will be using manipulatives to scaffold student understanding. Students who are working on grade level will use them independently, while you work with those who need additional help. The plan can note that those working at a higher level will use them as they create and solve each other's story problems.

Motivating Students Through a Growth Mindset

Having a genuine belief that every student can succeed, and communicating that belief to students and families, greatly affects children's own beliefs in their ability to learn. When students believe they can succeed, they put greater effort into their learning. Letting students of all abilities know that you do not expect them to be perfect, but that you do believe in them and expect them to try hard, provides motivation for them to make the effort. Motivated students have a passion for learning, are willing to take on challenges, and actually flourish in the face of obstacles.

Psychologist Carol Dweck suggests that one of the greatest ways a teacher can influence students is by motivating them to learn. This motivation, however, may look different from what some teachers are used to. Commenting on students' intelligence or ability (for example, "you are so smart") can actually hinder performance (Dweck 2008). This can lead students to avoid tackling difficult problems out of fear that having to work at a solution will cause others to view them as less intelligent, or that failure would mean they are really not that smart. In contrast, noticing *effort* promotes positive effects. Students whose efforts and process are acknowledged often seek out more difficult challenges to tackle. Therefore Dweck recommends helping students develop a *growth mindset.* A growth mindset motivates students to pursue mastery and improvement and to value learning, not simply accomplishing a task. This mindset does not result in a need to prove how smart one is or believe that everything should be easy.

Promoting a growth mindset can enhance teachers' work with children at all levels of ability. Help all students understand that they can succeed by working hard, reading, using study skills and strategies, learning from their mistakes, and continually trying to improve. This truly gets to the heart of the skills called for in the Common Core State Standards—problem solving, looking for multiple solutions, explaining and defending reasoning—and helps students avoid focusing on just getting the right answer. Cautioning against using labels such as *gifted* with children, Dweck suggests that teachers discuss with students who are gifted and talented that they will be able to accomplish a great deal if they, like other students, work hard over time.

Promoting Learning—and More—Through High-Quality Teacher–Student Interactions

High-quality teacher–student interactions are critical to student learning and development and an important part of best practice. Children who experience warm interactions in a caring environment have higher achievement in both math and reading (Pianta et al. 2008). There are many approaches that examine teacher–student interactions; one is the Classroom Assessment Scoring System (CLASS), which outlines 10 dimensions of interactions that have been shown to make a difference in student outcomes (Pianta, LaParo, & Hamre 2008). Although some programs use the CLASS as a classroom evaluation tool, you can use the 10 dimensions to help you grow professionally, to improve your teaching and students' learning (Teachstone Training 2011). We'll discuss each of the dimensions here.

First is creating a **positive climate.** Research shows that students learn more when they feel comfortable in their environment (Pianta, LaParo, & Hamre 2008). They are more motivated to learn when they are happy and feel connected to others. In classrooms with a positive climate, teachers and students enjoy being with one another. They have positive relationships and are respectful of each other. Teachers create a positive climate by

- Having a sense of humor and laughing at their own mistakes
- Holding back-and-forth conversations with students
- Encouraging students to respect and support each other and form positive relationships
- Showing enthusiasm for teaching and learning
- Celebrating students' accomplishments

Effective teachers also avoid creating a **negative climate.** Use of anger, yelling, threats, harsh punishment, sarcasm, teasing, bullying, or humiliation all make it more difficult for students to learn. Emotions play an important role in the acquisition of knowledge; children's brains learn best when they are challenged but not threatened (Caine 2008).

When teachers anticipate students' academic and social needs and provide support, they show **teacher sensitivity.** Effectively addressing students' questions, concerns, and needs helps students see you as a resource they can come to for guidance. This enables them to feel comfortable sharing ideas and challenging themselves academically. In the classroom climate created by these conditions, students are likely to be comfortable working on their own and in groups, attempting to solve their own problems, because they know that if a question arises they can go to you for help. When you are understanding and are sensitive to students' individual needs, you can effectively differentiate and scaffold student learning.

Teachers demonstrate a **regard for student perspectives** by encouraging children to share their ideas, listening with genuine interest, and showing that they value students' points of view. They think about planning activities and topics of study around students' interests. They set up the classroom and schedule to enable children to make some decisions and be independent. Such actions can motivate students to learn. Having regard for student perspectives means giving students responsibilities, such as simple classrooms jobs, and supporting students' autonomy and leadership roles. It also means being flexible and allowing reasonable freedom of movement during activities.

In primary classrooms with good **behavior management,** or guidance, children understand teachers' expectations and rules. Teachers are proactive, anticipating problems and working to avoid them. They notice and respond when students show signs of needing to move or take a break. They redirect inappropriate behaviors to more appropriate activities. Teachers are consistent and use cues to help redirect a child's attention, such as walking near a student who is off-task. The feedback they offer to a student is constructive and focuses on the student's positive behavior. In classrooms that are engaging and full of interesting things to learn and do, children are more likely to stay focused and less likely to exhibit challenging behavior.

Teachers who remember that every moment of the day is an opportunity to learn are more likely to be **productive.** Increase your productivity by taking care of managerial duties and disruptions efficiently and helping children learn expectations and routines so they are able to move easily from one activity to another. Prepare all activities and materials before students arrive. Provide engaging activities for students throughout the day, and offer options for when they finish their work. Plan so transitions are smooth and minimize the time students need to wait. Turn transition times into learning opportunities by engaging in activities such as brainteasers and practicing math facts. As students prepare for lunch each day, help them learn new vocabulary by introducing a "word to walk by." Describe the new word as they are getting ready for lunch, and ask them to think about a synonym, an antonym, or a way they could use the word in their daily activities. Have them share their response with you one at a time as they walk down the hall or arrive at the lunchroom.

Instructional learning formats include the use of a variety of auditory, visual, movement, and hands-on opportunities. Use interesting, creative materials, such as student-made books, balance scales and other measuring tools, and microscopes if possible. Use effective questioning techniques that prompt higher-level thinking with words such as "how" and "why." Actively engage with students, which will encourage them to be more actively involved as well. Help students focus on the learning objective of lessons. Begin lessons by asking them to recall what they already know about the topic, make predictions, and use graphic organizers such as story maps or charts to record new learning. Share your excitement, interest, and enthusiasm for content and lesson activities.

To promote **concept development,** teachers support students' higher-order thinking skills and focus on understanding and application of material, not simply memorization of facts. Ask *why* and *how* questions, and provide opportunities for children to solve problems, predict and experiment, and classify and compare. Students need experiences that enable them to be creative, brainstorm, generate ideas, plan, and develop their own constructions. They also need opportunities to apply concepts to the real world, make connections between concepts and activities, and connect new knowledge to what they already know. Furthering students' concept development will also help them meet the challenges set forth in national standards.

Quality of feedback is important in helping children stay engaged in learning activities and gain a deeper understanding of concepts. Increase the quality of your feedback by providing support and hints when students struggle with a concept and by responding to students' comments and questions in ways that scaffold their understanding. If students are comparing seed sprouts they have planted in soil and other media, and one student responds, "The soil ones are taller," you could follow up with, "Why do you think that is happening?" When the student responds, "Because the soil holds the seeds in tighter," you could ask, "What other experimental conditions could we set up to test your theory?" Engage in frequent feedback loops with students, providing specific information and exchanging comments that help a student expand his knowledge. Help children focus on the process of learning, not just on getting a right answer. Ask students to explain their thinking, and encourage their efforts and persistence. Make it a goal to engage each student in meaningful back-and-forth discussions at least once each week.

When teachers provide **language modeling** for students, they consistently immerse them in rich language activities and engage in meaningful conversations with them. Language modeling helps students use and develop language skills, which will facilitate both academic and social success. Language modeling is especially critical for children who have not had a wealth of language experiences at home. High-quality language modeling includes asking open-ended questions and using advanced vocabulary ("Do you see the *feline* in the book with her kitten?") in a variety of contexts. You can also broaden students' vocabulary by responding to their inquiries with slightly more advanced academic language. Map your actions by using words to explain what you are doing, and map students' actions by describing what they are doing. When you engage in conversations with students, repeat and expand on their statements and encourage them to converse with each other. This will facilitate skills needed to meet a wide array of standards, including oral language, fluency, speaking, listening, and vocabulary.

Improving teacher–child interactions will assist students in meeting standards, lead to better academic outcomes for them, and build relationships that foster their social and emotional development.

In a Nutshell

The primary grades are a critical time in students' educational lives. These years help form the foundation for all later learning. A welcoming environment that promotes active, engaged, meaningful learning will help students form connections in their brains that lead to greater understanding and application of the material they learn. Encouraging and scaffolding students' efforts, motivation, and willingness to solve challenging problems will also enable them to learn and to meet the state and national standards, including the CCSS, which require students to use strategies, look for multiple solutions, problem solve, and explain their reasoning.

Learning is most effective when it

- Relates to students' everyday lives
- Builds on what students already know

- Is challenging but achievable
- Involves hands-on, concrete materials or experiences
- Is enjoyable so that students want to pay attention and persevere with the task

Standards outline *what* students need to know. Teachers make decisions about the *strategies* and *approaches* that are most likely to help students learn based on what teachers know about child development and learning, their students as individuals, and each student's social and cultural context. Authentically assessing students' progress and building relationships with students guide teachers in planning a differentiated curriculum that helps all students meet standards. Working to continually improve interactions with students will also lead to higher outcomes. Teachers can do this by focusing on creating a positive climate, being sensitive to students' needs, providing choices, valuing students' interests, setting clear expectations, providing a variety of interesting materials and activities to actively engage students, offering opportunities for higher-order thinking and creativity, providing quality feedback, and modeling language through meaningful conversations and language-rich activities.

Fostering Students' **Positive Approaches to Learning** and **Social and Emotional Development**

2

Children's social and emotional development has a tremendous impact on their academic progress and learning. How students approach learning—their disposition toward it—influences everything they do in school. This chapter describes ways to help students become eager and engaged learners as well as ways to nurture their social and emotional development. One criticism of state and national education standards, including the Common Core State Standards (CCSS), is that they do not address students' social and emotional development or their approaches to learning (NAEYC 2012). Yet students with a strong sense of emotional well-being, ability to relate to others, and a positive approach to learning are more attentive, focused, and interested in learning. They will have the self-confidence to attempt challenging tasks, such as those outlined in the Common Core, and be more willing to continue trying when the work is difficult.

Positive Approaches to Learning

The way children approach learning has a profound effect on their success as learners. In a study of more than 20,000 children conducted by the National Center for Education Statistics (Denton & West 2002), first-graders who demonstrated a positive approach to learning on teacher ratings were more than twice as likely to score in the top 25 percent on reading and math tests as their peers who did not demonstrate a positive approach.

Hyson (2008) developed a framework for describing approaches to learning consisting of two key dimensions: *enthusiasm* and *engagement*. Each of these has underlying components. Enthusiasm for learning, or the emotion/motivational dimension, includes interest, pleasure, and motivation to learn. Engagement in learning is the action/behavior dimension and consists of attention, persistence, flexibility, and self-regulation. Other components of approaches to learning are independence, organization, and an ability to follow rules (Forum on Child and Family Statistics 2013).

Hyson's Framework for Approaches to Learning

According to Hyson (2008), there are two dimensions to approaches to learning:

- Enthusiasm, or the emotion/motivational dimension
  - -Interest
  - -Pleasure
  - -Motivation to learn
- Engagement, or the action/behavior dimension
  - -Attention
  - -Persistence
  - -Flexibility
  - -Self-regulation

Students who become deeply *engaged* in learning give their full attention to an activity and persist at it even amid distractions. Their memory and comprehension improve, and they are more motivated as they become *enthusiastic* about learning. When problems arise, or they face new challenges, these children adjust their thinking. They are flexible and consider other options. Instead of giving up when a subtraction problem is challenging, they might look for more examples in the textbook or ask for help in solving it. With encouragement from adults, students develop self-control and better manage their thoughts, words, and actions while learning (Hyson 2008). One way to encourage persistence is to provide an area in the classroom to store unfinished work so students can return to a project and work on it until it is completed. Persisting at and completing projects help create feelings of competence and satisfaction, which in turn motivate children to seek additional challenges.

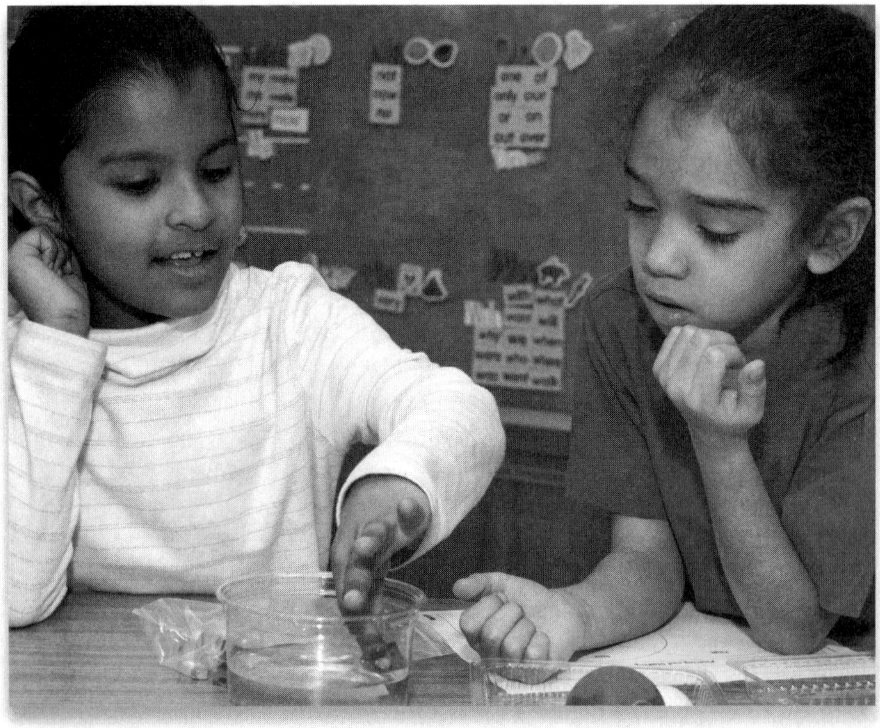

Developing Positive Approaches to Learning

In *The Global Achievement Gap* (2008), Wagner describes skills that today's students will need in the workplace. These include problem solving, curiosity, imagination, critical thinking, teamwork, and leadership. After reviewing vast amounts of research, Galinsky (2010) compiled and described seven life skills all children need to be successful: focus and self-control, perspective taking, communicating, making connections, critical thinking, taking on challenges, and self-directed, engaged learning. Both sets of skills match up well with those reflected in national standards. Some of these skills are part of the *executive function* of the brain, which includes the development of self-regulation, or being able to pay attention and control impulses. Children with good self-regulation skills remain persistent and focused in the classroom and can control their emotions and behavior. Executive function, which also enables children to be creative and solve problems using what they already know, may actually be a better predictor of school success than IQ (Bodrova & Leong 2007). Many students come to school without these essential skills, but students can acquire them if educators intentionally teach and nurture these competencies. Doing so will help students both learn what they need to succeed in the present and discover how to continue learning throughout life.

Promote a positive approach to learning by building on students' individual interests, providing a supportive environment and encouragement, and offering opportunities to practice skills. Avoid criticism and punishment—which typically discourage children and deprive them of constructive feedback—as well as indiscriminate praise (saying "Good job!" for everything students do). Instead, help students learn to evaluate their own efforts, determine where they need to improve, and generate possible solutions to implement.

Learning a process for problem solving gives students skills to tackle challenging problems and situations, so necessary for meeting math, literacy, social studies, and science standards. It also helps them think of actions they can take when they feel frustrated or angry in the wake of difficulties. This can be especially helpful for children with behavioral challenges. A class meeting is a good time to talk about the steps in problem solving (see the box) and to work on solving a variety of problems together that involve the whole group.

Post the problem-solving steps to help students tackle a difficult math problem, decode a new word, plan and carry out a science experiment, or solve a challenging social situation. Encourage students to view mistakes as opportunities to learn. Thomas Edison described each of his unsuccessful attempts—of which there were many—as learning one more way *not* to make a light bulb.

Students who find learning difficult are, like all students, much more likely to experience success if they are interested, motivated, and willing to persist at tasks. To foster these traits, build on children's interests and begin where they are, scaffolding them to each successive level. For example, encourage a student who is having difficulty with writing to begin by illustrating what he finds interesting. Ask him to describe the picture. Then provide support as needed in sounding out the words and adding additional descriptions, which could include settings or additional background information, depending on the student's abilities. Positive approaches to learning also benefit those children who tend to finish their work more quickly than their classmates. Willingness to take on additional challenges stretches them and helps them learn at higher levels. Offer these students activities that expand their thinking rather than simply give them more of the same work. Encourage students who have already mastered concepts to explore related topics that interest them. Students could gather data or research topics of interest with the help of a school librarian, parent volunteer, or other school resource personnel.

Try This!

Take brain breaks throughout the day to help children regain focus. Play some energizing music and have everyone get up and do exercises, stretches, yoga poses, dance steps, or whatever refreshes you and the students. Galinsky (2010) suggests playing games like *Simon Says*. Students can take turns leading the game, substituting their names for *Simon*. Students might count by fives while doing cross-body toe touches. These exercises provide practice in attention, flexibility, self-regulation, and thinking before responding.

Steps in Problem Solving

1. What is the problem? (Identify the problem.)
2. What are some of the ways I can solve this? (Think about several solutions.)
3. What shall I try? (Choose a solution.)
4. Give it a try. (Experiment and test it out.)
5. Did it work? (Decide if it solved the problem.)
6. If not, what else could I try? (Start the steps over and try another solution.)

Nurturing Students' Social and Emotional Development

Healthy social and emotional development includes experiencing, expressing, and managing emotions and establishing relationships with others in positive ways. Students with a healthy sense of self-worth and self-efficacy believe they can succeed, take on challenges willingly, and recover more quickly when things don't go as planned. Although the primary curriculum seems overloaded already, intentionally supporting children's social and emotional skills is critical, as this support may result in improved academic learning and fewer classroom disruptions.

Developing Social Skills

With a healthy self-concept and strong sense of self-worth as a person and a learner, children learn to respect others and have positive interactions with them. Teachers support students' sense of self by valuing children's interests, families, culture, and unique characteristics. Developing a positive cultural identity is a critical factor in children's sense of who they are; therefore, it is important that classrooms reflect students' home languages, cultures, and ethnicities through books, posters, materials, topics of study, activities, and other aspects of the curriculum. Provide examples of scientists, inventors, writers, leaders, and other individuals who have made a positive contribution to society and whose backgrounds are similar to the children's (Oertwig & Holland 2014).

Make the curriculum relevant and meaningful to students' lives by incorporating aspects of their cultures, home lives, and interests. Here are some examples:

- Give students math problems that include elements they can relate to from their daily lives, such as story problems that include classmates' names, sports they like, and favorite foods.
- Provide bilingual books with text in English and in students' home languages.
- Invite family members to create bilingual books with simple words and story lines. This will help all the students learn new words and broaden their cultural understanding.
- Ask family members to help you and the class learn a few key phrases in the students' home languages. This demonstrates respect for families' languages and cultures and helps build children's self-esteem.

Provide opportunities throughout the year for students to write about themselves. They might write a book or poem about something they enjoy, entitled *This Makes Me Smile!* Margaret Wise Brown's *The Important Book* provides a template for students to follow to describe their important attributes. For example, a dual language learner might write that what's important about *her* is that she speaks Korean *and* English. After students read biographies and autobiographies about historical figures, promote their writing and social skills by having them write their autobiographies. Work with them to plan topics for each section or chapter. They might even dramatize a section of their story.

The power of relationships. Fostering relationships with students and their families promotes students' social and emotional development, as well as positive approaches to learning. When students know that teach-

Try This!

Ask students to write and illustrate a book about themselves and their families. This activity is particularly helpful during the first few weeks of school, when students are getting to know each other. Describe your expectations for the book in a short rubric. Have students share their books at morning meeting for a few weeks to help everyone get to know each other. Create your own book to help students get to know you as well. Update it each year as needed—for example, after you get a new dog or take part in a triathlon. Share the books at teacher–family conferences as a conversation starter and to become better acquainted with families.

Try This!

Ask students to include a short "about the author" feature in all the books they write, along with their photo. This can promote a positive sense of self and provide motivation for writing and revising.

ers care about and respect them as unique individuals with their own strengths and interests, and when students have a positive relationship with their teachers, they are more likely to care about what teachers have to say. Children with disabilities or behavioral challenges benefit greatly from supportive teacher–child relationships (Tomlinson 2014). Taking time to understand the strengths and needs of individual students helps teachers differentiate instruction effectively and make decisions that will help students progress.

Andrea Peterson, the 2007 National Teacher of the Year, believes that the three Rs for teachers are *relationships*, *relevance*, and *rigor* and that these concepts flow naturally in this order. First, teachers establish relationships with students, which enables them to make curriculum meaningful and relevant for students. When learning is relevant, students are motivated to work hard and meet expectations (McDonald & Hershman 2010).

Engaging in two-way conversations with children about things that interest them is a key way to build relationships. Converse with children as they arrive in the morning, while they are waiting in line, at lunchtime, while they are engaged in the classroom interest areas, or at other times during the day. Focus your attention on them as much as possible during these conversations. Let them know you value them as individuals. For example,

> On the playground, Mr. Brooks, a second grade teacher, greets Kennedy, a student with autism. "Kennedy, I hear you are going to visit your dad this weekend! What do you like to do with your dad?" Kennedy shrugs but smiles. Knowing Kennedy is fascinated with animals and shows on the Animal Planet network, Mr. Brooks continues, "What kind of animals do you think they might be featuring next on Animal Planet?" Kennedy's expression brightens and he suggests, "Cheetahs." Mr. Brooks asks Maggie, another student in the class, to join the conversation, "Maggie, tell Kennedy about the bat your family found upstairs last week."

Relationships between students also contribute to their understanding of others and awareness of being part of a community. Provide an emotionally safe environment that promotes social interaction between children. Discuss ways members of a community treat each other, and plan activities throughout the year that will help students get to know and respect each other. Have children interview and gather data about each other. For example, they can create graphs to display data such as classmates' eye and hair color, favorite books, characters, activities, and foods. Foster students' appreciation and acceptance of diversity by pointing out the worth of each child's unique characteristics. Some primary teachers like to spotlight an individual child each week and ask all students to write the individual a positive message, highlighting their qualities, which could include friendliness, their skills, or special interests. Help children learn to respect each other by encouraging them to listen to classmates during group discussions and individual conversations. This will also help students meet listening standards and understand that everyone's voice is valued in the classroom community.

Have students work with a variety of partners and small groups throughout the year. Working in small groups enables students to learn to collaborate, cooperate, problem solve, plan, and organize their work. For some children, working with others makes it easier to participate and focus, stay engaged, and persist on a project than when they work on their own.

> Results from over 600 research studies that have investigated learning in cooperative, competitive, and individualist goal structures have indicated students learn more, are more highly motivated to learn, enjoy learning more, feel more positive toward the subject being studied, have increased positive regard for their teachers, and are more accepting of one another when they work together with peers as opposed to working competitively or individually. (Oertwig & Holland 2014, 114)

Think-Pair-Share

Think-pair-share is a helpful strategy for involving all students in a class discussion about a topic or question. After providing the topic or question, students

- **Think** individually about the question or topic
- **Pair** with a partner and take turns speaking and listening to each other's ideas
- **Share** with the class something from their discussion

Alanis (2013) recommends pairing dual language learners with students who are fluent in English for different activities throughout the day. During whole group activities, students can think-pair-share with each other. Taking a little time to think about a question and then share their ideas with a partner is very helpful for dual language learners, who may need additional time to frame a response. Alanis also recommends having partners collaborate at centers. Working with partners enables children to practice their developing language skills in a safe environment where they do not have to fear making mistakes. To help students work effectively together, model and role-play how partners interact.

When you group children for activities, include children with a variety of abilities so they learn from each other. Change the composition of groups throughout the year so students can see that everyone has strengths in different areas. Perhaps Melissa struggles with writing, but she's a whiz at addition and subtraction facts.

Friendships. Forming friendships is very important to primary grade children. Intentionally teaching pro-social skills will give children the tools they need to build friendships not only in the present but also throughout their lives. Address the theme of friendship, and other personal and social situations children face, through topic studies by reading a variety of books on the issue. Such topic studies will also help meet learning standards (Lanning 2013). During a class meeting discuss qualities that children look for in a friend. Together make a list to post in the room, along with photos of the children or pictures they have drawn portraying these qualities. Create a title for the list, such as *In Our Class, We Do Friendship!* Role-play scenarios about initiating a friendship, defending a peer facing a bully, and other situations typically encountered in this age group. Build vocabulary as you and the students suggest words they could use in those situations. Referring to students as *friends* ("Okay, friends, time to gather") and encouraging them to help each other will help promote a feeling of relatedness.

Relatedness. Relatedness, or connectedness, is a significant component of social and emotional well-being. Relatedness is considered to be one of three basic human needs, along with autonomy and competence (Oertwig, Gillanders, & Ritchie 2014). Creating a community of learners in which students feel valued, have a sense of belonging, and view themselves as contributing members of the community fosters their interest in learning and reduces disruptions. Students are more likely to support each other when they feel they are part of a learning community.

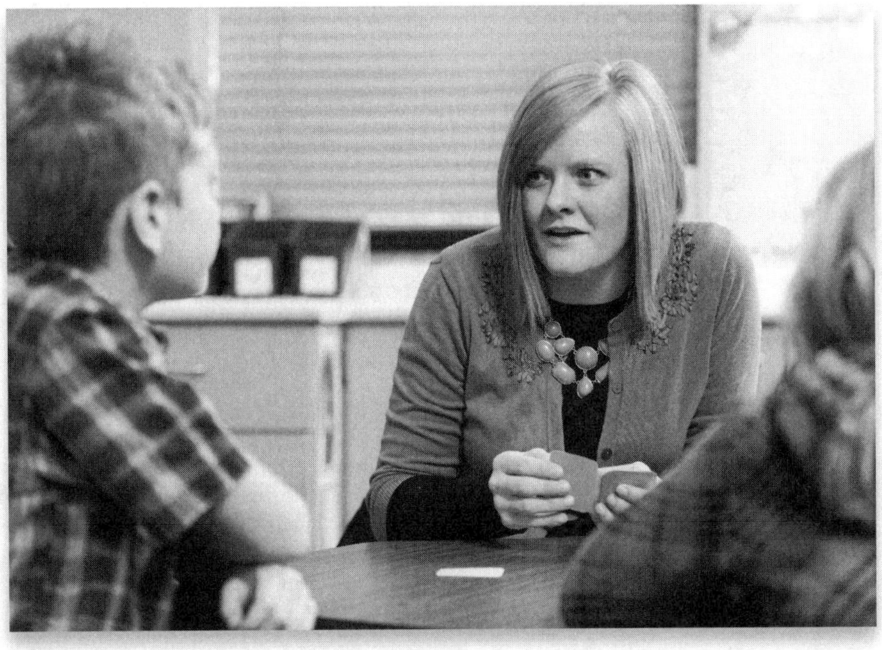

Build a sense of relatedness by demonstrating caring and respect and encouraging students to do the same. At a class meeting, ask students to generate a list of classroom jobs, such as keeping pencils sharp, watering plants, organizing the class library, distributing homework and memos, and taking messages to the office. Children with behavioral and academic challenges may shine in leadership roles, which give them an opportunity to make a positive contribution to the class.

Distinguished teachers demonstrate genuine respect and caring for their students as individuals and as a group and create an environment of respect and rapport (Danielson 2010). To further this atmosphere of respect, let students know how much you appreciate their kindness and collaborative work with each other.

Supporting Emotional Development

Emotional competence includes the awareness and constructive expression of one's emotions, picking up on cues to others' emotions, and expressing sympathy and empathy for others. Emotionally competent individuals can self-regulate to moderate and handle unpleasant emotions, and they understand that they have control over their feelings and can change the way they feel (Hyson 2004).

Support children's emotional development by creating a secure, accepting classroom atmosphere in which children can share their ideas and feelings. Have cozy nooks where students can be alone or curl up with a book when they feel the need to decompress. Provide stability balls and time outside, if possible, to help children who need more opportunities to move. Discuss emotions during class meetings and enrich children's vocabulary with a variety of words to express their feelings. When you see children attempting to regulate their emotions, acknowledge their efforts. Let them know you understand that it can be difficult to not act on their feelings, and reassure them that you are there to assist them. Help students channel their emotions into more positive pathways. Some teachers and students develop a prior agreement with each other to provide an outlet for students who need one. They put together a container of materials, such as buttons, rocks, or other manipulatives. When a situation arises where a child is having difficulty handling emotions, the teacher can ask the student to take a break and count or sort out a certain number of the materials to deliver to the other teacher. This gives the student a task, and an opportunity to move and get away from the situation for a short time. When a student is having a particularly difficult struggle, when appropriate, help the other students understand that that child needs their understanding and kindness.

Unique, interesting activities that prompt a positive emotional response, enthusiasm, and interest can help children process and retain information. Plan lessons and activities that will help children associate learning with positive emotions, such as tasting apples before writing poems about autumn or creating a map of their school neighborhood as they walk around the block, enjoying the time outside while helping to meet social studies standards.

Emotional competence plays a significant factor in learning. Students who are able to regulate their emotions will be able to spend more time on focused learning and less time distracted by negative feelings. Children's self-esteem grows as they experience the satisfaction of accomplishment, so design and scaffold lessons that are challenging but achievable. With confidence born of success and ever-expanding skills and knowledge, students seek new challenges to conquer and experience the joy of learning.

> Like interest, joy and happiness also foster learning and development. People are more empathetic, more generous, and more creative when they are feeling joyful. Feelings of joy are accompanied by confidence, vigor, and self-esteem. Joy opens our minds and hearts to new experiences, making our mental processes more creative and flexible. (Hyson 2004, 113)

Kindness. Cultivate children's empathy—their ability to understand others' emotions—by noticing their acts of kindness and talking about how it feels when someone is kind to them or they show kindness. Read books about the subject, such as *Hey Little Ant* (Phillip and Hannah Hoose), *The Kindness Quilt* (Nancy Elizabeth Wallace), or *Have You Filled a Bucket Today? A Guide to Daily Happiness for Kids* (Carol McCloud). Talk about the fact that when we do or say something kind to others, it has a positive effect on both the giver and receiver. Doing or saying something caring is comparable to filling people's "buckets," but being hurtful empties the buckets of both the giver and receiver. Suggest that students symbolically put a lid on their buckets when someone is treating them unkindly so the negativity bounces off. Encourage students to be bucket-fillers with classmates, family members, and others they encounter. For resources and more ideas on this concept, see www.bucketfillers101.com.

Discuss ways students can be kind to others, including forming friendships and being respectful to children in their school with sensory or academic challenges. They can also write thank-you notes to school staff, other teachers, and administrators who contribute to their school experience. They might make cards for children in hospitals or for residents of nursing homes (perhaps after reading Mem Fox's *Wilfrid Gordon McDonald Partridge*). They could take part in school or community projects or events such as National Make a Difference Day, the largest national day of service (see www.makeadifferenceday.com). What other ideas can they think of?

Resilience. Researchers describe protective factors that help children become *resilient*—adapting successfully when faced with trauma, adversity, or severe stress—when their lives are disruptive or unpredictable. Resilient children are better able to cope when facing stressors. Resilience factors include

- Attachment (strong, mutual relationships with significant adults in the child's life)
- Initiative (a child's ability to meet needs independently through thought and action)

- Self-regulation (the ability to manage one's thoughts, feelings, behaviors, and impulses) (Sperry 2011)

Teachers can help build resilience in children by nurturing these qualities. For example, positive relationships with teachers offer a significant source of resiliency for students. Promote children's initiative by providing opportunities for them to make meaningful choices and decisions throughout the day, such as choosing books to read and activities during center time or giving students a choice in how they present information they learned in a book they have read, such as making a poster, writing a skit, or composing a song or rap. To help children strengthen self-regulation skills, develop classroom rules together and discuss the need for controlling and adjusting their actions so everyone has a positive learning environment. Have students role-play scenarios that require self-regulation and conflict resolution. For example, students could role-play how to respond when they are not chosen first for a team or partnered with their best friend or how to handle disagreements on the playground. There are a number of resources devoted to promoting resilience, including those from the Devereux Center for Resilient Children (www.centerforresilientchildren.org/). The website *Growing Sound* (http://shop.childreninc.org/) offers music CDs and other resources that promote social and emotional skills, including resilience.

Integrate discussion of social and emotional topics throughout the curriculum. When choosing read-aloud books, occasionally choose those that prompt a discussion about issues students face. For example you might read *Gimme-Jimmy* by Sherrill S. Cannon or other books about bullying and then lead a discussion about how to respond to bullying behaviors aimed at themselves or a classmate. Talk about other challenging situations, letting students know that everyone has stressors they must cope with. Talk about who they can turn to for help, such as teachers and other school personnel, parents, grandparents, or other trusted adults.

When reading literature and informational text, ask students to consider the characters' emotions and motivations. Occasionally ask them to choose a character and write from the perspective of that person. This will increase their ability to see issues from another's perspective and to empathize. Another activity for perspective taking is Readers Theater, which involves cooperative dramatic reading from a text. Reading aloud and interpreting a character's words gives the reader—and listeners—a deeper sense of the character's viewpoint and feelings. Scripts and tips for conducting Readers Theater can be found at several websites, including www.aaronshep.com/rt.

Home<—>School Connections

Forming supportive relationships with families helps teachers understand students. To engage families as partners in supporting their children's social and emotional development and encouraging children to have a positive approach to learning, let families know the ways you are supporting children in these areas throughout the year. Initiate conversations with families and encourage them to share examples of their child showing initiative, self-regulation, and other social and emotional skills at home. Schedule enough time during conferences to get to know families better and allow time for them to share their insights about their children's strengths, interests, and needs.

Use home–school communication vehicles, such as your classroom newsletter and website, to suggest activities families and children can do together at home to help foster these skills. Children can help carry out daily routines such as cooking and cleaning up, and families might read together, engage in conversations, take walks, and share the wonder of the world around them. Families can incorporate math and literacy skills in daily activities, such as reading the cooking instructions on a box of macaroni and then measuring the water and other ingredients. Suggest that families create or designate a space at home where their child can read, write, and do artwork and homework, and that they help their child take responsibility for organizing both the space and the projects. Send home books or suggest books with positive social messages that families can read together. Ask families to suggest books to read with the class at school.

Remind families that children are still developing their skills and need our patience and encouragement. Suggest that modeling qualities like respect, listening, and resolving conflicts in a fair manner are some of the best ways for children to learn these behaviors.

In a Nutshell

Positive approaches to learning and social and emotional skills establish a foundation for students' learning in all curriculum areas. Primary teachers need to intentionally address these skills. Students with positive approaches to learning are enthusiastic and engaged learners, and those who have strong social and emotional skills exhibit healthy self-esteem, emotional understanding, empathy, self-regulation, and social competence. They respect others and enjoy the company of classmates and friends.

When teachers form respectful, reciprocal relationships with students and their families and support relationships between classmates, students feel valued and respected. This in turn promotes social and emotional development and positive approaches to learning—and results in students who are interested in and enjoy learning.

Meeting the Common Core State Standards for **English Language Arts**

3

A major focus for students in the primary grades is learning to read and write. Providing experiences that promote a love of reading and writing and that boost students' self-confidence will encourage them to read and write more. This strengthens their skills and increases their success. The cycle can continue throughout their lives.

There can be no doubt about the critical importance of literacy teaching in the early grades. Failure to read on grade level by fourth grade is a strong predictor of students dropping out before completing high school. Most children who are not reading on grade level by grade four do not catch up (Annie E. Casey Foundation 2010).

Engaging Young Readers in Literacy-Rich Primary Classrooms

The Common Core State Standards (CCSS) have increased expectations for students and teachers. Students need to accurately analyze text, make high-level inferences, and provide evidence for their thinking. They are expected to read a balance of informational text and literature as well as use academic language that cuts across disciplines. The CCSS challenge teachers to bring *all* children to a high level of literacy. To do this teachers need to know the skills of each child in addition to knowing what is typical at each stage of development, and to set challenging goals that are within the child's reach.

When the National Reading Panel was convened in 1997, members were charged with finding the best ways to help all children become successful readers and writers. After thoroughly examining the research that met their strict criteria, panel members found that good readers and writers have several characteristics in common: good ***comprehension;*** command of a strong ***vocabulary*** and good ***oral language skills;*** good oral reading ***fluency; phonemic awareness*** and ***alphabet knowledge; phonics*** skills and good ***word recognition;*** and ***motivation*** to read and write (National Institute of Child Health and Human Development 2000). Additional research has verified these findings as well as the unquestionable importance of high-quality teaching to help children learn these skills (Reutzel & Cooter 2013; Shanahan 2005). These skills are also critical in achieving the expectations of the CCSS.

Reading in the Primary Classroom

Opportunities to help students acquire the essential skills to be successful readers and writers and to meet standards are present throughout the school day, beginning as soon as students enter the room.

Begin the Day With Opportunities for Reading

Daily routines for students typically include signing in, greeting other students and the teacher, and answering a posted question of the day, which can be intentionally planned to foster literacy and vocabulary development. While students wait for everyone to put away backpacks and complete other morning tasks, they can choose a book to read or add an entry to their journals. Sing or play a favorite class song as the signal to come together on the rug or designated area for morning meeting.

At the beginning of your literacy block—the time set aside for literacy learning—sing songs or recite poetry from charts to provide practice in phonemic awareness, rhythm, and word skills, as well as strengthen the community of learners' atmosphere. Shared reading with big books or text on the whiteboard can follow. This enables you or a student to point to text as the class reads along, building foundational skills of fluency, decoding, and word recognition. Repeated readings of text everyone can see provides the modeling and support students need to become more confident readers. This is especially helpful for children who are beginning to acquire reading skills or who have difficulty learning to read. Dual language learners also benefit from repeated readings. Each repeated reading should have a specific focus. The first reading might focus on prediction and enjoyment of the text, while the next builds comprehension skills. A third shared reading might center on expanding language and vocabulary. Additional readings could address decoding, fluency, and deeper understanding of the craft and structure of texts as called for in the CCSS. The Teachers College Reading and Writing Project, whose aim is to build skilled readers and writers, offers numerous resources for teachers' professional development. See www.readingand-

How to Select Appropriate Texts for Students

According to Fountas and Pinnell (2001, 223) there are several criteria to consider when choosing texts for young readers:

- Readers' present strategies
- Readers' interest and background knowledge
- Text complexity in relation to readers' current skills
- The language of the text in relation to readers' experience
- The content of the text in relation to readers' background knowledge
- The appropriateness of the content to the age group
- The representation of gender, racial, ethnic, and socioeconomic groups in positive ways
- Your own assessment of the learning opportunities inherent in a text and their match to your instructional goals
- The quality of the text: language, illustrations, layout, writing style

For more information see *Guiding Readers and Writers, Grades 3–6: Teaching Comprehension, Genre, and Content Literacy* (Fountas & Pinnell 2001) and *Teaching for Comprehending and Fluency: Thinking, Talking, and Writing About Reading, K–8* (Fountas & Pinnell 2006).

writingproject.com/resources.html for booklists—including big books appropriate for the primary grades—and other resources related to the CCSS.

Readers' Workshop

Research clearly indicates that the amount of time children spend in actual reading makes a difference in developing reading skills (Calkins, Ehrenworth, & Lehman 2012). These authors recommend that students read books they find interesting and can fluently read with 96 percent accuracy and comprehension for at least 45 minutes in school and spend additional time reading at home. Although there are many ways to provide this time for students to read in school, many teachers use a 60- to 90-minute block of time in a readers' workshop (Calkins, Tolan, & Ehrenworth 2010; Miller 2013) or a similar approach, such as the Daily 5 (Boushey & Moser 2014). The readers' workshop often consists of several mini-lessons, with time given to individual or pairs reading and other activities between the mini-lessons. The topics for the mini-lessons are based on strategies required in the standards. Teachers assess students on an ongoing basis to determine their strengths and their needs. The workshop begins with the teacher presenting a mini-lesson to the whole group, focused on a strategy the students then put into practice. For example, checking for understanding by asking oneself questions about the words and meaning of the text. During the five- to ten-minute lesson, the teacher models and shares her thinking aloud. After the lesson, the students choose texts from individual or class book boxes and read independently, employing the strategy they have learned (Boushey & Moser 2014; Calkins, Tolan, & Ehrenworth 2010; Miller 2013).

Helping Students Select Their Own Just Right Texts

Use the Goldilocks method (McDavid 2007) to help students choose their own *just right* books:

> **Too Easy Books** are books I have read many times and can retell easily. I know most of the words and can read it smoothly.
>
> **Too Hard Books** have five or more words I don't recognize on a page and the story is confusing. I need help reading it and can't read it smoothly.
>
> **Just Right Books** interest me even though I haven't read them yet. I can retell the parts I have read. I may need help with a few words.

This description can be put on bookmarks for children to use when selecting their own books. For more information on helping students choose appropriate books, see www.readwritethink.org/classroom-resources/lesson-plans/choosing-right-book-strategies-916.html?tab=4, and for a poster (McDavid 2007) with this information see www.ourclassweb.com/center_activities/readers_workshop/rw_poster_goldilocks_rules.pdf.

For the strategy of checking for understanding, students might comment on their reading in their reader's notebooks or on sticky notes, using prompts such as *I'm wondering about . . . , I noticed . . . , I don't understand this part . . . ,* and *I think ________ will happen next.* Students can place the sticky notes in the book or attach them to a notebook page, or they can write their notes directly in a notebook along with the page number and title of the book they are reading. To encourage interest, provide a variety of shapes, colors, and sizes of sticky notes, and perhaps also an assortment of colored paper or cardstock for students to make bookmarks to use for writing their comments.

The second part of the workshop time often begins with another mini-lesson to introduce a new concept or to work with the whole group or a small group of students who need help with the previously taught strategy. This is a good time to introduce or reinforce skills students need to read increasingly complex text. After this mini-lesson the students might read with a partner, taking turns or reading in unison and periodically asking each other questions about the text. Reading with partners is a good way to acquire skills needed by successful readers. Partners sit near each other during the mini-lesson and are ready to discuss their readings with little time lost to transition. Discuss and model strategies for listening carefully to partners and encouraging them to expand on what they are thinking. When Ms. Roerig begins her partner reading time she explains the procedure, "Face your partner and give your partner your attention. You each drew a number at the beginning of the week. Those who drew the number 1 will begin reading. Number 2 partners listen carefully without talking while their partner reads. Then switch roles. Today, let's have each partner read a page."

A third mini-lesson might be for the whole group or a small group who need assistance on another skill that builds on the strategies you are targeting that day. After this lesson, students can engage in several literacy-building activities in a reading work time. Give this time an engaging name, such as "Readers' Workout Time." During this time, students might read independently or with a partner, listen to audiobooks in small groups to improve fluency, and work with words at literacy centers. Give students a choice of activities or assign activities based on students' needs. Between mini-lessons, as students are working, the teacher confers with individuals or works with small groups. This might include guided reading, an instructional approach in which teachers work with small groups of students with similar abilities, using the same text to focus on learning reading strategies they can successfully use independently (Fountas & Pinnell 2006). It could also include Response to Intervention (RTI) groups, which offers "a hierarchy of support that is differentiated" according to students' needs (DEC, NAEYC, & NHSA 2013, 5).

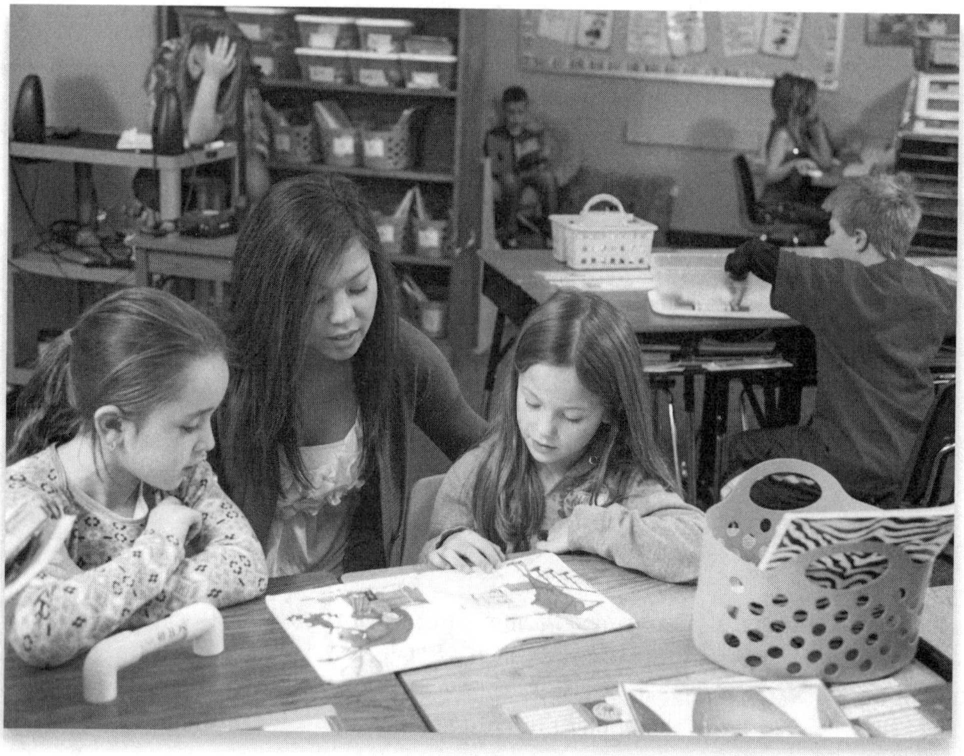

The amount of time students spend reading between the mini-lessons varies with their age and ability. Gradually increase this time over the course of the year to help students improve their ability to focus and engage in sustained reading.

Conferencing and assessing. Working with individuals, partners, or small groups while other students are absorbed in their reading allows teachers to document progress and determine how best to help each reader. Keep a calendar of the times you meet with each child, the strategy you worked on, and the next meeting with the child. This documentation ensures that you allot time to meet with each student weekly or more often. Conference with children who need additional support as frequently as possible.

Conferences are generally brief and focus on specific strategies. Listen to students read a short passage and ask them to briefly retell what they read. Take notes on their strategy use, fluency, and comprehension. End the conference with words of encouragement or a discussion of a particular skill or strategy for the student to use in future reading. If other students want to talk with you while you are conferencing, Miller (2013) suggests they write their requests on a sticky note and place it at a designated spot near you. You can address their concerns as soon as you finish.

Conferences are an effective way to individually assess students, as we listen to them read and retell what they have read. There are several free online tools that help you make rubrics for retelling and offer pre-made rubrics as well (see, for example, http://rubistar.4teachers.org). The Teachers College Reading and Writing Project (www.readingandwritingproject.com/resources.html) has free assessments and other resources, including running records, assessments for concepts about print, and rubrics for retellings at various levels of text complexities. This site also has informal reading inventories to help determine children's individual reading levels.

When you notice that several students find the same strategy challenging, conference with them in small groups. You may discover additional strategies that the whole class could benefit from in future mini-lessons.

Readers' Workshop Components

Component	Description
Opening Mini-Lesson	Teacher models a reading strategy in a whole group.
Independent Reading	Students choose texts from book boxes to read independently. Teacher listens to individuals read.
2nd Mini-Lesson	Teacher reinforces previously taught strategy or introduces a new concept during a whole or small group.
Partner Reading	Students read in partners. Teacher listens to individuals read and confers with them.
3rd Mini-Lesson	Teacher introduces or reinforces another skill that builds on the strategies she is targeting that day during a whole or small group.
Readers' Workout Time	Students read independently, read with a partner, or work in literacy centers.
Closing Reflective Time	Several students share strategies used during the workshop. Teacher reinforces teaching points, helping students make connections.

Concluding the readers' workshop. Bring everyone back together to reinforce teaching points, making connections to previous lessons that will help students apply the day's targeted strategies. During the closing of the readers' workshop, several students can share what they have worked on.

Teachers can combine the readers' workshop model with other approaches to literacy instruction to ensure that children have extended opportunities for reading. With any approach, the procedures should be simple and predictable. Students will need to see procedures modeled and then practice them multiple times at the beginning of the year, along with additional practice throughout the year. As the year progresses students will work and read with increasing fluency and independence. End each reading block with the assurance that you have confidence in their efforts to be active, thoughtful readers.

Integrating Literacy Throughout the Day

A high-quality block of time for reading each day is critical to ensuring that students spend sufficient time reading and working on literacy-related activities. The rest of the day, too, is filled with opportunities for reading to, reading with, and reading by children, as well as time to write and study words. Designate a time each day to read aloud to students, perhaps after lunch or recess as a calming way for students to settle back into the day. Use read-aloud times to introduce students to a variety of genres and complex text and to demonstrate strategies used by good readers. Making it an enjoyable experience will build the classroom community and promote children's love of literacy.

Students will be meeting standards during the readers' workshop and read aloud times. The remaining sections of this chapter discuss the CCSS for reading, followed by the CCSS for writing, listening, speaking, and language, and additional ways to address them with engaging activities throughout the day. Although the CCSS are used as examples, these activities can be used to meet other early learning standards as well.

Engaging Learners With Literature and Informational Text

The CCSS for reading place a strong emphasis on reading for meaning. One of the major differences between the CCSS and previous standards is the increased emphasis on comprehension of both literature and informational text. In fact, the CCSS recommends that 45 percent of all reading in grades K–8 consist of informational texts (Calkins, Ehrenworth, & Lehman 2012). Developing skills and strategies to read for meaning and to discuss informational text will help students comprehend the material they read in science, social studies, and other content areas. It also prepares them for lifelong reading, which will include newspapers, manuals, ballots, and transportation schedules. The standards for both literature and information text are grouped into the following areas: Key Ideas and Details, Craft and Structure, Integration of Knowledge and Ideas, and Range of Reading and Level of Text Complexity.

Key Ideas and Details

A number of research-based teaching strategies help students identify and understand key ideas and details in text and categorize the material, such as story mapping and other graphic organizers. These tools promote lasting recall. Work with students to develop your own creative maps and organizers, or use an app (such as *Popplet*) or software (such as *Kidspiration,* www.inspiration.com/Curriculum-Integration/Kidspiration). The International Reading Association (IRA) and the National Council of Teachers of English (NCTE) offer numerous interactive tools, printables, and lesson plans on the ReadWriteThink website (www.readwritethink.org). One of these tools is an interactive story-mapping tool that enables students to make story maps that focus on various aspects of the story.

There are other ways students can summarize what they have read. Ask them to retell stories, making sure they incorporate the main ideas and key details. To help in their retelling, students could use the illustrations found in the text, flannel board characters, pictures they draw, or puppets they make. Several resources, such as www.janbrett.com, provide ideas for imaginative puppets and masks students can make to add interest and enjoyment to story retelling.

Comprehension. Describing the main idea and supporting details of a text involves higher-level comprehension skills. Students interact with and construct meaning from a text by applying skills in phonemic awareness, phonics, oral language, and fluency; background knowledge, motivation, and interest are also important for comprehension.

Reading materials with familiar content increases motivation and comprehension, especially for dual language learners (Oertwig, Gillanders, & Ritchie 2014). When students have comprehension skills they can ask and answer questions about the text, retell stories, identify main topics and key details, and describe characters, events, and settings. Help students develop deeper comprehension skills by asking questions such as *Whose point of view is this story told from?, Whose point of view is missing?,* and *How did this text make you think more like a scientist/mathematician?* Students need to learn these comprehension skills by third grade so that they are able to reflect on their reading, providing insights such as character motivation and feelings and explaining how key details support the main idea of a text as the CCSS requires.

The National Reading Panel (Shanahan 2005) found evidence to support teaching several comprehension strategies:

1. Asking questions—posing questions about what students are reading
2. Monitoring—verifying that they understand what they read
3. Summarization—assimilating concepts read and summing up what the text is trying to convey
4. Answering questions—responding to questions asked by the teacher, who provides prompt feedback
5. Graphic organizers—making visual representations of what they are reading using graphic and semantic organizers, including story maps
6. Cooperative grouping—learning and using comprehension strategies with other students

The panel recommends the *gradual release of responsibility model* in teaching these strategies. This *I do it—We do it—You do it* approach begins with the teacher providing explicit instruction on how to use a particular reading strategy, such as stopping periodically to ask oneself what is happening in a story. After the teacher demonstrates the strategy, the students practice it along with the teacher. Once students seem to understand the strategy, they practice it with the teacher's guidance. Finally, the students use the strategy independently in reciprocal teaching, other small groups, or individual work. In *The Book Whisperer: Awakening the Inner Reader in Every Child,* Miller (2009) describes the importance of a gradual release of responsibility: "Every lesson, conference, response, and assignment I taught must lead them away from me and toward their autonomy as literate people" (16). Although each of these strategies in isolation aids comprehension, the strongest benefit comes when students use multiple strategies in their reading (Shanahan 2005).

Reciprocal teaching. The panel also suggested the use of *reciprocal teaching* to help students learn comprehension strategies (Shanahan, 2005). Years of research have verified the benefits of reciprocal teaching, including an increase in students' reading level and greater retention (Oczkus 2010). In reciprocal teaching, students learn and gradually take on the role of the teacher in reading group discussions by using four strategies: prediction, questioning, clarification, and summarization (see the box). To achieve maximum benefit, focus on a single strategy for four or more weeks before introducing a new strategy (Shanahan 2005). Reciprocal teaching can be used with a wide variety of texts, including literature, informational text, poetry, and read-alouds, and in small group settings including guided reading and literature circles.

Monitoring and regulating one's thinking and learning—that is, metacognition—facilitates the learning process. Reciprocal teaching helps children acquire metacognition as they learn to monitor their own comprehension and use strategies to improve it. For example,

> To develop his students' metacognition, Mr. Donelan encourages his students to activate their prior knowledge. Before reading an informational text about fossils, he asks each student to write and draw a picture illustrating what they already know about fossils or dinosaurs. As they begin reading individually, he reminds them to think about the reading strategies they have discussed, such as reading the captions associated with the illustrations and looking in the glossary for any of the bolded key words they don't understand. When they finish reading he asks them to reflect on the strategies that were most helpful to them.

Oczkus (2010), a leading expert on reciprocal teaching, recommends the use of symbols, puppets, and other props to help students remember to use the four strategies, which she calls "The Fab Four." You can use her symbols and materials (www.lorioczkus.com) or develop your own. For example, you might use an image of a wizard or groundhog for predicting, an investigator for asking questions, a librarian for clarifying, and a reporter for summarizing. Oczkus also provides charts and graphic organizers to record students' results. Provide materials for children to make bookmarks with these symbols and their meanings to use in their reading. You can find bookmarks, charts, and additional suggestions for reciprocal teaching at the Reading Rockets website: www.readingrockets.org/strategies/reciprocal_teaching/.

It's important to frequently model your own use of the reciprocal teaching strategies and remind students to use them. *Anchor* charts are posters made collaboratively with students that outline or describe strategies or procedures on a particular topic. They are an effective way to help students anchor and retain the new information or strategies they are learning. These charts help to make the new learning visible by recording the strategies, processes, and thinking you have discussed with students. Display an anchor chart listing the reciprocal teaching strategies, including the acronym *PACS* to help students remember the strategies.

Four Reciprocal Teaching Strategies

P Predict. What could this be about? What might happen next? What clues can I use to think about what might happen? I wonder if/about. . . . (wizard image)

A Ask Questions and Connect. Am I understanding what I am reading? Have I experienced anything or anyone like this? What do I wonder about? (investigator image)

C Clarify/Clear Up. Are there words or ideas I don't understand? What strategies can I use to find out? (librarian image

S Summarize. So what is this about? What is the main idea? What did I learn? (reporter image)

Using the strategies in small groups of four is especially effective. Here is how it might work with Mrs. Nash's class who is reading *Moonshot: The Flight of Apollo 11,* by Brian Floca.

> Mrs. Nash prints sheets for each group that have all four strategies, including the name, symbol, and a short description of each strategy along with space for the group's response to that strategy. She cuts the sheets, so that each student in the group has one strategy and will be in charge of, or the teacher for, that strategy. She asks each student to choose one of the strategies. Katrina is responsible for *predicting* (the wizard or groundhog) for her group and asks them to predict what the story or book might be about and records their ideas on her paper. Tomas, who is responsible for *asking questions and connecting* (the investigator), asks questions about the text as the group reads and asks the others if they have questions or connections to make, and also records their questions and responses. Kim, the librarian, who is

> in charge of *clarifying/clearing up*, suggests words or ideas the group may need to research further and reminds the others to do the same. She also asks the group to think about strategies they could use in their decoding. Jay, the reporter, helps the group *summarize* their discussion points and records the main idea and key details.

This activity can be used weekly or more frequently to reinforce skills and increase students' ability to read for understanding. Vary the groups and the roles students take; readers who struggle will benefit from the support others in the group provide. Teachers can incorporate reciprocal teaching strategies in other literacy practices, including guided reading groups and within the RTI framework. With younger primary students you may want to use reciprocal teaching primarily when you are working with a small group. Older primary students can work in groups on their own after you have modeled it with them several times. For a number of reasons, dual language learners may have difficulty asking questions in class. Research shows that reciprocal teaching with small groups of four children can boost their confidwence and skill in doing this. Focusing on the questioning and clarifying aspects of reciprocal teaching, for example, is effective in helping dual language learners become more confident questioners (Williams 2010). Reciprocal teaching fits well with the *gradual release of responsibility model* in teaching reading.

Craft and Structure

Reading aloud to children every day is one of the most beneficial activities teachers and families can do to help students acquire literacy skills (Trelease 2013). It is especially effective when children actively participate in the reading, asking questions and discussing what is happening in the text. Reading aloud provides an avenue for talking about the overall structure of a story, which you can do after reading the story or as you are reading it. To help students apply their new knowledge, you can ask them to write their own stories, including writing about the structure of a story structure. For example,

> After talking about how the beginning of a story introduces the plot, Ms. Frost asks her students to start writing a story with a beginning that clearly presents the plot. Each day she introduces another aspect of story structure and asks them to incorporate that aspect into the piece they are writing. By the end of the week the students have finished their stories with strong endings that provide a conclusion to their plot.

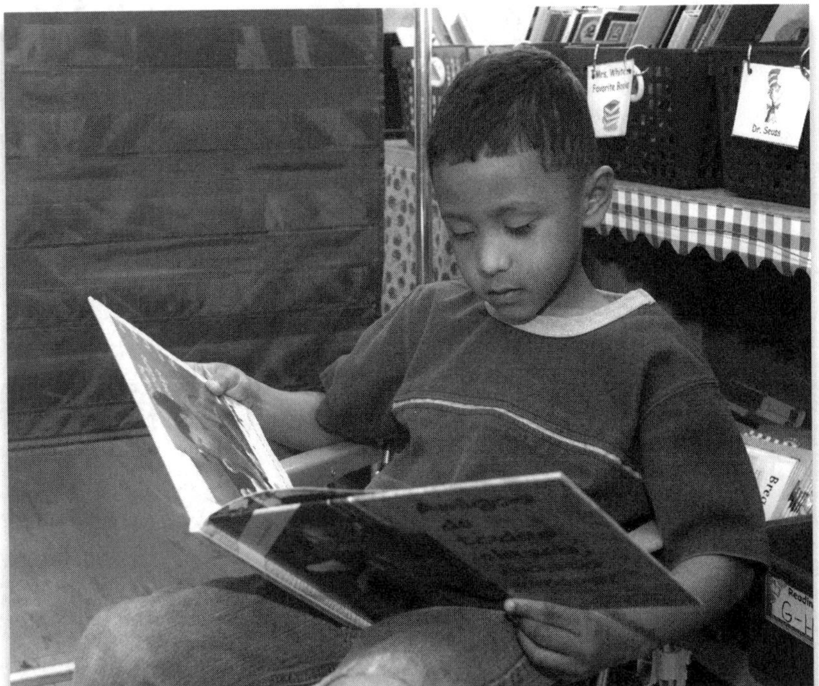

Ask children to visualize a story's or poem's characters, setting, and events as you read it aloud to them. They can also sketch images evoked by the reading. Reading to children using different voices for each of the characters will keep students' attention, help them comprehend the story, and enable them to identify the characters in the story. Hearing the frequent use of different voices gives students a model for doing this when they read aloud. Ask students to think and discuss why characters respond differently in a story. They could then act out parts of the story, portraying the characters' perspectives, using suitable voice and tone to emphasize the characters' feelings.

Integration of Knowledge and Ideas

To help students meet the standard of integrating knowledge and ideas, encourage them to examine the illustrations, photographs, charts, and diagrams in the texts they read. *National Geographic for Kids, Ranger Rick*, and other children's magazines provide rich illustrations and graphics, as do digital resources such as www.pbs.com. Ask students, "What information did you learn from these illustrations [or graphics]?" Give them opportunities to illustrate their own writing and ask them to describe the information their illustrations convey.

Pete the Cat: Rocking in My School Shoes		***Pete the Cat and His Four Groovy Buttons***
DIFFERENCES	**SIMILARITIES**	**DIFFERENCES**
Pete sings about shoes. Pete wears shoes. Pete is at school.	Pete is a blue cat. Pete says, "Goodness, no!" Pete is always happy. Pete loves to sing. The story is fiction.	Pete sings about buttons. Pete has no shoes. Pete is at home.

Graphic organizers help students think about and record their comparisons of texts on a similar topic or by the same author. After students read two texts on a topic, have them list key points found in each of the texts. They can record the similarities in a column between the two other lists (see the chart).

Venn Diagram for Comparing Characters in Three Cinderella Stories

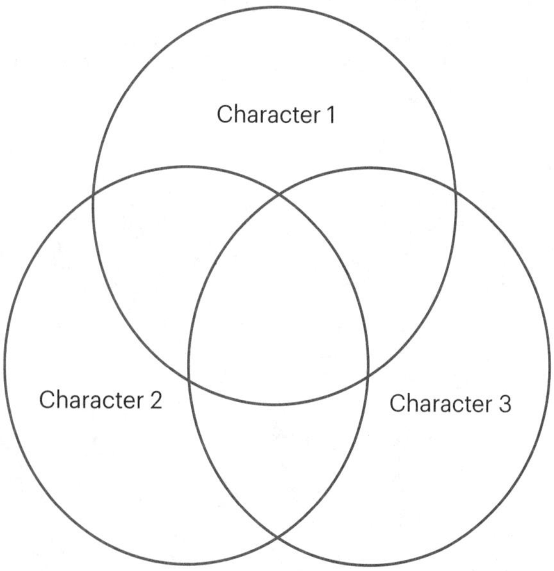

Add interest to this activity by providing illustrations related to the topic to record their findings. For example, when comparing two texts on polar bears or the Arctic, students could write similarities between the two texts on a picture of an iceberg and the differences on outlines of polar bears. You can find images to use on the Internet, such as at http://images.google.com.

A Venn diagram is a graphic way for students to represent similarities and differences between two or more topics. The diagram uses two or more overlapping circles. Similarities are recorded in the section that overlaps; differences are recorded in the areas of the circles that do not overlap. The diagram provides a supportive format for comparing similar texts, such as different versions of fairy tales. For example, students might read the traditional Cinderella tale along with *Yeh-Shen: A Cinderella Story From China* (retold by Ai-Ling Louie) and a Native American version, *The Rough-Face Girl* (Rafe Martin). They could write their comparisons on a three-part Venn diagram like that illustrated here, inserting characteristics that are similar in the overlapping spaces. They can also draw unique characters or story elements from each of the books in the corresponding circle. The ReadWriteThink website (www.readwritethink.org) has an interactive tool that you can use to make Venn diagrams with your class or that students could use on their own.

Another research-based strategy to integrate knowledge and ideas is to encourage students to use their prior knowledge to think about connections between what they are reading and other texts they have read, their own experiences, and what they know about the world (Pardo 2004). Here are some prompts and questions to get them started.

Text-to-text—Compare and contrast this text to something else you have read.

Have I read something similar in another book or story?

What differences are there in this text compared with another text?

What evidence from the text can I give to support my comparisons between the texts?

Text-to-self—Compare and contrast this text to something you have experienced.

Has something similar happened to me?

Have I felt or experienced this before?

Can I identify with the characters? In what ways?

Text-to-world—Compare and contrast this text to something else in the world.

Have I seen or heard about this somewhere in the world?

Is the setting a place or time I have heard or read about?

Range of Reading and Level of Text Complexity

Reading aloud increasingly complex texts is an effective way to introduce students to more rigorous reading challenges as you model and teach the skills they need to understand such texts. Discussing themes, characters, plot, and organization of more advanced texts will enhance students' capacity to tackle them on their own.

Another important way to increase the level of text complexity is to encourage students to read a large number of high-interest texts at their current level. As they become proficient, provide support and coaching to help them gradually advance to more difficult texts.

To expose students to a wide range of interesting texts, provide equal numbers of informational text and literature in multiple genres that will appeal to both boys and girls. Gather books on topics of interest to the students as well as topics that are part of your social studies and science curriculum. Knowing that science standards include knowing about animals and how they survive, if some of the students in your class are interested in learning more about endangered animals, you might locate books about these animals by talking with your school or community librarian. Also have a selection of books in children's home languages. Building a diverse classroom library takes time. In addition to the books you buy yourself, seek the assistance of families and community members who might be willing to contribute books. Supplement your own supply with books from your school and community libraries. Be selective about the books you offer to students, however, making sure they have high-quality content, story lines, and messages by choosing books in a variety of genres, including interesting informational text, engaging fiction, and appealing poetry and texts that represent positive, non-stereotypic gender

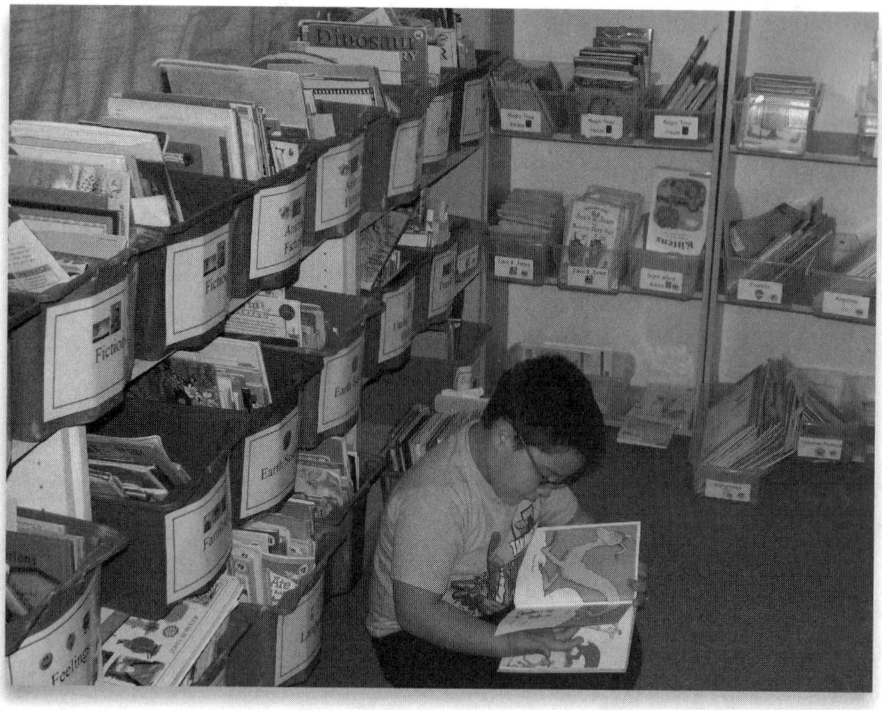

roles, as well as cultural, racial, and linguistic diversity (Machado 2013). The Association for Library Service to Children has lists of books that have won the Caldecott, Newberry, and Pura Belpré awards at www.ala.org/alsc/awardsgrants/bookmedia.

Sort books by topic, genre, or reading level and store them in labeled plastic containers or book baskets. Family members might enjoy helping with the initial organization and then volunteer weekly to help the students reorganize the books. Students could decorate the boxes with pictures from calendars, magazines, or their own art. Label the boxes in English and in children's home languages, and cover the label and decoration with clear contact paper.

It is important for students to enjoy the books they are reading. Studies show that influential factors in students' reading success are having easy access to *high-interest* books and having a *choice* in their selection of books. These factors increase the amount of time students want to spend reading, and the *time* students spend engaged in reading makes a significant difference in their reading development (Calkins, Ehrenworth, & Lehman 2012). Primary teacher Melissa Sweger has a box of "Friday books" that includes joke and riddle books and similar high-interest books. Only being able to access them once a week makes these books and reading seem like a special treat.

Research-Based Strategies Related to Text Complexity

Supply books that are at a slightly more difficult level for students but that they are highly motivated to read, and provide supports such as those that follow (Calkins, Ehrenworth, & Lehman 2012).

- Introduce the book, providing some background and what readers should look for as they read. Activate their prior knowledge by helping them make connections between the topic and their own life experiences. Ask them to predict what might happen in the book.
- Read aloud the first chapter of more difficult texts and discuss them with students to get them interested and gain a basic understanding of the storyline or topic. Talk about the plot, characters, setting, and the author's point of view. Make these texts available in the classroom library for future reading.
- Provide an audio version of the book for students to listen to.

To encourage children to read a variety of text types, Reutzel and colleagues (2008) suggests using a genre wheel with several different genres, such as mystery, sports, fantasy, biography, and poetry, listed on the pie-shaped segments of the wheel. Students have their own genre wheel and color each segment after reading a book corresponding to that genre, with the expectation that they will color the entire wheel by a certain time. Students can also keep track of their reading in a simple log containing columns for title, author, genre, and their comments about the book. Exposing students to a wide variety of topics and genres helps them learn what they love, which can lead to a desire to read and learn more. Motivation to read is one of the best gifts teachers can help a child discover; it is essential to becoming a competent reader.

Assessment. This is a critical component of teaching that helps students meet standards. The process of assessment identifies students' current skills, knowledge, and reading levels so teachers can help students read texts of increasing levels of difficulty. Once you know the areas in which a student is struggling, you can work with the student individually and in small groups to address the challenges. The sooner you identify and address the need, the easier it is for the child to make progress. Taking notes as you listen to students read, conferencing, observing, using running records, and keeping anecdotal notes on children's progress are all authentic assessments that help inform teaching. Many districts use standards-based report cards that list key standards students must meet at each grade level. The report card can serve as a checklist of skills that need to be assessed.

Assessment data helps teachers identify students who are ready for more advanced work as well as those who need additional help. Make sure that all students have texts at their current level to boost fluency and confidence as well as books just beyond their current reading level to help them comprehend text with increasingly higher levels of complexity. Let students know what they can work on when they finish their current work so they always have something to do that will help them develop their reading abilities. Options for independent work can be shown on a chart hanging in the room or in a work folder students keep with them. The folder might include a calendar or checklist that includes items such as check your work, write in a journal, research a topic of interest, or work in centers or on special take-to-your-seat center activities. Each student's folder could also contain an individualized booklist with texts at their current reading level, as well as one level beyond to support and deepen the level of text complexity they are reading. Change the items on the list weekly or monthly as appropriate.

CCSS Foundational Reading Skills

The Foundational Skills section of the CCSS contains standards for Print Concepts and Phonological Awareness, Phonics and Word Recognition, and Fluency. The standards for Print Concepts and Phonological Awareness are written for kindergarten and first grade only. The other standards are for kindergarten and first, second, and third grades (as well as fourth and fifth grades).

Engaging Learners With Print Concepts and Phonological Awareness

Beginning readers need to have a basic understanding of the organization and features of print, as well as the connection between sounds, syllables, and words. Once children have these skills, usually by the end of first grade, teachers typically do not need to spend much time on this instruction.

Alphabet, alphabetic principle, and phonological awareness. To successfully read and write, students must know the alphabet and understand the alphabetic principle, the idea that letters and letter combinations have sounds associated with them. They also need to learn phonological awareness, the understanding of the sound structure of language, including being able to segment words into syllables and blend syllables into words, as well as hear and produce rhymes. Most children master these skills through shared reading experiences, games, and songs, with additional small group instruction in segmenting and blending.

Phonemic awareness. The ability to hear and manipulate individual sounds in spoken words—phonemic awareness—is a subset of phonological awareness. To help students acquire phonemic awareness, the National Reading Panel recommends using enjoyable activities that will enhance students' motivation to learn: "This instruction should seem like play, and songs and games can easily be part of the phonemic awareness routines in the classroom" (Shanahan 2005, 10). Create simple bingo cards, placing an initial sound, blend, ending sound, or other feature in each square. Playing this version of bingo is a fun way for children to practice the alphabet and phonemic awareness. Students can play with a partner or in small or large groups. You could also ask students to sit in a circle and play a sound game focusing on initial and final sounds in words. For example, focus on the letter "T" and ask students to jump up when you say a word that beings with a /t/ sound and give one clap if it ends with a /t/ sound. They can sit if you say a word that does not begin or end with the /t/ sounds. Switch sounds the next time you play the game.

Rhythm and rhyme. Have a different student serve as line leader each day. As the other children get in line, they use the beginning sound in their names to rhyme with the leader's name (for example, if the leader is *Felipe,* Sam would say *Selipe,* and Tanya would say *Telipe).* Rhyming songs that incorporate children's names are especially inviting and effective in promoting children's phonological awareness. Make your own big book of rhyming songs that you and the children enjoy singing. Laminate the pages; point to the words as you sing together. Store the book in the classroom library where children can continue to sharpen their skills and enjoy playing with the sounds of language.

Frequently read rhyming books and encourage children to join in on the rhymes. Judy Sierra's *Wild About Books* has enjoyable rhythm and rhyme, along with a story children love that focuses on the joy of reading. It is also available in Spanish: *¡Qué locura por la lectura!* Another book with wonderful rhythm is *Take Me Out to the Yakyu* by Aaron Meshon. Integrate phonological awareness activities in your daily routine throughout the day, such as practicing tongue twisters together when you have a few extra moments.

Engaging Learners With Phonics and Word Recognition

One of the major goals of phonics instruction is to help students develop the letter–sound concepts they need to read and write. These concepts begin with phonemic awareness, which enables students to decode words by blending sounds and segmenting spoken words into sounds, which they can then write. The National Reading Panel recommends that phonics instruction be integrated with other reading instruction, including a focus on fluency and comprehension strategies, to create a comprehensive reading program (Shanahan 2005). The panel states that it is critical for teachers to understand that phonics instruction be entertaining, vibrant, and creative. They suggest that systematic phonics instruction is particularly helpful through second grade, with review later as students encounter more challenging words. Children who experience decoding difficulties, however, will need additional help until they have mastered these skills.

Word and picture sorts. One effective and enjoyable way to help students practice phonics skills, as well as enhance their vocabulary and spelling proficiency, is through word and picture sorts. A word sort uses cards that have different words (for readers) or pictures (for emerging readers) printed on each card. The students sort the cards, using the words or the pictures, into categories based on a certain characteristic such as the number of syllables, blends, or those containing short vowel and long vowel sounds. This activity heightens students' awareness of words and helps them attend to the critical features of words. The teacher might suggest how to sort or students can use critical thinking skills to determine how to sort the words. Make word or picture cards using words from grade-level reading and spelling texts or from lists available on the Internet, such as those found at www.carlscorner.us.com/sorts.htm. The readwritethink.org website from IRA and NCTE have interactive online word sorting activities students can do. There are also word and picture cards, game boards, and many innovative ways to do the sorts in the *Words Their Way* (Bear et al. 2012) text and program, which supports foundational reading skills.

Prefixes and suffixes. Learning about prefixes and suffixes helps students meet the CCSS related to phonics, word recognition, and vocabulary. To make this enjoyable for students, explain that prefixes and suffixes are clues to use in their detective work of decoding and reading words. Focus on a new prefix or suffix each week, reviewing those already learned by playing charades. Students will enjoy acting out words they know, such as ***re****wind,* ***un****wrap,* ***dis****connect, throw****ing****, or strong****er****.* Make a visual display to which you add each new prefix or suffix along with its meaning and some examples. Be creative with the display—for example, display a large picture of a bike on a bulletin board or chart and label the front tire prefixes and the back tire suffixes. Add each new prefix or suffix and its meaning as a spoke on the appropriate wheel. Learning prefixes, suffixes, and common root words will help all children, especially dual language learners whose home language has similarities to English.

Sight words. Decoding skills alone are not sufficient to help students read fluently. Almost half of the words in the English language do not fit phonetic patterns and therefore need to be memorized as sight words. There are also a number of high-frequency words that are used repeatedly in text. Helping children learn these high-frequency words will greatly improve their ability to read (Graves et al. 2014). Jan Brett (www.janbrett.com) has free mini-posters with high-frequency words that you can use to make word sorts and other word games for students.

Engaging Learners With Fluency

Being able to read fluently is one of the characteristics of successful readers. Fluency also aids in comprehension, another critical factor in reading.

Practice and rereading. As with so many other skills, practice strengthens fluency. Rereading favorite books and poems to the class helps students when they read those materials themselves. Predictable books and books with patterns, such as *Compost Stew: An A to Z Recipe for the Earth* (Mary McKenna Siddals) and *Do You Know Which Ones Will Grow?* (Susan A. Shea), provide support for emergent readers and children who have difficulty reading. Having students reread texts at their independent reading level also supports fluency. Students can read texts multiple times to themselves, to peers, or to older students. Asking classroom volunteers to listen and provide support to individual children reading can be especially helpful for children who struggle with reading.

Singing. Singing is a natural and enjoyable way to practice fluency. Write the words of favorite songs on a large piece of chart paper or a whiteboard and point to words as you sing the songs together. You can also use high-quality trade books that have words to songs, such as *Sing . . . Sing a Song* (Joe Raposo and Tom Lichtenheld), *I'm in Love With a Big Blue Frog* (Leslie Braunstein), and *Maria Had a Little Llama/María tenía una llama pequeña* (Angela Dominguez). Singing also provides the practice and repetition dual language learners need to read English. Make charts of captivating poems to use in the same ways.

Personal readers. Students' personal readers offer abundant opportunities to practice fluency. Make them by printing copies of poems and songs you have enjoyed together as a class, as well as passages from familiar books, and binding the pages together. You can personalize each child's reader by adding materials at their independent reading level, or make them the same for the whole class. Personal readers can be kept in students' book boxes, in their desks, or on classroom shelves.

Readers Theater. In Readers Theater students read from scripts they have practiced but not memorized, which enhances fluency and comprehension and motivates children to read. You can choose from numerous scripts available in books and online, such as those at www.teachingheart.net/readerstheater.htm and www.thebestclass.org/rtscripts.html. Students can also rehearse and read material they have written themselves, which provides added incentive for writing. Vasinda and McLeod (2011) found that combining podcasting with Readers Theater produced significant gains in reading scores for second- and third-graders who struggled with reading. Students were excited to podcast their productions and practiced a great deal to put on a quality event that their families and friends could later listen to.

Echo reading and choral reading. To provide a good model of fluency and expression for students, try echo reading. Read aloud a line of text, then ask the child to read the same line. Continue taking turns to help the student read more fluently and expressively. Choral reading—when individuals and small or large groups read together—also provides models for children to follow and decreases the anxiety some children feel when reading aloud by themselves.

The National Reading Panel found that repeated oral reading and pairs reading with texts at students' instruction level with one-on-one feedback during the reading from a teacher, parent, or peer has a positive impact on fluency, word recognition, and comprehension. This is true for students at all levels. The panel also found these practices to be more effective than round-robin reading, in which children take turns, which shows a benefit only to the child reading (Shanahan 2005).

Nurturing Young Writers

Reading and writing skills develop at the same time and strengthen and support each other. As children progress in understanding the mechanics of reading, they also gain a better understanding of the writing process; the reverse is also true. With improved writing skills, students express their thoughts more effectively and are able to document what they are learning in other areas of the curriculum.

Writers' Workshop

To become better writers, students need to write frequently. Set aside time each day for a writers' workshop to ensure that students have adequate time to study mechanics and to write. Writers' workshop is done in a similar format as the readers' workshop, allowing teachers to differentiate and help students develop writing skills, build confidence, and enjoy the writing process. Many teachers like to plan a literacy block that includes a writers' workshop after a readers' workshop or reading time.

Writers' Workshop Mini-Lessons

As with readers' workshops, a writers' workshop often begins with a mini-lesson focusing on specific skills and strategies. This whole group lesson, typically lasts five to ten minutes depending on children's ages and the skill addressed. These mini-lessons are designed to add new tools to each student's writer's toolbox, as well as reinforce previously introduced writing strategies. Establish a signal to let students know it is time to gather at the meeting area for a mini-lesson to begin the writers' workshop. While demonstrating a writing skill on chart paper or a whiteboard, express your thoughts aloud to help students learn to put the skills into practice more easily.

Here are some possible topics for mini-lessons:

- Stretch out words to help students listen for the individual sounds. To give students a visual image, stretch out a slinky while you explain the technique.
- Construct a story map together that serves as a guide for later writing.
- Address writing in different genres, adding dialogue, working on stronger beginnings and endings, adding details, or writing so others can understand the message.
- Teach children how to decide on a topic or make mental plans for writing.
- Make a class list of strategies good writers use.

Teach writing skills in meaningful and motivating units of study (Calkins, Tolan, & Ehrenworth 2010) designed around concepts students can relate to. For example, Pomperaug Regional School District 15 in Connecticut uses unit titles such as *I'm a Reader and Writer, Getting to Know Characters, Making Friends—Keeping Friends,* and *Ingredients of a Mystery* for the primary grades, integrating a variety of genre, concepts, and processes (Lanning 2013). In a character study, students can acquire and strengthen a variety of reading and writing skills. They learn about different genres, including biography and autobiography, by reading and writing in these genres. They make inferences about characters based on evidence from the text and use that evidence in their writing. They also discover more about character trait development through their reading. A character study is an excellent way for students to learn how to add dialogue to their writing.

Independent Writing

Setting up the writers' workshop requires careful planning to have a consistent routine that students can follow with ease and continue working independently while you work with other children. It works well to follow the mini-lesson with 15 to 20 minutes of individual writing or longer depending on student interest and ability. At the beginning of the year you might allot less time for writing and increase it as students progress. Let students choose where they want to write, or have them go to an assigned writing spot. Meanwhile, you will be available to work with individual students to scaffold their writing and help them gain strategies that will build their confidence as writers.

During the writers' workshop students might continue working on a prior piece of writing or start a new topic—either one they choose or a prompt that you assign. The prompt could relate to a book they are reading, social studies and science concepts they are exploring, or a situation related to their own lives: "Imagine you are living in the time of . . ." or "You just witnessed a volcanic explosion . . ." or "A new family just moved into your neighborhood . . ." Inviting students to choose their topic at least some of the time can motivate them to do more in-depth writing. Young writers who have difficulty getting started may find it helpful to start by illustrating what they are thinking, and then describing what they have drawn. Assure students that writers do not always know how to spell every word they want to use, and encourage them to put down their thoughts and edit later. Provide tools, such as writing dictionaries, to support them. Writing dictionaries can be purchased commercially or made by stapling or binding paper together to make a book with one page for each letter of the alphabet. During the writers' workshop throughout the year, help individual students add words they want to use in their writing but are having difficulty spelling to appropriate pages. You could also add a new word to the writing dictionary each day with the whole group to increase their vocabulary.

Partner talk. If students become restless during the writing time, you might refocus their attention by asking them to talk with a partner for a few minutes about a specific writing skill. You could also suggest something specific for them to work on, such as adding descriptive words that give the reader a better visual image of the topic. This helps students get back on track. If students finish writing before the end of the workshop, encourage them to add a few more details. They could also add an illustration, proofread for clarity or grammar, or apply another strategy you have introduced.

Writing portfolio. Keeping a collection of students' writing is an excellent way for teachers to evaluate students' work—not only their writing but also their reading skills (Calkins, Ehrenworth, & Lehman 2012). It also encourages students to review and assess their development as writers. Students can store their writing in a two-pocket folder or other type of portfolio. Ask students to begin each piece of writing by writing the date or using a date stamp. This will help both you and the student see the writing progress made over time. Students may also write on a computer or other device. Their writing can be dated and stored in a labeled digital folder.

Writing conferences. As children write, the teacher's role is to support, encourage, and help them learn and expand their writing skills. Writing conferences with individual students give you time to focus on one child and allow you to differentiate your teaching to meet students' specific needs. Set up a weekly schedule, assigning each student to a day of the week so you are sure to check in with every student. Make a chart such as the one shown in the figure "Sample Writing Conference Schedule," listing students' names and goals to document the individual sessions. Review the goals for each student to determine the mini-lessons that would be most beneficial for the whole group and to organize small groups of students who need to work on the same skill. As other students are writing independently, you could occasionally work with small groups in a guided writing format, jointly composing a short piece of writing and providing modeling and support for those who need it.

Sample Writing Conference Schedule

Student Name	Current Goal	New Goal
Monday		
Tuesday		
Wednesday		
Thursday		
Friday		

Vygotsky (1978) talked about the early years as a time when children are able to understand increasingly complex ideas as their teachers and peers scaffold their learning in their *zone of proximal development* (ZPD). He suggested that adults start with what children can do independently and help them to more advanced levels one step at a time. To find this zone for each child, you must continually observe and do formative, authentic assessments to find students' levels of functioning and their gaps in understanding. Use this information to inform your instruction and decide on next steps to build on children's current knowledge and skills. Writing conferences are an ideal way to authentically assess children and then scaffold their writing progress. Involving students in self-assessment makes them more aware of the learning process and more invested in setting and reaching new learning goals. Students actually score higher on content tests when they have had the opportunity to assess themselves (Combs 2012).

Mrs. Santiago begins her writing conference with Nili by asking her to describe what she is writing. Mrs. Santiago listens carefully, knowing that this will help her learn a great deal of information about what Nili is thinking and where there are gaps in her understanding. She points out the descriptive words Nili is using and other positive aspects of her writing. Then she asks Nili what she thinks she can do to elaborate on her topic, and adds one quick teaching point she thinks will help Nili advance her writing at this point. Mrs. Santiago and Nili look at Nili's current writing goal, and she asks Nili to show her how she has demonstrated that goal in her writing. Together they discuss and agree on a new target to take Nili's writing to the next step. Mrs. Santiago knows that goal setting is a critical skill for children to learn, one they will need the rest of their lives. She provides a goal sheet for each of her students to keep in their writing portfolios to help them remember the goal they are working toward (see "Sample Student Writing Goal Sheet"). She also uses it as a record for evaluating her students' progress. Mrs. Santiago ends her writing conference with Nili with words of encouragement and begins a conference with another child.

Sample Student Writing Goal Sheet	
Week	My Writing Goal

Author's Chair

Writing is more meaningful and motivating for students when they share it with an audience. Close the writers' workshop with an author's chair, in which students share their work with the whole group. Students sign up to share their work in the author's chair, two to three students per day. Be sure that all students have an opportunity to share over the course of a week or two. Peers may comment on what they like about the piece, make constructive suggestions, or ask questions to clarify the writing. Explain that it is important to provide only positive and constructive comments. Modeling this yourself will help students understand how to support each other's efforts. To reinforce specific writing skills, ask students to watch for a particular feature in the writing that is being shared. Partners can also read their work to each other and provide constructive feedback and encouragement as a variation on the author's chair.

Writers' Workshop Components

Component	Description
Opening Mini-Lesson	Teacher models a writing strategy with the whole group.
Independent Writing, Conferences, and Small Group Mini-Lessons	Students write independently. Teacher confers with individuals and provides mini-lessons to small groups as needed.
Author's Chair	Several students share a piece of writing they have been working on during the writers' workshop. Teacher reinforces writing strategies student authors have demonstrated.

Celebrating Students' Writing

An Author's Celebration, held at the end of each quarter, unit of literacy study, or other times, provides motivation for students to work on their writing. The celebration could be a Meet the Authors Day when family members, the principal, or another class come to admire the writing samples. Ask the authors to write a short autobiography to post next to their writing. The class could also host an Authors' Tea or Poetry Party with children's work displayed on a bulletin board or simply placed on each desk for guests to read. The celebration could be for the class, with students taking turns reading their work to each other in partners, in small groups, or to the class.

Engaging Learners With Writing

The CCSS put equal emphasis on writing and reading. The goals of the writing standards include students being able to think critically and deeply about topics and write clearly with well-defined main points and relevant details. Young students begin this process as they learn that one thing can represent another—one letter can stand for a sound, a group of letters can stand for a word, and a group of words can represent a thought, an idea, or a concept. They come to understand that the purpose of writing is to convey a message that makes sense to the reader. These understandings are best accomplished through authentic tasks, such as writing letters, thank-you notes, and invitations to real events.

Try This!

Upload videos to your class web page of students reading their writing for family members to view and share. Students might write about a regular featured topic, for example, animals or history facts that students find interesting or hard to believe. Encourage students to decide on a clever title for the feature, such as "Believe It or Not!"

The CCSS call for children to use reading, writing, speaking, language, and listening skills in an integrated fashion. Students learn these skills most effectively when the skills are taught in collaboration with each other. Having children write from their own experiences and *encode* their thoughts is a successful way for them to learn how to *decode* and read. Writing is emphasized in the Common Core "as a tool that develops children's critical thinking and learning across subject areas" (Evenson et al. 2013, 45). Writing also helps students build foundational skills and a deeper understanding of the basic features of print.

Text Types and Purposes

Before students can express themselves in all the formats required by the CCSS, they need to read and discuss a variety of texts to experience what authors do to convey meaning. An excellent teaching tool is the use of *mentor texts,* which are writing samples that provide a good model of the type of writing you are trying to teach. Examples could come from texts all students have, classroom or library books, or a portion of an exemplary text displayed on poster board or an interactive whiteboard. Draw students' attention to the features of good writing by asking questions such as "What makes this a good example?" and "What do you like about this introduction, ending, and style of writing?" Reading from mentor texts is also an engaging way to introduce a new genre.

Opinion writing. Opinion or persuasive writing presents the author's view on a subject. It provides facts to support the reasoning and may try to convince readers to change their mind on a topic. Young readers learn to express and broaden their thinking as they write and draw in response to a text they have read (Pinnell & Fountas 2007). This could be done in a Reading Response Journal or on a form that asks for reflections on specific topics. Students might make predictions, inferences, and character comparisons and provide evidence and examples from the text to validate their opinions. In addition to writing in response to texts they have read, encourage students to write opinion pieces on a variety of topics, which might include why an important person in their lives is special to them or why they like a certain sport or event. You might also ask them to write an opinion piece for a school newspaper or a letter to school administrators, trying to persuade them to do something the student believes would improve the school.

Informative/explanatory writing. Informative or explanatory writing provides the what, how, and why of a topic. Another way to introduce students to writing different types of text and gain experience in informative writing is through the use of Meet the Author studies. Students read multiple texts by an author to learn more about a particular genre and discover that author's style. Many authors have websites students can explore, such as Mo Willems's site at http://gomo.net. To gain experience in writing informative or explanatory texts, students could write a report on the life of their favorite author. They can read books by the author, read about the author's life, and even write a letter to the author, explaining what they like about the author's style and asking for more information. You might also help the class compose an email to favorite authors.

Writing autobiographies can be an appealing way to gain experience in explanatory writing. Mrs. Chang, who teaches second grade, began a study of autobiographies by reading a mentor text, *The Moccasins* by Earl Einarson, an autobiographical account of a young Native American foster child, that portrays different types of families and the love they have for each other. After reading the autobiography, she asked the students to draw something they treasure. The following day, she brought in a small wooden top her grandfather had played with as a child, one of her treasured possessions. She wrote her own short autobiographical sketch on the whiteboard, including the day her grandfather had given her the top and how proud she felt when she could make it spin. Then she asked the students to write about the treasured objects they had drawn the day before, using rich descriptions of the object and why they valued the object.

Narrative writing. Narrative writing tells about something real or imaginary that happens, including a beginning, middle, and ending in sequential order. One technique to strengthen students' ability to write descriptive narratives is to ask them to write about different times of the day using as many colorful words as they can. For the morning's first activity one day, ask them to describe a morning. Another day after lunch, have them write a description of an afternoon setting. Homework one night can be to imaginatively describe an evening before bed. Try this during different seasons. Go to various places in your school on different days, asking students to describe the classroom, the library, lunchroom, or playground. If possible, take them to a natural setting or view various settings online and ask them to write a description of what they see. Students can keep these descriptions in their writing portfolio and use them in future narrative writing.

Story maps and other graphic organizers help children organize their thinking for narrative and other types of writing. The organizer might be as simple as writing *First, Next, Then, Finally* or *Setting, Characters, Problem, Solution* on the whiteboard. Next, lead the class in writing a short narrative together on the board, following these prompts. This group activity helps students better grasp how to do this on their own. You could also create a simple graphic organizer form for students to fill in or use one of the interactive online story mapping tools at www.readwritethink.org. Students can use the form as an outline for their narrative, adding in description and detail. Using these forms on a regular basis helps students become more familiar and comfortable with the process.

As a way to grow in their ability to develop characters, students can write a response to a book they have read from the perspective of one

Try This!

Make descriptive writing engaging by making it part of a weekly game. Have students write a description of something without naming it. Encourage them to add details and use descriptive words. Then have students take turns reading their descriptions aloud while their classmates guess what they have written about. This can be a motivating activity that students look forward to each week. Throughout the week, students think about what they will describe and write notes in a journal. Some weeks have designated topics, and other weeks are writers' choice. Students help determine topics for the following week, which might correspond with books they are reading or units of study.

Another activity is for students to write their descriptions on a piece of paper folded in half, with the description on the front and the answer folded underneath. Post these descriptions on a bulletin board or hallway for other students to guess what is described.

of the characters. They might also look for different types of hats or headpieces—a helmet, hardhat, baseball cap, crown—on the Internet, draw or create one themselves, and write a story from the viewpoint of someone who might wear that hat. This would make an intriguing bulletin board or hallway display to highlight children's writing skills for families, administrators, and other classes.

Writing collaborative stories is an enjoyable way for students to practice writing narratives and hone their descriptive skills. One student begins by writing the description of the setting of an invented story and then hands it to a partner, who adds a description of the characters. They pass the story back and forth or give it to a third person, as they add a conflict and then a solution. Writing scripts to perform in Readers Theater or as a play is another motivating way for students to practice composing narratives.

Dual Language Learners

Dual language learners may be able to write fluently in their home language. If this is the case, help them translate their writing into English by working with an adult or with a peer or independently by using a picture dictionary or word wall. Websites by well-known dual language learner experts Larry Ferlazzo (www.larryferlazzo.edublogs.org) and Judie Haynes (www.everythingesl.net) provide resources and guidance for teaching dual language learners in elementary school.

Poetry writing. Writing poetry is another way for students to express opinions and write narratives or informative pieces. Writing poetry can also deepen students' understanding of the genre itself. Similarly, reading poetry provides inspiration for students' writing. Write poems together as a class occasionally. Ask students to use their senses and write about the way something looks, sounds, smells, feels, and/or tastes. Students can write simple, vibrant poems about the sounds, smells, and sights of their neighborhoods and then use this experience to write about other objects, sounds, or events they encounter.

Katharine Walmsley likes to read poetry to her primary students from books such as *Silver Seeds* by Paul Paolilli and Dan Brewer, in which the authors create poems by using each letter of a word. Students can try writing this type of poem using their names or words related to a study topic or their interests. For example, Magdalena wrote a poem about the sky:

> **S**ilvery clouds slipping by
> **K**issing the earth
> **Y**ellow sunflowers against the beautiful blue

This type of poetry provides a structure that facilitates writing. It would also be motivating for young writers to contribute to a class book of poetry that is added to the classroom library and shared with families.

Production and Distribution of Writing

Students need to revise, edit, and add details to their writing. Encourage them to think about what they really want to communicate, and ask open-ended questions that help them include more details and descriptive language.

Focusing on a topic. Pictures from nature calendars or magazines and interesting science objects fuel students' ideas for writing and offer opportunities for honing their descriptive skills. There are also many short videos on the Internet, such as those about animals, geography, and science or other countries and cultures. Ask students to describe what they see using vivid language that allows the reader to picture it, even though they cannot see it. Or, students could take digital photos, print them, and write text captions to describe what appears in the photos. Have the class create a book containing each student's photograph and accompanying text.

Organizing ideas. Primary students can benefit from illustrating their writing. They often add details in their sketches that they can then describe with words. Sentence frames and patterned writing, which provide a model for students to follow and require them to fill in just a few words, can be especially helpful for writers who struggle.

> To kick off a social studies unit on communities, Mr. Sherlock provides his students with this sentence frame: What I like about living in ________ is _______. The next day he takes the students to a neighborhood fire station. When they return, each student fills in the sentence frame: At the fire station they have _______ to ________. If I worked at the fire station, I would like to ________. He binds their pages together in a class book that students take turns taking home to share with their families.

Students could also dictate a short story or description that you transcribe, talking out loud as you write their words and add punctuation. Children can then practice reading it back to you several times. You may find that these strategies help dual language learners with their writing. Encourage all students to elaborate on their writing, adding descriptive language to help their readers visualize the ideas they are trying to communicate.

Display anchor charts around the room to serve as writing references, such as one describing the stages of the writing process:

1. Planning and prewriting
2. Drafting
3. Revising
4. Proofreading and editing
5. Publishing and sharing

If you develop these charts with student input, students will find them more meaningful.

Adding details. Create anchor charts with questions students ask themselves and each other to help elaborate on their writing. Here is an example.

After writing your informative draft, ask

What else did you learn or do you know about your topic?

What other details could you add?

What other describing words could you use to help others understand your topic?

After writing your narrative draft, ask

Is there anything else about the setting you could add?

What else can you tell the reader about the character?

What other details could you add?

What other describing words could you use to help others feel like they are watching your story?

Revising. To meet the CCSS, revision needs to be a natural part of students' writing process. Help students become comfortable and effective at revising by making it a positive experience. Encourage students to find ways to improve their writing, and talk about the fact that this is what authors do. Some teachers provide special editing pens or pencils as a motivation to make revising and editing more enjoyable. Students might even use multiple color pens for different aspects of their editing. For example, they might use a green pen or pencil to revise their punctuation, blue to add additional descriptive words, and purple to edit spelling and grammar (this would not all be done at once!). Emphasize the importance of rereading what they have written to identify where, for example, dialog sounds off or they have not explained something sufficiently. They should ask themselves questions like "Does this sound right?" and "Is something missing?" Revising will be more effective and allow students to stay more motivated and creative if you limit the number of pieces you ask students to revise.

Using technology to enhance writing. Some students enjoy writing on a computer, tablet, or other digital device instead of on paper. Using a computer or digital device also makes the revision process easier and more routine. To be college and career ready, as the CCSS expects, students need to use digital tools effectively. Google Apps for Education, a free service for schools, provides a suite of tools that are especially helpful, including tools for word processing and creating, storing, and sharing presentations and videos. Schools can sign up at www.google.com/enterprise/apps/education, but individual teachers can access most of these tools simply by signing up for a free Google account. In his book *Google Apps Meets Common Core* (2013), teacher Michael Graham describes how these tools can help students meet standards. View his helpful resources, links, and videos online at goo.gl/Envlf.

Google Drive enables teachers and students to store and share documents with each other, which greatly facilitates the editing process. In Google Drive and in other word processing programs, you can edit a student's work electronically and return it with immediate feedback, including adding comments. The *StoryBuddy* app (available for Apple and Android devices) can boost students' interest in writing and make the revision process more enjoyable. Search for free sites students can use to make word clouds, an excellent way to motivate students to use more descriptive words. Students type words or paste a previously written piece about themselves, a character, or a setting into the word cloud program, resulting in an attractive cloud of words they have created. For example,

> Mrs. Nash's third grade class creates a word cloud about their class. One day during writers' workshop, Mrs. Nash asks each student to write descriptive words about their class. The next day she asks them to highlight one of the words that would best describe their class and check

for correct spelling in their dictionaries. She asks Peter, who is good at keyboarding, to type in the words on the laptop connected to the interactive whiteboard as each child shares and spells a descriptive word. Once the word cloud is completed, she prints and hangs it outside their classroom door.

3rd Grade Word Cloud

Once a month Teacher Kayla Loecker supports her first grade students by working in small groups to write stories on an interactive whiteboard. Depending on their ability, each child dictates or types one or more sentences to add to a story. Afterward, she provides each child a printed page with his sentence to illustrate, then binds the completed pages into a class book.

Students enjoy creating PowerPoint presentations related to study topics or story narratives. Many students find the smaller space on each slide to be less intimidating than filling an entire blank page. You can print two or four slides to a page and collate them into a small book.

Publishing. Publishing their writing, either individually or in class books, provides a strong incentive for students to revise and edit. Provide cardstock or construction paper for students to make covers for completed, edited stories. For a more durable and decorative cover, they can cover the cardstock with wallpaper, colored duct tape, or wrapping paper. Students can practice using their best penmanship to write their published works or use a computer. Place the finished books in the classroom library and celebrate the authors!

Research to Build and Present Knowledge

The CCSS include the expectation that primary grade students will research a topic using multiple sources, analyze the information, and base their writing on facts and evidence they have read and documented. To model the report-writing process, offer several science and social studies topics and ask the class to choose one that interests them. Together, create a list of questions or facts they want to learn about the topic. For example, if students choose the topic of marsupials, they may be interested in knowing which animals are marsupials, how long babies stay in their mothers' pouches, and where they live. Demonstrate how to use a form such as the one shown in the figure "Sample Form for Organizing Research" to organize research on the topic. Together, look up information from a number of sources, such as http://kids.nationalgeographic.com/kids/, a nonfiction book on marsupials, and a *Ranger Rick* magazine article. Show the class how to look up the information needed and record it on the form. Then use a whiteboard to collaboratively compose a short research report based on the information collected. Finally, ask for suggestions on editing for grammar, punctuation, and clarity. The Florida Center for Reading Research has additional forms and suggestions at www.fcrr.org/studentactivities/writing.htm.

On another day develop an anchor chart together that lists the steps in writing a research report or essay. Your list might including the following:

1. Choose a topic.
2. List questions and areas you want to learn more about.

3. Read from several trusted sources.
4. Organize the information you read.
5. Start with a topic sentence to interest the reader.
6. Include the information you found.
7. Close with a strong summary sentence.

Sample Form for Organizing Research

TOPIC: ______________________

	Question or Subcategory #1	Question or Subcategory #2	Question or Subcategory #3
Reference #1 Title ________			
Reference #2 Title ________			
Reference #3 Title ________			

Rubrics help students understand the expectations for research reports and assignments and gives them specific objectives to work toward. Encourage students to use rubrics to evaluate their writing on their own and when working with partners. Identifying and evaluating specific points in another's writing can help students do the same with their own. Education Northwest, a regional educational laboratory, developed the 6+1 Trait Writing Model of Instruction and Assessment, a writing model that describes a framework and rubric that define quality writing. They offer a crosswalk between the traits included in the writing rubric and the CCSS, grade-specific lesson plans, scoring guides, and other resources at http://educationnorthwest.org/traits.

Rubrics can be differentiated for individual learners. Students who find writing challenging can focus on fewer key points, and those who are ready for additional challenges can use more advanced skills and do additional research and presentations on topics that interest them.

Range of Writing

The CCSS include an expectation that third grade students will be able to write for a variety of purposes and for multiple types of audiences. To meet this standard students need many opportunities to express their thoughts in writing and to cite facts and details to support their opinions. They also need a sizable vocabulary to assist in word choice. It is important that teachers help students increase the complexity of their writing rather than focus on perfection, which can hinder that growth (Calkins, Ehrenworth, & Lehman 2012). Most students will improve their writing if they have ample opportunities to write every day. Even short periods throughout the day will help, combined with longer periods when they are researching a topic. The amount of time spent will depend on students' age and purpose for writing.

Try This!

Make an anchor chart with the students to remind them to think about strategies good writers use as they write. You can use the 6+1 Traits as a framework. Your chart may look like this:

I write clearly with a main idea and supporting details. (IDEAS)

I arrange my writing with a good beginning, middle, and ending that help readers understand my meaning. (ORGANIZATION)

I write so my audience wants to keep reading my unique words. (VOICE)

I use new and amazing words that create pictures in my readers' minds. (WORD CHOICE)

I vary my sentences, and my writing flows when I read it out loud. (SENTENCE FLUENCY)

I use correct capital letters, punctuation, and spelling. (CONVENTIONS)

I write neatly, and it is easy to read. (PRESENTATION)

For example, teachers might have third-graders write a

- Skit, research report, or short book on a specific topic
- Play about pioneers or inventors after researching a topic on the Internet and in books
- Fictional story or an autobiography with chapters on various details and events in the character's or student's life—family and home, town, important events, and so on
- Variety of letters to diverse audiences

Promoting Effective Communication Skills

Teachers want all students to become confident communicators who can express their thoughts clearly through both spoken and written words. The best way to make this a reality is by giving students many opportunities to speak, listen, and write throughout the day. For example, to promote students' speaking and listening skills, begin the day with a morning meeting and provide time for both whole class and small group discussions in different subject areas. Being able to communicate effectively, which requires an extensive vocabulary and strong speaking, listening, writing, and language skills, is one of the twenty-first century skills necessary to function successfully in the world (Partnership for 21st Century Skills 2010).

Engaging Learners With Listening and Speaking

The Speaking and Listening section of the CCSS is divided into two areas: Comprehension and Collaboration, and Presentation of Knowledge and Ideas.

Comprehension and Collaboration

Students need to have good listening skills to work collaboratively with others and understand their points of view. Listening skills also help children comprehend what they hear in text read aloud or other media. Reading time is an opportunity to focus on fostering students' comprehension and collaboration. Designate time for students to read with a partner and discuss the text. Encourage them to ask each other questions, including questions about the meaning of the passage, why their partners believe what they do, and what evidence they found in the text to support their belief.

Improve students' listening skills by giving them reason and motivation to listen. Let them know about special projects or activities they will do after they hear the directions. Model good listening skills yourself as you engage in conversations with students and as they provide answers in class. Provide plenty of time for dual language learners to listen and not feel forced into speaking before they are comfortable.

Presentation of Knowledge and Ideas

Students need to communicate in a clear, concise manner. Give them opportunities to discuss topics with partners, small groups, and large groups, nurturing their self-confidence and ability to share their ideas as well as listen to others. Opportunities for students to share their writing with peers, such as an author's chair or reading to a partner, provide a meaningful context for them to present their ideas. Students can also plan presentations on books they have read, which could include a short skit, poem, mock newscast, song, or other creative approaches. This will help them meet the standards for listening and speaking as well as reading and writing. Creating presentations using PowerPoint, Prezi (www.prezi.com), Google Drive, or other digital options can enrich students' presentation of their knowledge and ideas. Digital media presentations can provide support for dual language learners who can include clipart and photos to help explain their ideas. It will also help them to work with a partner who is more fluent in English and to have ample time to prepare and give their presentations.

Provide books with jokes, riddles, and silly songs, such as *Wise Crackers: Riddles and Jokes About Numbers, Names, Letters, and Silly Words* by Michael Dahl in your classroom library. Students can use the riddles in these books as inspiration in helping them create a Class Brainteaser of the Week. Each week several students pose their riddle or brainteaser, taking turns so each student has a turn every month. Establish ground rules with the class to ensure that classmates treat each other with respect and encouragement as they work on their presentation and listening skills. When students present or simply ask or answer a question, remind them to speak to the whole group, not just the teacher. This improves their skill at presenting information in a routine, nonthreatening way and makes listening more engaging for the other students.

Engaging Learners With Language Development

The Language section of the CCSS is divided into Conventions of Standard English, Knowledge of Language, and Vocabulary Acquisition and Use. Teachers can integrate experiences that address language standards throughout the day along with other reading and writing work.

Conventions of Standard English

Students need to correctly use language and grammar in both their speaking and writing. To help students meet the expectations of the Common Core, Ruday (2013) recommends teaching grammar in the context of writing to help students see the practical use of grammar and to make it more interesting. He also suggests using literature to illustrate the ways language and grammar concepts are applied. To teach the individual grammar concepts required by the CCSS, such as correct use of pronouns, commas, and quotation marks, Ruday recommends that teachers

- Clearly describe the concept and how it can be used as a tool for clear writing
- Provide models from literature that use the concept
- Discuss why the concept aids understanding of that piece of literature
- Ask students to use the concept in their own writing
- Support students in a think-pair-share reflection on ways the concept helped their writing

Grammar. Ruday (2013) recommends assessing grammar concepts by providing short passages from a text that contain a concept, asking students to underline the concept in the text, and then describe how it improves the text. For example, a teacher might ask students to underline pronouns used in a sentence from a text and then explain why the author may have used them. You could provide correct and incorrect examples and ask students to choose the correct example and compare the two sentences, explaining why the chosen sentence is correct. Next, students can write a short piece that contains the concept being assessed, underlining their example of the concept and describing how it helps the writing. With younger children teachers might do this one-on-one and ask them to point and describe their answers verbally. As students progress in their skills they can write responses on their own. Provide a short rubric to guide them.

Spelling. Spelling is an important language skill and helps in the development of reading and writing. Early readers learn to read words before they can spell them. Once children know how to read words, they begin to see patterns in words and apply this knowledge to the spelling of multiple words. Doing activities like word sorts can help students become better spellers in the early grades. Students can use an interactive whiteboard or file cards to sort words by characteristics such as short vowel sounds versus long vowel sounds or contractions versus the full words.

The National Reading Panel concluded that invented-spelling activities—encouraging children to listen to the sounds in words and spell them according to the sounds they identify—support the development of phonemic awareness and phonics learning (Shanahan 2005). With practice, encouragement, and numerous exposures to words in print, students will continue to improve their spelling over time. Focus on high-frequency words and words students choose to use in their writing.

Differentiate the spelling instruction and activities you provide. Challenge students who are gifted with more advanced words; focus on fewer, key words with students who struggle with spelling. However, vocabulary building needs to be handled differently from spelling. All children will benefit from hearing increasingly more advanced language to build their vocabulary.

Knowledge of Language

Inject an element of playfulness when talking about the differences between informal conversational language and more formal written language. For example, ask students to dictate something they might say to a friend. A third grade student might suggest something like "Hey, what's up?" Then talk with the students about how that same phrase might be written more formally, such as "Maria asked Shanise what was new with her." Students might enjoy finding words and phrases for effect, such as, "Paulo pounded his fist on the table to make his point." Placing emphasis on *applying* language skills will help students use them more accurately.

To help students meet the language expectations of the CCSS, Calkins, Ehrenworth and Lehman (2012) recommend that instead of the workbooks and methods often used in the past, educators "teach students the skills and strategies that will make them independent word solvers and writers and speakers who are able to apply meaning, structure, elaboration, and conventions as craft moves to their writing and speaking. The ultimate teacher is you, responding to the needs of your students as they progress along this continuum of expectations, not a series of prepackaged words or disconnected activities" (176).

Vocabulary Acquisition and Use

One of the first grade CCSS language standards is "With guidance and support from adults, demonstrate understanding of word relationships and nuances in word meanings." To help students meet this and other standards related to vocabulary acquisition and use, they need to become word solvers—using strategies to figure out the meanings of words, such as looking at prefixes, suffixes, and context and recognizing smaller words they know in an unknown word. Research shows that vocabulary is strongly related to reading ability, general intelligence, and academic success (Benjamin & Crow 2013). In reviewing studies, the National Reading Panel concluded that the larger the reader's vocabulary, the easier it is to make sense of text. They recommend teaching vocabulary through multiple methods, both indirectly and directly, making sure to actively engage students in the instruction. Reading storybooks and text on computers, listening to others, and studying words before reading text are all effective strategies. The panel members also suggest that enjoyable re-reading of text, as well as learning through everyday experiences and meaningful contexts, such as acting words out, engage the brain more effectively (Shanahan 2005).

Vocabulary is critical to students' success in both reading and writing. The classic study by Hart and Risley (1995) found that children who grow up in families with low incomes know far fewer words when they get to school than their more affluent peers. This difference tends to increase over the years in school. Teachers need to work especially hard to help children who come to school without the benefit of a rich vocabulary. Hands-on experiences, pictures, and video assist with focus and retention. Pre-teaching words that will appear in new stories, using pictures from the book as well as other visuals, will especially benefit students who need more help in building vocabulary. Emphasize high-frequency words students will need in multiple settings but also provide repeated exposure to higher-level vocabulary in context throughout the day in activities and conversations.

After using visuals and other materials to teach vocabulary, encourage students to picture the meaning of new words in their minds. Both YouTube and TeacherTube (www.teachertube.com) have engaging sight word songs that pair music and visuals to help children learn and remember words. Boost speaking skills and oral vocabulary by encouraging student presentations and conversations with you and other students.

Oral vocabulary. Neuman and Wright (2013) emphasize that because oral vocabulary is the foundation of reading, children need to have command of a large, ever-growing vocabulary. To help students meet the expectations of the CCSS, these authors recommend intentionally teaching about 15 words each day in the context of rich science investigations, mathematical problem solving, and other subject areas. These meaningful content-related contexts are the perfect place to teach strong, academic vocabulary in multiple subject areas, such as *compare, contrast, predict,* and *observe.* Children need many opportunities to

Try This!

Neuman and Wright (2013) suggest using word and picture sorts to increase students' vocabulary growth. They recommend using a puppet they call *Picky Peter* to provide additional motivation for the word sorts. You can use your own puppets or stuffed animals for this activity, using names such as *Selective Selena* or *Discerning Diego*. Working with a small group, tell the children that *Selena* is very *selective* and only wants words in the box next to her that are related to a certain topic you are working on. Ask children to name the picture or word on each card provided, and tell if it belongs in the box, providing a rationale for their choice. They can sort a stack of word or picture cards by word meaning, affix (prefix or suffix), or other characteristics. This will help students not only with vocabulary development but also the critical skills of providing evidence and constructing effective arguments.

learn and practice words in meaningful contexts before they become a permanent part of their vocabulary. Having multiple texts on a topic and teaching words in categories and through units of study accelerates word learning.

Rimes and word families. Working with word families promotes students' language skills in a variety of areas. Frequently used rimes that can be used to develop word families include the following:

ack, ain, ake, ale,	aw, ay, eat, ell,	ing, ink, ip, it, ock,
all, ame, an, ank,	est, ice, ick, ide,	oke, op, ore, ot,
ap, ash, at, ate,	ight, ill, in, ine,	uck, ug, ump, unk

Each week introduce a different word family, such as *ad,* and make a chart with words in that family—for example, *bad, dad, fad, had.* Use one color for the base of the word (rime) and another color for the initial letters to help children better understand the concept. Children can make word family books, adding a new page each week for each word family as you make the list together on chart paper or an interactive whiteboard.

Try This!

During a project or study, work with students to create charts with words related to your study. Post them in the room. Make lists of synonyms to broaden vocabulary with words such as *walk, stroll, saunter,* and *stride.* Give each student a copy of these word banks to store in their writing folders and use to enhance their writing. You could hang the charts on clothes hangers with clothespins or clips in an area called *Our Word Closet.* Learning words in categories can assist in retention and aid long-term storage of meanings. (For tips on using word walls, see Wingate, Rutledge, & Johnston 2014.)

Brain-friendly activities. In *Teaching the Brain to Read: Strategies for Improving Fluency, Vocabulary, and Comprehension*, physician and classroom teacher Judy Willis (2008) provides suggestions from neuroscience research as well as her experience as a teacher. She suggests that brain-friendly activities such as conversations, word games, and using words in rich, meaningful contexts help students to build a powerful vocabulary. She recommends engaging multiple senses with audio, video, and hands-on activities, which stimulate multiple regions of the brain. For example, create a vocabulary bulletin board by taking photos of students dramatizing words, along with additional pictures of the word if necessary for clarification. Using pictures, objects, and actions helps students to build a mental model of words. Because the brain responds well to choice, Willis encourages teachers to provide a choice of reading material with topics of interest, and have students prepare presentations and posters on topics they select. She recommends using cross-curricular units, such as a study of migrating birds that could include science, social studies, and math, or collections of rich thematic books, such as biographies or books about friendship, to help build vocabulary and content knowledge. This helps the brain see the patterns in the information and words, allowing better storage in long-term memory. Rehearsing words and concepts and connecting them to previous knowledge through motivating activities in multiple settings also enable words to move from short-term to long-term memory and strengthen neural pathways. For example, when studying energy, ask students to brainstorm words they associate with energy. Prompt additional words by encouraging them to think about experiences they have had with batteries, motors, electricity, wind, or solar energy. Students can work in teams to make illustrated word cards that can be displayed on a poster throughout the study. During writers' workshop one day, ask students to write about a topic related to energy and use some of these words. At science time, offer activities that allow students to explore energy and then write about their explorations. Willis points out that stress can be overpowering, causing children to give up if they become too frustrated. She suggests encouraging *participation,* not *perfection.*

Interactive experiences. Focus students' attention and promote learning by making vocabulary lessons interactive experiences. For example, give each student a small erasable whiteboard or clipboard and paper when you teach new words. As you introduce a word, ask students to draw a picture of it and hold it up. Occasionally ask them to draw the opposite of the word. Take students outside with clipboards and brainstorm words in categories, asking students to list words related to plants or vehicles. The more portions of the brain that are engaged and involved in processing the word, the more likely it is that the word will become a permanent part of a child's vocabulary. Benjamin and Crow (2013) recommend thinking about the updated version of Bloom's taxonomy by Anderson and Krathwohl (2001) when designing activities to help children truly learn vocabulary. The higher up the taxonomy, the more in-depth processing the brain does, and the greater the retention and ability to use the words. Simple memorization helps children remember in the short run but does little for long-term retention.

Bloom's Revised Taxonomy by Anderson and Krathwohl

Higher-Order Thinking Skills

↑ Creating
Evaluating
Analyzing
Applying
Understanding
Remembering

Lower-Order Thinking Skills

Provide a meaningful way for students to *apply* a new word by asking them to find ways to relate the word to their lives. Determining word meanings by examining prefixes and suffixes allows students to *analyze* words. Compare and contrast activities require students to *evaluate.* Inventing skits, illustrations, and posters about word meanings allow students to be *creative*, requiring more thinking and in-depth processing. Engaging activities that promote children's curiosity about words will enhance their vocabulary skills. Encourage students to be *word detectives* who analyze and evaluate the clues they find in new words.

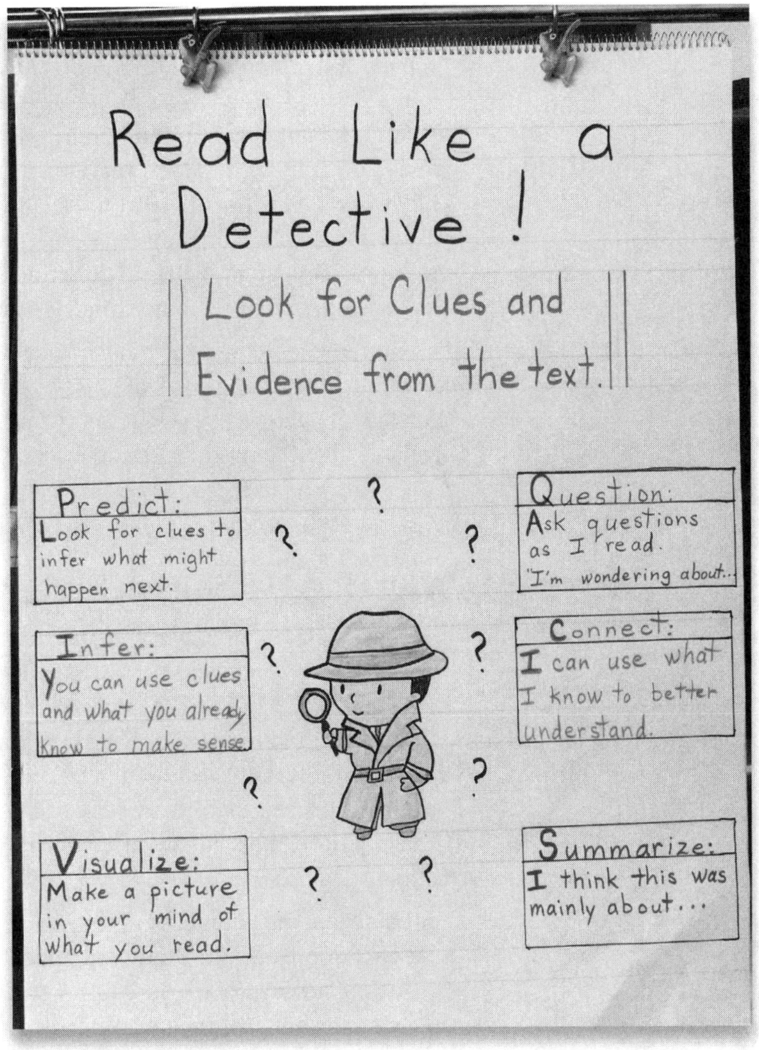

Ask students to describe new vocabulary in their own words to assess their understanding of these words. Having them use the new words in their writing also provides an authentic assessment and reflects the goal for students to increase the working vocabulary they use in speaking and writing.

Learning vocabulary needed for functioning successfully in everyday life is a key to success for dual language learners. Make sure that children know words they need to navigate daily activities. Back-and-forth conversations with students are an excellent way for them to build this vocabulary and practice English. There are a number of games to build vocabulary at www.vocabulary.co.il/, including

Try This!

Make a class dictionary, adding words as you introduce or read about them. For example, after you have read a book about forests, add the words *forest* and *trees* to the dictionary. Consider making a class thesaurus as well. At least once a week choose a frequently used word, such as *said*, *ask*, or *happy*, and invite students to brainstorm synonyms for the word.

Keep the dictionary and thesaurus in a three-ring binder, or store them on the computer connected to an interactive whiteboard in a PowerPoint book you add to over time. Students could also have their own printed or electronic version that they add to as you add to the class version. Having students draw illustrations for each word helps them process the words at a deeper level. These tools will help all students increase their vocabulary and enhance their writing as they meet language standards.

games specifically designed for dual language learners. Provide opportunities for all students to research, write, and share short pieces about their home cultures. This can promote pride in their heritage and provide an opportunity for classmates to learn more about each other's cultures. Be sensitive, however, in asking students to share their pieces; some students, including dual language learners, may be hesitant to do so if they do not feel confident in their English skills.

Creating Engaging Literacy Centers

As Fountas and Pinnell suggest in their classic books, *Guided Reading: Good First Teaching for All Children* (1996) and *Guiding Readers and Writers Grades 3–6: Teaching Comprehension, Genre, and Content Literacy* (2001), literacy centers are an effective, research-based approach to helping students meet standards. Although literacy centers are a natural fit with guided reading, they can enrich any approach to teaching literacy. They work well with the word work, listening to reading, and writing required in The Daily 5 approach (Boushey & Moser 2014) and can supplement basal reading and other programs (Goldstein & Bauml 2012). They can be used as an integral part of your daily literacy program or as motivating activities at other times of the day.

Literacy centers, or literacy stations, provide a productive way to differentiate instruction as students work at their own pace, applying and practicing the skills they are learning. Provide for varying ability levels by having a variety of materials and activities available in the centers. Students can be working in centers while the teacher works with individuals or small groups on guided reading, RTI, or a variety of literacy strategies.

Why Use Learning Centers and Stations?

Well-designed learning centers and other approaches to hands-on learning and exploration are effective ways for children in the primary grades to learn. Piaget describes the ages of about 7 to 11 as the stage of concrete operations; in this stage students need to experience and investigate materials firsthand in tangible ways in order to learn. Literacy centers also fit well with a balanced approach to literacy instruction, providing varied opportunities to read, write, and learn more about words in an engaging setting. The work done by students at centers provides a window into their learning and informs teaching practice.

Using learning centers can motivate students to read and write. The National Reading Panel and other national experts have cited motivation as one of the qualities needed by successful readers and writers. "Motivation has been shown to be among the most important considerations in students' willingness to persist and put forth the necessary effort to learn to read and then love to read" (Reutzel & Cooter 2013, xxii). Learning centers provide students with *choice*, which is one of the most powerful motivators. The use of centers also reflects what we know about the way the brain processes information, providing students opportunities to learn through meaningful activities and problem solving, with multiple senses, focused attention, physical movement, and practice. Dopamine is an important neurotransmitter that enhances attention and executive function networks, and it is released when the brain finds an activity pleasurable or rewarding. The brain can even start releasing dopamine in anticipation of activities it finds enjoyable and involves some opportunities for choice, such as being able to choose from a variety of literacy centers or which word game to play on the computer. Our brains pay attention to new things, so occasionally changing books, activities, and materials at the centers will help keep children focused and interested. Including a sign describing the skills and standards students learn at each center can help parents, administrators, and students better understand all the learning that takes place.

Examples of Literacy Centers and Stations

Think about standards as guides for planning centers. Provide engaging activities that students can work on independently to learn, practice, and master the skills required by the standards. An individual center or workstation could have one assignment or several activities students choose from, all focused on similar goals.

Consider the number of centers you want and where to place them. Some areas, such as a computer center that needs electrical outlets, will have limited options. It is helpful to have art materials near a sink if one is available. Place quieter activities near each other. Centers can be set up in a variety of locations around the room. The side of a file cabinet provides an excellent surface for magnetic letters and words. Windowsills, cubbies, cabinets, corners, and carpet squares are all potential center locations. Include center materials that are stored in a container with a 2'×2' square of fabric to mark out a space on the floor to work.

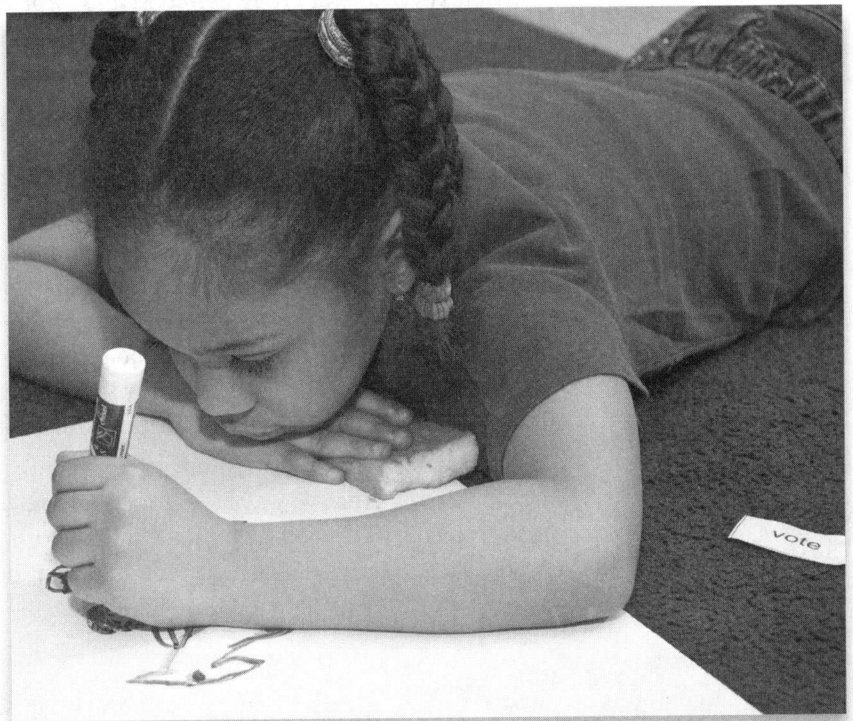

Materials for centers can come from a variety of sources. You may already have many materials, such as alphabet and word cards, magnetic letters, books, CD players, computers, and tablets that would promote hands-on learning at the centers. Teacher guides for student textbooks often provide a number of suggestions for enrichment activities that can be done effectively at centers. Some literacy centers, such as a library area, may be set up all year, while others change throughout the year. You can store center materials in plastic containers, backpacks, or large envelopes that students can access and bring to desks or tables. Several ideas for literacy centers are described below.

Library Center

The expectations in the CCSS make a library area with high-quality literature and informational text more important than ever. A well-designed library encourages students to spend time engaged in reading. Ideally, the area includes a bookcase with books attractively displayed to invite young readers. Rotate books regularly to reflect study topics and children's skills and interests. Be sure to include books in children's home languages and books that reflect diverse cultures, including those of the children in the class. If space permits, locate book baskets with leveled books here as well. Cozy seating, such as pillows, beanbags, a rocking chair, or other creative seating options, add to students' enjoyment of the space. You could include posters that promote books and poetry, as well as a chart with sections for fiction and nonfiction books where students put sticky notes about books they recommend and why. Alternatively, include a display area for student-made posters promoting a book they have read. Display books from a variety of genres after you have introduced them to the class. Include children's magazines, student-authored books, and tablets with ebooks in the area to inspire additional reading.

Enlist students' help in setting up the library. Take children on a tour of the school library to see how books are sorted there. Ask students to share what they notice about the categories used to sort the books, and solicit ideas for organizing the classroom library. They might start by separating literature from informational texts and then divide the informational texts into categories such as science, biography, and geography. If students help set up the classroom library at the beginning of the year, they may be more inclined to keep the area tidy and return books to the appropriate shelves and baskets.

Listening Center

Listening and reading along with audio versions of books help students increase the level of text complexity they can read and improves fluency, comprehension, and vocabulary. This is especially true for dual language learners. It's easy to set up a listening center on a small table, the floor, a mobile cart, or almost any available space and add a CD player and headphones. Audiobooks are also available for a variety of devices, such as tablets and laptops.

Many school and community libraries lend children's books on CDs. Students love to record themselves reading books as well—these can become favorite choices at the listening center. A classroom volunteer could help students make a recording of themselves reading. Several children can take part, with each child taking on a different character or section of the text. Rehearsing before recording builds fluency as well as comprehension. Families, too, might be interested in recording books at home to share with the class. In addition to CD players, there are several free software programs that allow students to use a computer or tablet to make recordings.

Both the library and listening centers can be stocked with clipboards and response forms outlining creative ways for students to respond to what they read, focusing on a variety of skills. This could include making story maps, drawing pictures of the setting and characters, and writing a recommendation or advertisement of the book explaining to peers why they would enjoy the book.

Writing Center

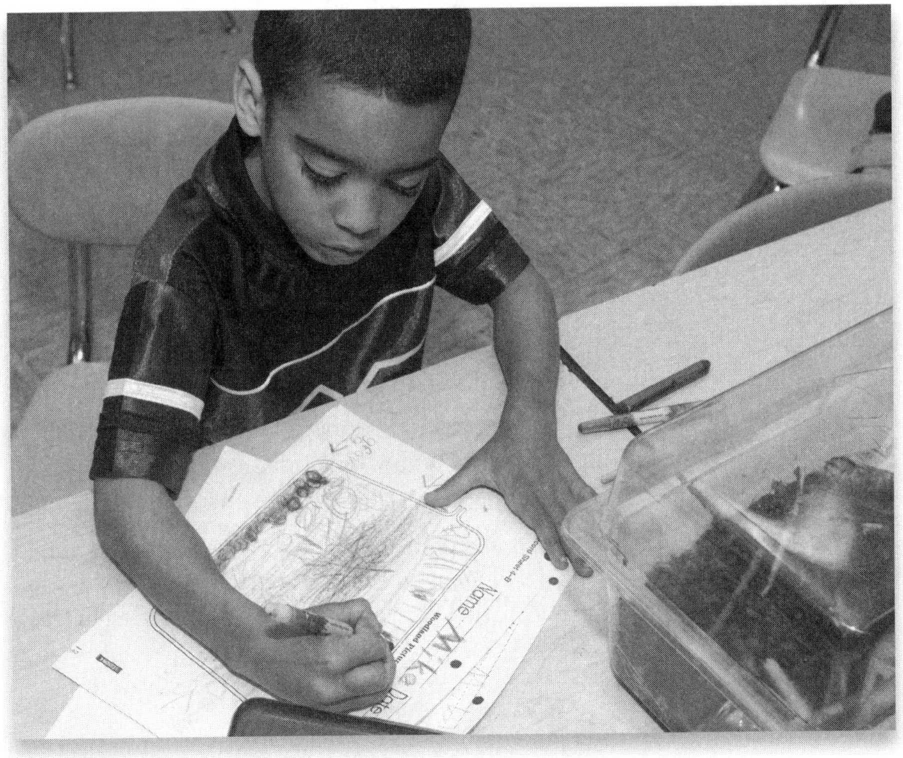

In the writing center students can practice a wide range of skills required by standards and gain experience writing routinely for a range of tasks, purposes, and audiences. Stock the writing area with a variety of writing tools such as pencils, pens, erasers, markers, and crayons as well as a variety of paper, envelopes, and dry-erase boards. Students can make their own stationery with rubber stamps or other creative art materials. Include clipboards and other surfaces for writing, as well as tablets and laptops if available. Alphabet charts, lists of high-frequency words, a children's dictionary and thesaurus, and writing dictionaries are also important items in this center.

Students can work on a variety of tasks at the center, including writing stories, autobiographies, letters, journal entries, and content-related informational pieces. The writing area can have space for several students to work or primarily be used as a place to store writing utensils, paper, and other writing tools that students take elsewhere to do their work. The Balanced Literacy Diet website has information on writing centers and many other literacy-related topics at www.oise.utoronto.ca/balancedliteracydiet/Recipe/50142/.

Try This!

In the writing center students can work on individual pages for class books—for example, adaptations of books you have read with the class such as Laura Joffe Numeroff's *If You Give a Moose a Muffin.* Students create their own page, following the pattern the author uses, such as *If you give a bird a bagel . . . , If you give a camel a carrot . . . ,* and so on. Your class's version might be something like *If you give a first-grader a _______.* Specify that their sentences need to contain rhyming words or other types of words you are studying. Students can write and edit their own books on topics of interest at this center as well.

Poetry Center

Set up a poetry center to invite students to explore this literary genre in depth. Students could choose from teacher-made task cards with activities such as highlighting important words in a poem, dramatizing a poem with a partner, comparing poems using a Venn diagram, illustrating poems, writing their favorite poems in a journal, and making a list of interesting words found in the poems they are reading. You might introduce one new poem each week, making copies for each child. Students could illustrate the page and add it to their individual poetry books. Read the poem of the week together each day, occasionally reviewing previous poems to build fluency, vocabulary, speaking, and other literacy skills. The poetry area can also be used as a place to write poetry or to house poetry books such as *Here's a Little Poem.*

Comprehension Center

The comprehension center is stocked with materials to help students retell stories, such as flannel board characters, puppets, or plush book characters (Clifford, Curious George, Pete the Cat, and Junie B. Jones). Students could also make their own props at this center.

Another center activity might provide questions on cards about stories that students can answer in their journals or on sheets of paper they deposit in a designated box at the center. Questions could include

- Describe the setting of this story.
- Describe three of the main characters.
- If you had to choose one of the characters to be in the story, which would you choose and why?
- What was the final outcome of this story?

Students could also draw scenes depicting main events or a make a cartoon strip with a sequence of events. There could be additional activities for informational text, such as listing interesting facts they learned in the text.

Read the Room Center

The read the room center might be housed in a container and have imaginative pointers such as silk flowers, flyswatters in unique shapes, or back scratchers. Use hot glue to attach to the end of a dowel stick a small object or foam shape that corresponds with books you are reading or units of study. Add unusual glasses purchased at discount stores or fairs. Students can wear the glasses and use the pointers to guide their reading as they read posters, poetry and song charts, inspirational sayings, anchor charts, graphic organizers, and other print around the room. Students could make a recording of the print they are reading or simply practice their fluency and word skills by reading the room. When working on blends, attach foam letters with the blend to the top of a pointer and ask students to search the room for that particular blend. Students can record the words they find on paper attached to a clipboard.

Rhyming/Word Family Center

The rhyming center can offer students a variety of activities:

- Practicing phonemic awareness skills by matching rhyming picture or word cards
- Playing rhyming games on a tablet or laptop
- Sorting word cards into rhyming word families
- Writing rhyming words in their journals that children find in stories and poems
- Using rubber alphabet stamps to stamp rhyming words in a particular word family the class is working on

Buddy Reading Center

Students work in pairs at the buddy reading center, reading to each other or in unison. They discuss the text and ask each other questions. Owocki (2005) suggests providing self-evaluation sheets for partners to fill out at the end of their session. Questions might include the following:

- Write something you learned in your reading today.
- Describe an important way you contributed to the discussion.
- Talk about what you did to be a careful listener.
- Tell what you can do to help you and your partner learn even better.

Word Study Center

Using words from texts they are reading or from spelling lists, students at the word study center complete a variety of activities to increase their vocabulary and other language skills. Here are some examples:

- Write words with dry-erase markers on individual whiteboards or chalkboards.
- Form words with magnetic letters or letters made of craft foam and other materials on the side of file cabinets.
- Do word sorts, alphabetize word cards, and write words or play word games, such as Scattergories or Password.
- Complete word activities on the computer.
- Work in pairs to draw sketches that explain the meaning of words and ask their partners to guess the word they have illustrated.
- Make word cards by writing the word on the front with a picture and definition on the back. Use these cards for word sorting activities, such as sorting them into word families.
- Help make word element kits, which consist of file cards with prefixes written in one color, suffixes on other cards in another color, and root words in a third color on another set of cards. The word elements can also be written on die-cut seasonal or unit-related shapes or on sticky notes.
- Write prefixes and suffixes on flat stones or other materials, then use the word elements to make, write, and illustrate words.
- Play a game by turning the word elements over and taking turns choosing a few and trying to make words.

Phenomenal New Words	
Word:	
Dictionary definition	
Synonyms	
Antonyms	
Comparison	
Real-life example	
Picture or symbol	
Act it out	

The National Reading Panel (Shanahan 2005) indicates that simply writing out definitions does not tend to be helpful because it does not require much thinking. Instead, panel members recommend using the research-based approach of filling in a chart such as the one shown with a motivating title such as "Phenomenal New Words." Students could choose three of the activities on the chart for each word. This could be done in the context of a word of the day, with students adding a new word each day to a binder of words used to enhance their writing. New pages could be put in alphabetical order. Students can do this activity in pairs at a center, each day as they arrive in the morning, or when they return from lunch.

Spelling Center

The spelling center provides options for practicing spelling, building vocabulary, and using high-frequency words in a variety of motivating ways. Provide a list of ways for students to practice words each week, adding new activities occasionally to enhance interest. Third grade teacher Angie Bickett offers her students these options: "Students may use Bendaroos (similar to Wikki Stix) or playdough to form the words; use pencils to trace the words in colored sand in a plastic container; make the words using magnetic letters, word tiles, or letter rocks; stamp out the spelling words; make Rainbow Words; use Boggle boards or Scrabble; and type their spelling words on a tablet or computer. Another thing I have done is entered all my spelling lists on the VocabularySpellingCity.com website. The students can access these lists from any computer, tablet, or digital device. There are different games to play using the words from each week's spelling list. I try to add a new idea every couple of weeks to keep the students engaged."

Computer Center

The computer center offers many possibilities for practicing literacy skills. Students can read ebooks, listen to audiobooks, and play literacy-related games. The IRA/NCTE site www.readwritethink.org is a storehouse of interactive games and activities to help students learn essential literacy skills as they meet standards. Children can also write and illustrate stories, skits, and reports on a variety of digital devices.

Interactive Whiteboard Center

There are many literacy-related activities and games for students to play by themselves, in pairs, or small groups using an interactive whiteboard. Students enjoy this technology and the immediate feedback it provides. Small groups can listen to books read aloud, with full-screen pictures projected on the whiteboard. Students can make their own books on the computer or write and illustrate stories and reports on paper, take digital photos of the pages, and then project them on the whiteboard.

Managing Centers

Teachers may find that challenging behaviors often dissipate during this time because students are engaged with learning. Provide general instruction cards at each center so students know what is expected of them, and model what students need to do at each center

ahead of time. This includes where to find supplies, where to put their finished and unfinished work, and how to clean up. Repeated modeling and practice at the beginning of the year, and reminders throughout the year, will assist students in becoming more self-sufficient. Once students have learned to work well at centers, you are free to work with small groups or individuals.

Think about the number of students that would work best at each center at one time. Students can work in small groups, in pairs, or by themselves depending on the activity. Some teachers form groups that rotate from center to center using a rotation board so students know where to start and how to proceed. Other teachers prefer to let students choose which centers they wish to work at.

To help her first-graders use centers, teacher Jenna Gilkyson uses keys and key rings with transparent tags containing each student's name. Labeled signs in inexpensive frames hang at each center with the number of hooks that correspond to the number of students that ideally fit at the center. At center time, which takes place at the end of the day, she calls students individually and hands them their keys. Once they receive their keys, students hang them at the center of their choice and begin work. When students finish a center they move to another open center and place their keys there.

Another approach is to give each student a center guide sheet at the beginning of each week. Each center is listed on the guide, along with a graphic if children need a visual cue. Students cross off each center as they complete the tasks there. Let students know your expectations for completing the centers—for example, they need to visit all centers by the end of the week. You can also use a center management board with pictures and names of the stations along with an indication of how many students can work there. Students can use a clothespin or Velcro tag with their name and picture to indicate the center where they wish to work.

Many helpful books and online resources offer innovative ideas for centers. Karen McDavid's site has directions, photos, forms, and templates as well as ideas for transitions, assessment, and differentiation she uses in her third grade centers; visit www.ourclassweb.com/sites_for_teachers_new_learning_center_research.htm.

Home<-->School Connections

According to the classic report *Becoming a Nation of Readers: The Report of the Commission on Reading* (Anderson et al. 1985), one of the most important things parents can do to help their children read successfully is read aloud to them. The report also recommends that families encourage reading as a free time activity and set reasonable limits on activities such as TV viewing and use of digital devices. Encourage families to read to their children every night before bed or some other time each day. Stress the importance of making reading enjoyable for both the parent and child. Suggest they read a variety of books, including informational text. Recommend that they help their children make connections between what they are reading and their own lives: "Remember when that happened to us?" They can also ask their children to predict what a book might be about before reading it and, later, predict the ending. Suggest that they talk about the words and ideas in the books.

Encourage parents to have their children read to them as well and to show patience and provide encouragement and support during this process. Let families know how important it is that they let their children know they are proud of them and care about them. In addition, suggest that they set aside time for their children to read on their own. One strategy many families find to be successful is to set a bedtime for their children that is about half an hour before they feel lights need to be out and then let children read for 30 minutes before turning out the lights. This makes the reading time seem like a special treat.

Encourage families to visit the library together if possible and send home notes describing the location of nearby libraries and how to obtain a library card. In addition to their school libraries, many primary teachers set up their own classroom lending library, allowing students to check out books as they return those they have previously borrowed. Taking turns as classroom librarian is a job many primary students enjoy. There are also many free books online now, such as those available at www.gutenberg.org. Look for free printable books online and read them with the class, then send them home for families to read together. You can also write books as a class, print them, and give them to families to read. Propose that families play word games together, such as Scrabble Junior. Suggest websites, such as www.pbskids.org, that offer word games families can play together.

Ask families at the beginning of the year how they would like you to communicate with them. This could be part of a survey that also includes asking family members how they might like to contribute throughout the year (for example, coming in or sending in a video as a guest reader, boosting vocabulary by talking to the class about a special interest they have, making blank books that students can use for final drafts, helping during writers' workshop, or other ideas they may share). Consider setting up a classroom blog where families can share ideas with each other, recommending books, games, and apps their children have enjoyed.

Send notes home in the preferred method of the family, discussing ways they can strengthen children's communication and language skills at home. For example, families help children develop understanding and vocabulary just by talking about everyday tasks as they do them together, and they build essential background knowledge by visiting places together and even doing activities around the house as they talk and listen to each other. Emphasize that children learn a great deal by simply watching the adults in their lives. Taking time to listen to children provides a model children can follow, and having reciprocal conversations strengthens children's language skills and builds family bonds.

Suggest that parents write letters to friends and family with their children and record family experiences. Invite families to attend Author Celebrations at school to celebrate children's writing. Students may read their poems, books, or other writing to the whole group, even using a karaoke machine if one is available. Make a video of students reading to show at a family event or upload to a class website. Reading Rockets has a special section for families as well as helpful guides they can read at www.readingrockets.org/guides/other/.

You can also offer families resources to help children with language acquisition. Refer them to websites where they can listen to books read aloud, such as www.awesomelibrary.org/Awesome_Talking_Library.html. This might be especially helpful for families of dual language learners. Send home simple books to read together, and encourage families to read to children in their home language. Dual language learners might enjoy helping other family members learn English and, in turn, learning new words in their home language from family members.

Meeting Standards—and More!

While you are working hard to help children meet standards, remember that it is vital to also help them love learning and understand how to apply all the skills and knowledge they're acquiring to their own lives. Reading can change children's lives. Being a proficient reader opens new possibilities and increases self-esteem. Reading also introduces children to new worlds or interests that may shape their futures. Make sure the texts students read include biographies of inspirational people who have made a difference, and provide books with topics of great interest and concern that may inspire your students, such as overcoming adversity, standing up for what you believe in, or new discoveries in alternative energy.

Many teachers begin the day with a morning message posted on a board near the classroom door. This is a great way to boost vocabulary and other language skills and a wonderful avenue for sharing words of encouragement and inspiration. Here are a couple of examples:

> Everyone worked hard yesterday on ________. Today we are going to tackle ____________.
>
> Being kind makes you happier and the world a better place.

Use messages like these when you model writing, too.

As you work with students on building language and listening skills, read inspirational stories and poetry to help them appreciate the beauty of diversity, such as *My People* and *The Dream Keeper and Other Poems,* both by Langston Hughes. Choose topics, themes, projects, or units of study that inspire children and help build character. For example, consider a project in which students research the topic of heroes. Read books about people who students might be able to relate and look up to. Ask students to research a hero of their choice—a family member or a more widely known figure. Brainstorm questions they could investigate, such as when and where the hero lived, what the person did that was important, why the student looks up to the person, and ways the person influenced others or what she did for others. Together make a list of words that describe a hero. Have students choose a format for their report, which might be a poster hung in the classroom, hallway, or cafeteria; PowerPoint slides; or pages in a class *Hero Book* that can be shared with other classes or at a Family Night.

In a Nutshell

Teachers can provide many engaging experiences for students that will help them meet reading, writing, listening, speaking, and language standards and become proficient communicators. Readers' and writers' workshops are an effective way for students to meet standards and can be combined with other literacy programs. In addition, teachers can integrate opportunities for reading, writing, listening, and speaking throughout the day.

Students need experience in analyzing texts, drawing inferences, and providing evidence from the text for their positions. Reading to students every day and making sure they have at least 45 minutes each day when they are engaged in actual reading both literature and informational texts will help them meet standards. To understand what students currently know and to scaffold their progress, use authentic assessment methods, such as having students read to you, collecting and reviewing their work in writing portfolios, and writing and giving presentations to other classmates. Confer frequently with students, providing high-quality feedback that helps them gain skills and nurtures their self-esteem as readers and writers.

Becoming effective, capable communicators in the primary grades will serve students well throughout school and life. Being able to express themselves clearly in speaking and writing and having the vocabulary and confidence to speak up for themselves and others is an invaluable skill.

Literacy activities that are meaningful and motivating, such as researching and writing about topics of interest, engaging in activities at literacy centers, and writing letters, will help instill in children a love of reading and writing along with joy in learning.

Meeting the Common Core State Standards for **Mathematics**

4

The primary grades are a vital time for students to build a firm foundation in mathematical concepts. Math is all around us, but students need to see the connection between the math they use in their daily lives and the mathematical concepts they are learning. Teachers and family members can help students understand that math is useful in everyday situations, such as knowing how much change they should receive when purchasing a toy, figuring out how to share a package of mini-figures with two friends, measuring the distance of a softball throw, or being able to double a recipe for trail mix to make with friends. Understanding this connection will motivate them to apply concepts, help them gain self-confidence, and improve their ability to grasp in-depth concepts. To gain a deep understanding of mathematical concepts, primary students need concrete examples and hands-on opportunities. As with other subject areas, it is most effective to teach math concepts by building on students' previous knowledge, connecting new learning to their lives and interests, and providing experiences to apply the new skills. "To *know* mathematics is to *do* mathematics. While mathematics content is very important, the mathematics *processes* (problem solving, reasoning, communication, connections, and representation) are equally significant for young children" (Copley 2010, 15).

The Importance of Mathematical Practices

The Common Core State Standards (CCSS) outline eight mathematical practices that cut across all grade levels and standard areas (see the box). Focusing on these practices in all the math experiences you provide for students will help students develop the higher-order thinking skills they need to meet standards in all areas of the curriculum. Establish a culture of thinking and reasoning by making questions part of everyday math conversations with students: "How did you figure that out? Could you draw a picture showing how you solved it? How else could you measure it?"

The CCSS emphasize using mathematical practices throughout the standards. Judith Jacobs, a 2007 recipient of the National Council of Teachers of Mathematics (NCTM) Lifetime Achievement Award, calls the mathematical practices one of the most important aspects of the CCSS. In describing the importance of the practices and the emphasis on students' use of strategies to solve problems, she notes that the CCSS do not even use the term *basic facts*. In light of this, she says,

> The traditional flash card or timed test approach in Kindergarten and Grade 1 and for most of Grade 2 must be modified. Students are expected to use strategies, not memory to come up with an answer. They will need more time to state the answer, and how they thought out the answer is as important as stating it. It is only by the end of second grade that students are expected to have the addition facts memorized. Notice that there is no call for memorization of the subtraction facts. (Jacobs 2011, 232–33)

This, along with the fact that stress can inhibit learning, calls into question the value of activities such as mad minute races, or minute math drills, in which students complete as many basic math facts problems as they can in a short amount of time.

Mathematical Practices From the Common Core State Standards

1. Make sense of problems and persevere in solving them.
2. Reason abstractly and quantitatively.
3. Construct viable arguments and critique the reasoning of others.
4. Model with mathematics.
5. Use appropriate tools strategically.
6. Attend to precision.
7. Look for and make use of structure.
8. Look for and express regularity in repeated reasoning.

National Governors Association Center for Best Practices (NGA) & Council of Chief State School Officers (CSSO) 2010b, pp. 6–8.

Cognitively Guided Instruction

Many primary teachers use the research-based method Cognitively Guided Instruction (CGI) to help students learn mathematics and integrate the mathematical practices. CGI is a problem-solving approach to mathematics education. In CGI, teachers make decisions about what to teach based on what students already understand about math. Children naturally try to make sense of their world and are curious about relationships, such as which of two containers holds more liquid and who in the class is taller than they are. By posing questions to students about their mathematical thinking and listening carefully to the responses, teachers discover what students know. They use this knowledge to plan what, when, and how to scaffold children's mathematical learning (Carpenter et al. 1999).

Problem-Solving Strategies

Plan problem-solving opportunities to help students learn concepts outlined in the standards through meaningful problems and questions that relate to their interests and everyday lives. Think about resources and questions that will help students explore mathematics content on a deep level. "Successful teachers pose questions and challenge students to think and reason. They also value interpreting students' mathematical ideas and misconceptions and using them as part of the lesson. Mistakes can be good things in the trajectory of a lesson" (Jacobs 2011, 66).

In CGI, students start with skills they already have to find solutions to math problems. Students who have beginning subtraction skills might solve a subtraction problem using manipulatives to model or they may be able to count backwards to determine the answer. Encourage students to devise their own strategies for solving challenging and interesting problems, which will help them better understand and retain the concepts. For example, when given a problem such as "If Meriah has 12 flowers and she puts three flowers in each vase, how many vases can she fill?" students might model the solution by using counters, drawing pictures of flowers in vases, or count by threes until they get to 12. With guidance and many opportunities to develop their skills, children will be able to construct these strategies on their own. Support their problem-solving strategies and ensure that all students stay engaged. One way to do this is to provide quiet think time after presenting a problem. After thinking about how to solve a problem individually, students can share their process with a partner and then with the group, using the think-pair-share strategy described in Chapter 2.

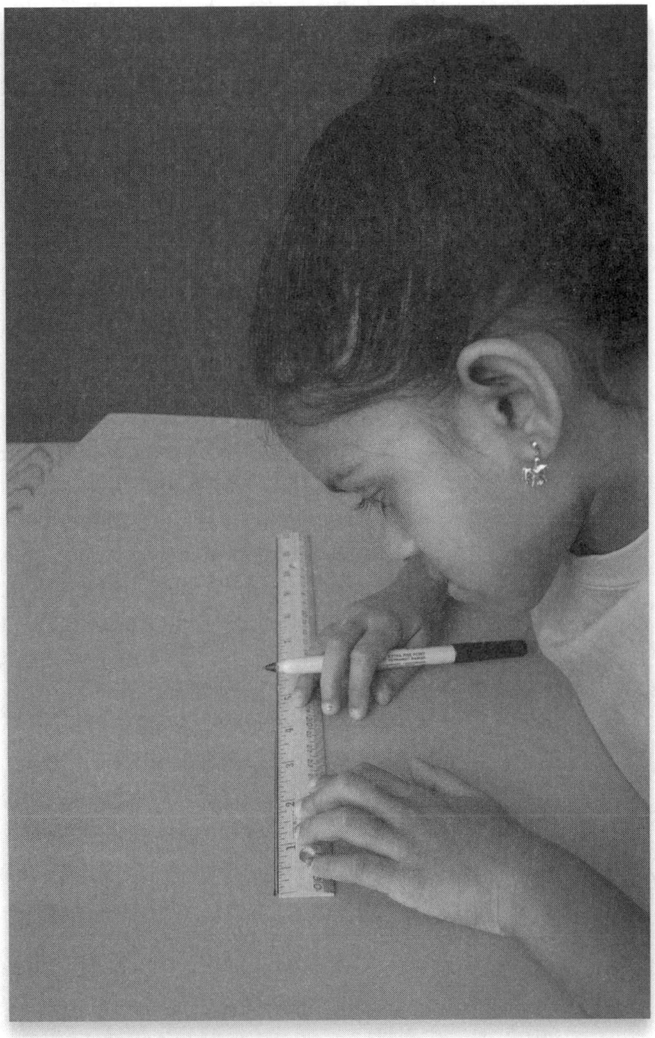

Students could also work in small groups to solve problems while you ask guiding questions. Solving problems with other students enables children to learn new strategies and ways of thinking through a problem that they might not acquire by working alone. Teach students to find multiple ways to solve the same problem as a way of confirming their answers and broadening their understanding of mathematics. Encourage them to discuss how the various solution strategies are alike and different. After students have had time to work together answering a question, ask a few pairs or groups to explain to the class how they got their answer and their evidence or proof that their answer is correct. Clarify and accentuate their points or share an additional way to approach a problem. As students continue to problem solve and communicate their thinking to others, they will view themselves as capable problem solvers rather than look to their teacher as the source of all the answers.

Manipulatives

Offer students many opportunities to solve problems with a hands-on and minds-on approach using manipulatives. Teach students how to use manipulatives to model mathematical problems and solution strategies. When students are working on CGI problems, they can think of manipulatives as tools to help them perform a task and solve a problem. Offer a variety of manipulatives so students can choose the ones that best fit their way of thinking about the solution. Help them learn ways to talk about their mathematical thinking and ways they can use the manipulatives to provide evidence for their answers. For example, after asking students to model how the number 12 can be divided into equal parts, encourage them to discuss with their group members how to solve the problem and use manipulatives to verify their thinking. One student may share his idea that their group could draw cat faces in three groups of four or four groups of three, while another suggests that they then use two sets of 12 counters to show that their work is correct. When you introduce manipulatives, give students an opportunity to simply explore them first. This will help students to focus better on actual problem solving later when they need to put them to use.

Manipulatives can help dual language learners see mathematical processes being demonstrated even if they do not yet understand all of the words associated with the concepts. As with all students, demonstrating the processes with concrete materials, drawings, and number lines will help students grasp the mathematical concepts.

Math Journals

Math journals can help students develop the math practices outlined in the CCSS. There are a variety of ways these journals can be used. Students can record their problem-solving process by drawing the way they used manipulatives or by writing their thoughts about how to solve the problem. Give students a CGI problem of the day to solve in their journals and show their problem-solving strategies. For example, you might write, "If Rashaun has seven eggs, how many more does she need to have a dozen eggs?" Provide similar problems over several days to reinforce a concept you are highlighting, such as comparing numbers. Write the problem on the blackboard or whiteboard at the beginning of the day or at other times of the day. For younger students, write out problems ahead of time that they can glue into their journals. At the end of a lesson, students can also write or dictate any questions they still have and explain why something was easy or difficult for them to learn. Writing can help students learn mathematics because it requires them to reflect and clarify the ideas they have developed. As they become more confident with math skills, the journal writing can focus more on confirming their answers. It is also a good way to strengthen literacy skills.

Six-Step CGI Method

First grade teacher Becky Holden, 2008 recipient of the Presidential Award for Excellence in Mathematics and Science Teaching, uses CGI to differentiate learning. She developed a six-step method for introducing concepts students need to be successful in CGI (2007):

1. **Math Read-Alouds.** Share stories that illustrate mathematical problems, such as Margaret McNamara's *How Many Seeds in a Pumpkin?* and Diane Johnston Hamm's *How Many Feet in the Bed?*
2. **Math Read-Alouds With Manipulatives.** After several days of read-alouds, students sit in a circle on the floor and individually use manipulatives to portray the math processes in the stories. They pretend the manipulatives are characters in the book, which helps them with the concept that one thing can stand for another—a symbol can represent a character, an object, or a number.
3. **Materials Protocol.** To help students use the manipulatives appropriately, Becky passes out paper or cloth workspace mats and manipulatives to children sitting in a circle and describes how to use the materials. She places the manipulatives at the top edge above children's workspaces and then children move them onto the workspaces as needed to represent a story. Additional manipulatives are in baskets around the circle to use if needed. Designated students collect the manipulatives in the baskets at the end of the lesson.
4. **Describing.** Students explain what they did with the manipulatives and why.

5. **Speaking and Listening.** As students share their strategies, Becky reminds the rest of the group to look at the student speaking and listen carefully. Students learn from each other that there are multiple ways to solve a problem.
6. **Recording.** Students go back to their tables or desks with paper to record what they were thinking as they worked with the manipulatives. Becky talks with them about using drawings, words, numbers, or other symbols to represent their work. As students work, she comments to the class about how various students are representing their thinking, such as drawing turtles, drawing circles to represent turtles, or using Ts to represent them.

This process prepares students to work with word problems and provides information about students' abilities. Using that information, Becky types out a word problem each day using students' names and topics of interest to them. For example, the problem might say, *Luis has ____ pretzels. He gave some to Aleah. Now he has ____ left. How many did he give to Aleah?* To differentiate, she provides three sets of numbers students can use to put in the blanks of the problem, each set being progressively more difficult. For example, the number pair choices for the Luis problem might be (4, 3), (11, 9), and (34, 8).

Students sit in a circle—which allows Becky to easily support them as they work—with their mats and manipulatives and glue the word problem strips in their math notebooks to solve. Students choose which set of numbers to use, depending on their comfort level. Once students have solved the problem using manipulatives, drawings, or words, Becky encourages them to try using another set of numbers provided. She makes sure to have problems with the unknown number first, in the middle, and at the end so students experience all three types of problems. Becky keeps track of the strategies students use on a recording form so she can scaffold individuals to develop/learn more rigorous problem-solving strategies (Holden 2007).

Math Centers

After working in large or small groups on CGI problems, students can work on math skills at a variety of math centers or with other activities designed to strengthen the concepts they are learning. The centers and activities provide multiple ways for students to practice skills with a variety of manipulatives and formats. Many teacher manuals and websites offer suggestions for math center activities to reinforce concepts. Additional center ideas can be found in this chapter beginning on page 88.

Engaging Activities for Meeting Mathematics Standards

The Common Core State Standards for Mathematics cover fewer topics at each grade level than previous state and national math standards, but those that are included go into greater depth and are more rigorous. To meet the standards, students need a deeper understanding of mathematical concepts and procedures. They must solve problems and provide evidence for their thinking, just as the Common Core State Standards for English Language Arts require. This means students work on fewer problems and focus on thinking through solutions and justifying their answers. These are the types of tasks students will encounter as part of the Common Core assessments being developed by the Smarter Balanced Assessment Consortium and Partnership for Assessment of Readiness for College and Careers (PARCC), two multistate consortia awarded federal funding to develop assessments aligned to the CCSS. Websites such as NRICH (www.nrich.maths.org) provide problems and activities in meaningful contexts appropriate for different age levels. Making the quest for evidence an everyday experience as students work on math problems fosters skills that will carry over into many other areas, including literacy and science.

Findings from brain research can help teachers understand how students comprehend mathematics and, therefore, help them make learning activities more appropriate and interesting. People are more likely to remember things that are linked to emotion. For example, you may still remember an enjoyable elementary school project as well as facts you learned about the topic of that project. Even now you may be tuned into that topic and eager to learn updates about it. Emotions focus our attention, and attention is necessary for learning to occur (Kaufeldt 2010). Students are also more likely to pay attention to new or interesting things. You could read a math riddle each day for students to look forward to solving, such as those in *Math Jokes 4 Mathy Folks* by G. Patrick Vennebush and Greg Tang's books, including *Math for All Seasons: Mind-Stretching Math Riddles.* Offer time to work outside occasionally. Movement and social interaction promote interest in learning and long-term storage of information (Sousa 2006). Provide hands-on activities that help to focus students' attention. Use a variety of manipulatives and drawings to illustrate concepts and encourage students to do the same. As students study more symbolic and advanced concepts, continue to use concrete examples and materials to help them understand the concepts and visualize the mathematical processes involved. When you or another student works on a problem in front of the class, have all students work on the problem on individual whiteboards, chalkboards, or clipboards so they can be actively engaged.

Everyone can do math. In order for everyone to experience success, however, you need to differentiate the curriculum. "The Standards should be read as allowing for the widest possible range of students to participate fully from the outset, along with appropriate accommodations to ensure maximum participation of students with special education needs" (National Governors Association Center for Best Practices & Council of Chief State School Officers 2010b, 4). When students have difficulty with a problem, encourage them to think about what they already know that will help them solve it. Challenge them to try to think about the problem on a simpler level. Can they break it up into smaller chunks to solve one piece at a time? Can they find a point of entry into the problem? Think about ways to offer additional challenges for students who are more advanced. Create Try This folders with experiences, explorations, and problems they can tackle.

When helping students meet math standards, first focus on their current level of understanding. Learning trajectories that describe the concepts taught at each grade level and how students' understanding progresses from one grade to the next will help you support students in their mathematical growth (Sarama & Clements 2009). Learning trajectories for the Common Core math standards can be found at www.turnonccmath.net/ and http://ime.math.arizona.edu/progressions/, along with detailed explanations of skills and how to help students gain these skills.

Look beyond textbooks for ways to help students meet the standards. There are many online resources, including The Illustrative Mathematics Project (www.illustrativemathematics.org) and Inside Mathematics (www.insidemathematics.org), that explain the standards and provide sample lessons that are searchable by grade level. The NCTM Illuminations site (http://illuminations.nctm.org/) offers lesson plans, activities, and interactive games for core mathematical areas outlined in the standards.

NCTM recommends combining math and science to promote children's problem solving in meaningful contexts (Evenson et al. 2013). For example, students can measure and graph the growth of an amaryllis bulb as they discuss what a plant needs to grow. Connect math to other areas of the curriculum too; have children read math-related books, write story problems, and use the scale of miles on a map to calculate distances. In-depth studies on topics of interest are another way to integrate math into the curriculum in a meaningful way.

The Common Core State Standards for Mathematics are divided into the domains of Operations and Algebraic Thinking, Number and Operations in Base Ten, Number and Operations—Fractions for grade 3, Measurement and Data, and Geometry. The following pages discuss engaging activities that will help students meet the standards in these domains.

Operations and Algebraic Thinking

The Common Core State Standards for Mathematics describe several *critical areas* to focus on at each grade level. In the domain of Operations and Algebraic Thinking there is a critical area for each of the primary grades:

Grade 1—Developing understanding of addition, subtraction, and strategies for addition and subtraction within 20

Grade 2—Building fluency with addition and subtraction

Grade 3—Developing understanding of multiplication and division and strategies for multiplication and division within 100 (National Governors Association Center for Best Practice & Council of Chief State School Officers 2010b, 13, 17, 21)

Students will progress in their understanding of Operations and Algebraic Thinking when offered many engaging experiences and materials, such as those mentioned below, that help to strengthen their grasp of the concepts.

Skip counting. The goal of the standards is for students to become increasingly fluent in addition and subtraction. Help children achieve this fluency by providing activities each day to teach and reinforce these skills. For example, during transitions and

Try This!

The rekenrek, developed in the Netherlands, is a math tool similar to an abacus that combines the benefits of number lines, counters, base-ten blocks, and other math materials in one tool. Rekenreks have two rows of 10 beads, each row made up of five red beads and five white beads. To begin, all the beads are pushed to the right side. Students push beads to the left to solve problems, developing their computation skills.

Students can make their own rekenreks by stringing five beads of one color followed by five beads of another color on a long pipe cleaner and then following the same procedure with a second pipe cleaner. Next, they attach the pipe cleaners to card stock or cardboard. If students store their rekenreks in their desks they can be used frequently, supporting students' understanding of number, addition, subtraction, and place value. For a virtual experience, try the Number Rack app, available as a web version and for Apple devices.

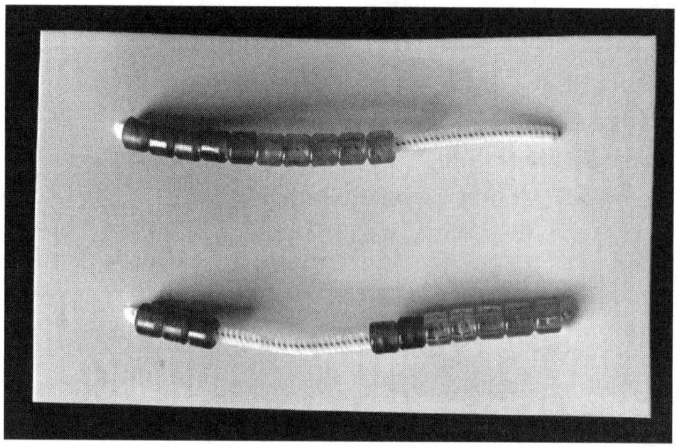

other times throughout the day, have the children skip count, beginning with 10s and moving to 2s and 5s as they become proficient. Older primary students can also count by 3s, 7s, and other numbers, both forward and backward. Skip counting helps with addition, subtraction, and beginning multiplication and division. Challenge students to find patterns in groups of numbers, such as 25, 50, 75, 100 or 6, 12, 18, 24, 30, 36.

Number lines. Use number lines to foster students' understanding of the relationships between numbers. Make and laminate individual number lines on sentence strips to use in counting, skip counting, adding, and subtracting. Post a large number line in the classroom where all students can view it. Create a number line with colored tape on the floor so students can physically move from number to number. Increase the complexity of these number lines throughout the year, beginning with 1–20 for younger students and including higher numbers and fractions for older primary students.

Manipulatives. Research by Sarama and Clements (2009) shows that when students use manipulatives and count on their fingers, they develop a deeper understanding of mathematical concepts. In addition, students who are most successful using these methods develop a better understanding of concepts more quickly than children who are not as adept at these methods, because they are more confident of their answers and can move on to more efficient strategies. To assist students, use a variety of math manipulatives, including Unifix cubes, base-ten blocks, ten frames (see p. 82 in this chapter), and pattern blocks.

Incorporate other number-related materials into math learning, such as dominoes, dice, coins, and playing cards, to pique interest and encourage practice in a variety of formats. Virtual manipulatives—displayed on a laptop, tablet, interactive whiteboard, or other device—are also very helpful. Once you have demonstrated virtual manipulatives in class, students can use them on their own.

The CCSS math standards call for primary students to solve problems using not only concrete objects but also drawings. Drawing a problem helps students visualize concepts, making them more understandable and enabling students to apply what they learn to other problems.

Mathematical symbols. It's important to provide ways for students to use mathematical symbols in conjunction with hands-on math materials. Talk about what the symbols +, -, and = mean as you show that 3 counters + 4 more counters = 7 counters,

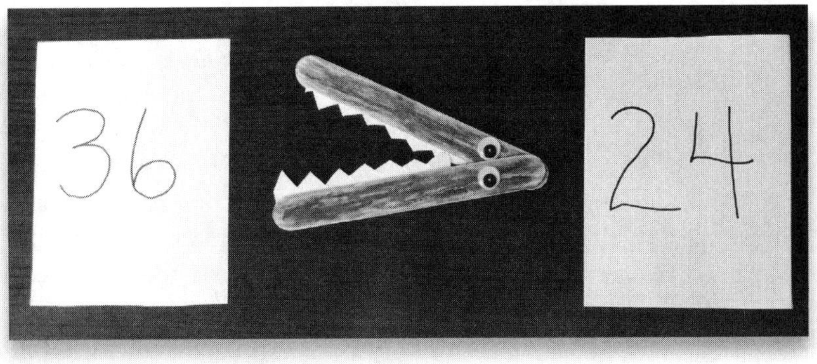

with symbols for the problem printed on cards underneath the materials. Use the symbols for greater than (>) and less than (<) in the same way. Help students remember that the wider part of the symbol faces the larger number. For example, students could think of an alligator with a wide mouth that wants to eat the larger number, so the wider part of the symbol would face the number that is larger. Students can make their own alligator face with two craft sticks, wiggly eyes, and paper teeth. Students who have difficulty with these kinds of concepts may need additional explanations and experiences. Access short video clips on the subject, such as www.teachertube.com/video/256262, which illustrates the concept of greater than and less than with visuals and music.

For more advanced symbol work, set up problems that use a symbol to stand for an unknown number (for example, $3 + x = 7$). Students will need to solve this type of problem with increasing accuracy in each successive grade.

Number relationships. Students need a deep understanding of number relationships and addition to learn multiplication and division when they reach third grade. Students can work with rectangular arrays using concrete materials, pictures, dots, and unit squares to help them see that 4×6 is equal to four groups of six, which is also equal to six groups of four. Students can enjoy making a variety of rectangular arrays on drawing programs, such as *Hello Crayon* by Raysoft, available on Apple and Android devices.

Memorizing multiplication tables is one way children can learn basic multiplication facts, but it should be accompanied by visual strategies that help students confirm that their answer is correct and makes sense. The brain does not easily remember facts that make little sense or that have little personal meaning (Kaufeldt 2010). Helping students see the meaning and usefulness in what you are teaching will lead to long-term storage of the information. Educational neuroscience consultant David Sousa (2008) describes the conditions that enable students to successfully retain facts like multiplication tables:

1. Students need to be motivated, see the personal meaning in the activity, and want to get better at the task.
2. Students must understand ways they can apply the new skill or knowledge.
3. Students need to analyze the results of applying the skill and understand what they need to change to improve their future performance.

Sousa also cautions that students need to practice over an extended period of time and suggests each practice time last 5 to 10 minutes. Limiting what you teach to that which is most relevant to the student is also important.

> **Solving Word Problems With the C.U.B.E. method**
>
> **C**ircle the numbers.
> **U**nderline important words.
> **B**ox the question.
> **E**liminate unnecessary information.

Word problems. Word problems help students learn how to apply mathematical concepts. To increase interest, use students' names and activities they can relate to in word problems, and encourage children to create their own word problems in their math journals about topics that interest them. Simplify word problems for students who need more support, adding symbols and pictures to represent the problems. Help students understand what operation a problem requires. For example, teach them to associate key words with the operation needed, such as *altogether, in all, take away,* and *are left.* Introduce the C.U.B.E. method for solving word problems to make them more manageable (see the box).

Number and Operations in Base Ten

Critical areas in the CCSS for Number and Operations in Base Ten are

Grade 1—Developing understanding of whole number relationships and place value, including grouping in tens and ones

Grade 2—Extending understanding of base-ten notation

Grade 3—Developing understanding of fractions, especially unit fractions (fractions with numerator 1) (National Governors Association Center for Best Practices & Council of Chief State School Officers 2010b, 13, 17, 21)

Hands-on activities can support students' conceptualization of place value and base ten, allowing them to visualize and solve problems with understanding. Several of these activities are presented below.

Ten frames. A ten frame has two rows with five spaces in each row. Students can place counters in the spaces to represent a number. Ten frames help students gain a firm grasp of the quantity of 10. They can be used in a variety of settings and with a variety of materials. Laminated paper or cardboard ten frames provide a good background for children to use with math manipulatives. You can also make ten frames from a soft plastic ice cube tray; simply cut off any additional cubes over ten. Virtual ten frames on a computer, tablet, or interactive whiteboard can also help students visualize quantities.

1	2	3	4	5
6	7	8	9	10

Using ten frames to keep track of the number of days in the school year reinforces the concept of base ten by helping students visualize the groups of ten that accumulate over time. In addition you can keep track of the days using a long roll of cash register tape stretched across a wall, and adding one number each day that school is open. This becomes a type of number line and can help students see the multiple ways to represent number values.

1	2	3	4	5
6	7	8	9	10

11	12	13	14	15
16	17	18	19	20

21	22	23	24	25
26	27	28		

Understanding 100. There are an endless number of activities that can strengthen students' understanding of 100 and place value. Consider making books of 100 together; each student brings in 100 of something, such as 100 LEGOs or 100 pennies, or gathers 100 cubes or counters from the classroom. Students take digital photos of each other with their 100 items arranged in 10 groups of 10. Once the photos are uploaded, students write something for their individual pages. Students could also draw 100 dots or other images for the book. Other books could include pages for 10, 20, 30, and so on—or even 1,000 for second- and third-graders.

Have students work in groups to list 100 facts they know about a certain topic: 100 famous people throughout history, 100 different animals, or 100 book titles, or other areas of interest or study. They could also write what they would like their life to be when they are 100 years old. Celebrate the hundredth day of school with 100 balloons! (But please don't release the balloons!)

Number charts. Throughout the year make a variety of number charts with students to help them see relationships and patterns in numbers. Once completed, use markers or highlighter tape to draw attention to columns in the number charts

Ideas for Having Fun With 100

- Count 100 objects by 2s, 5s, 10s, and so on.
- Measure and then run 100 yards.
- Plant 100 seeds.
- Make 100 fingerprints, then decorate to turn them into animals or other designs.
- Draw 100 things.
- Recycle 100 items.
- Find 100 combinations of numbers that can be added to reach 100.
- Measure 100 inches and 100 centimeters.
- Write a poem with 100 words.
- Estimate how far 100 steps would take you. Then walk to see how accurate your estimate was.
- Melt 100 ice cubes—estimate where you think the water level will be when they melt.
- Create a piece of art, such as a collage, with 100 items or creatively represent 100.
- Dribble a basketball 100 times (for older students).
- Count 100 items to build with, like LEGOs. Then build something with that 100.
- Fill several containers with a different number of items. Ask the students to estimate which combination of containers has 100 items and provide reasons for their estimates.
- Weigh 100 kernels of popcorn. Then pop them and compare the weights of the popped and unpopped kernels.
- Collect 100 items to donate to a shelter or food pantry.

and look at the relationship between each of the numbers in the column. Students can work in small groups, each discussing a different column, and then comparing their findings. They might notice that in a five-column chart, the number directly below a given number is always five more than that number. Students could use this knowledge as a strategy to fill in missing numbers on a chart and discover patterns.

You can create number grids, number lines, graph paper, and spinners at http://illuminations.nctm.org/ActivityDetail.aspx?ID=205. Have students use them as a model to create their own grids and graphs to help them solve addition, subtraction, multiplication, and division problems.

There are many online games to help students with the concept of place value, such as at http://gregtangmath.com/games.php. This website has many other games to reinforce a variety of math skills. There are also a number of high-quality children's books available that center on math and literacy skills, such as *One Is a Snail, Ten Is a Crab* by April Pulley Sayre and Jeff Sayre.

1	2	3	4	5
6	7	8	9	10
11	12			

1	2	3	4	5	6	7	8	9	10

1	2	3	4	5	6	7	8	9	10	11	12	13	14	15

Number and Operation—Fractions

The CCSS include an additional area that begins in third grade, Number and Operations—Fractions. Third grade students are expected to learn about fractions, the quantity they represent, where they fit on the number line, and be able to compare two fractions as equivalent or not. Post a large number line in the room and add fractions to it with the students. Having a daily visual image will support their learning.

Use intriguing, real-life examples. Ask questions such as "Do you think most people would prefer 1/2, 1/3, or 1/4 of our snack today?" After giving students a chance to think about their answer, ask for a volunteer to pass out a snack and have students divide their own snacks to reflect their responses. Have a discussion about whether any of them would like to change their answer. Because the activity is fun and tasty, students may understand fractions far better than they would by completing a paper and pencil assignment.

Students need many opportunities to work with fractions in meaningful situations. Use paper or felt pizza portions or actual apple and orange slices to help them visualize operations with fractions. Ask students to demonstrate 1/10, 3/10, and other fractions on a ten frame. Provide Cuisenaire rods for students to use in making models of fractions, such as using the smallest unit rod on top of the double unit rod to demonstrate ½. They can also use the rods in solving fraction problems, such as using the different lengths of rods to show equivalent fractions of 1/2 = 2/4 = 3/6. Encourage the use of higher-order thinking skills by asking questions such as "How much would this $15 book cost if the price were cut by one-tenth?" that allow students to apply what they are learning. Websites and apps, such as *Pizza Fractions*, can help students improve their skills.

Try This!

Make layered cards to help students understand place value. Use cardstock, poster board, or stiff paper to make these cards, or create virtual cards to use on an interactive whiteboard. For example, to show the number 24, display these cards:

2	4

Under the *4* card would be a card with a *0* to help students see that this is *20* with *4* more:

2	0

Under those cards, another layer of cards could show the number of dots represented by each number in the top layer:

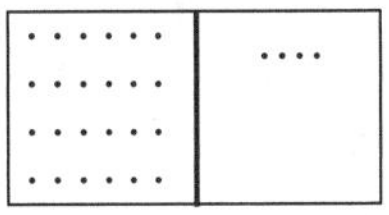

You could also include ten frames showing the amounts under the cards. Patterns for these cards and lesson plan ideas are available online at www.pinterest.com/pin/151785449913472027/.

Measurement and Data

Critical areas for instruction in Measurement and Data are

Grade 1—Developing understanding of linear measurement and measuring lengths as iterating length units

Grade 2—Using standard units of measure

Grade 3—Developing understanding of the structure of rectangular arrays and of area (National Governors Association Center for Best Practice & Council of Chief State School Officers 2010b, 13, 17, 21)

Students can meet standards in Measurement and Data area as they measure with a variety of tools, have hands-on practical experiences with time and money, and learn to organize and record data in graphs with activities such as those described below.

Measuring tools. To use measuring tools accurately, students must understand the idea of iterating—that is, a whole is made up of successive equal parts, one directly following after the next. For example, a ruler is made up of 12 equal parts called inches, and one inch directly follows the next. Students' experience with numbers and addition will help them understand this idea; for example, 4 is made up of 1+1+1+1. Give students opportunities to use many different measuring tools, such as rulers and metersticks, as well as objects to

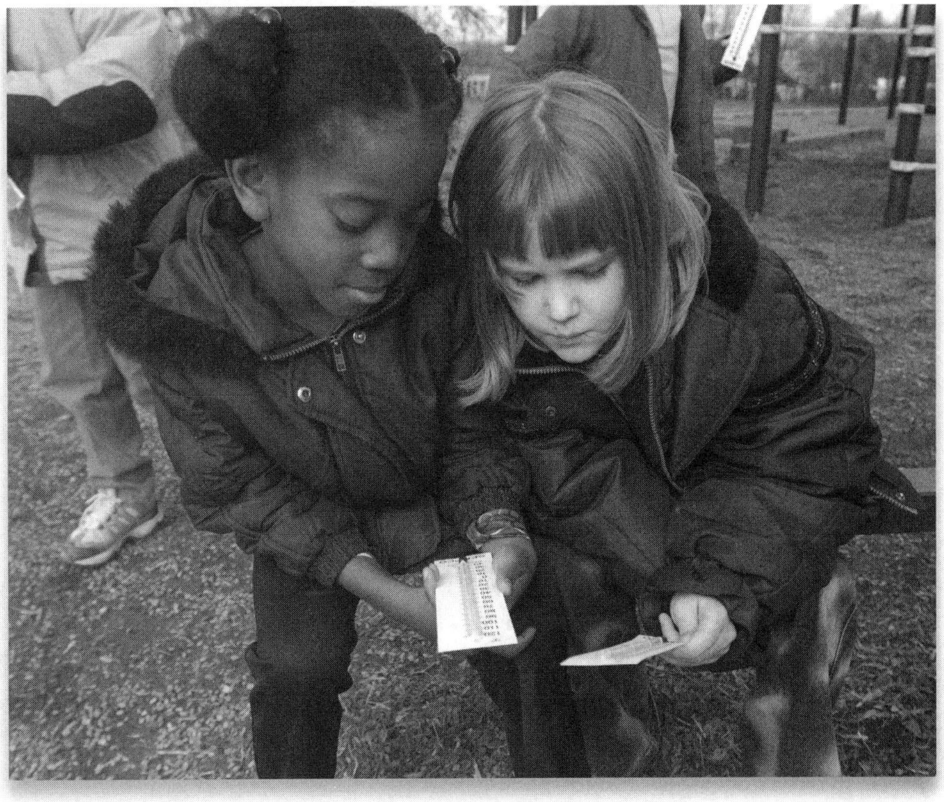

Try This!

Students can make their own inchworm rulers. First- and second-graders can measure and cut 12 one-inch lengths of paper and make them into unique inchworms by drawing a face and body on their inchworms. They can glue their inchworms onto stiff pieces of cardstock paper that is the same length. Third-graders can add 1/2-inch marks to their worms. Later in the year, second- and third-grade students could make a measuring centipede, marking out 30 centimeters on card stock 30 centimeters (about 12 inches) in length so they are able to use it like a ruler.

use as nonstandard measuring units, including paper clips, string, or cubes.

Help students understand the importance of using the same unit when comparing measurements. For example, ask students to measure the length of their desks or tables with their own hand span. Graph the results and talk about the findings. Ask, "Why are the numbers not the same and why that would matter when measuring items?" Discuss the difference between standard and nonstandard measurement tools and provide many opportunities to measure with both.

Estimating. Plan an "Estimation of the Day" that students can look forward to. Each day, provide a new item to measure or let the students choose something in the classroom to measure. Students estimate before measuring, recording both their estimate and the actual measurement. First- and second-graders can focus on length, while third-graders can begin to add in estimates of volume and mass. Sharpen students' skills by providing points of reference for comparison, such as a known quantity of the same item in a smaller container than the one being estimated: "This book is 10 inches long; how long do you think this book is?" and "This bottle holds one liter; how many liters do you think this pail holds?"

Integrate measurement with science. Have students measure the length of their feet, their shadows, and a variety of other objects and record their findings. Measuring and graphing the growth of bean plants is an easy way to give students hands-on math and science measuring experiences. Children will also enjoy measuring ingredients for a recipe, including doubling or tripling the recipe to cook something for the whole class

Graphs. Provide opportunities for students to collect data and make their own graphs. Encourage them to come up with their own questions to investigate, put their questions to fellow students and family members, record the responses with tally marks, and then graph the results. Teach students how to create different types of graphs, such as bar graphs, picture graphs, and line plots. The National Center for Education Statistics has a graph-making tool at www.nces.ed.gov/nceskids/createagraph/ that enables you and students to display data on a variety of graphs. You can also make a large, reusable graphing mat out of a shower curtain; mark graph lines with colored tape or permanent marker. Students can place objects on the mat or stand on the mat to graph data of all kinds, showing the measurements they have made.

Time. By the end of the school year, first-graders are expected to tell and write time using hours and half hours on both analog and digital clocks, and by the end of second grade they should be able to tell time in five-minute increments and understand the meaning of *a.m.* and *p.m.* By the end of third grade they need to be able to tell and write the time to the minute. The *Todo Telling Time* app, by Locomotive Labs, (available for Apple devices) provides an enjoyable way to practice all of these skills. Ask students to make a schedule of their daily activities and display each major event with the time on a clock.

Money. Second-graders learn to solve word problems using dollars, quarters, dimes, nickels, and pennies as well as how to correctly use the dollar and cent signs. Challenge students to identify what they would buy with different amounts of money: "What would you buy if you had ten dollars? ten dimes? five nickels?" This makes problem solving more meaningful and personal for each child. It also strengthens money skills, as well as addition, subtraction, and place value skills.

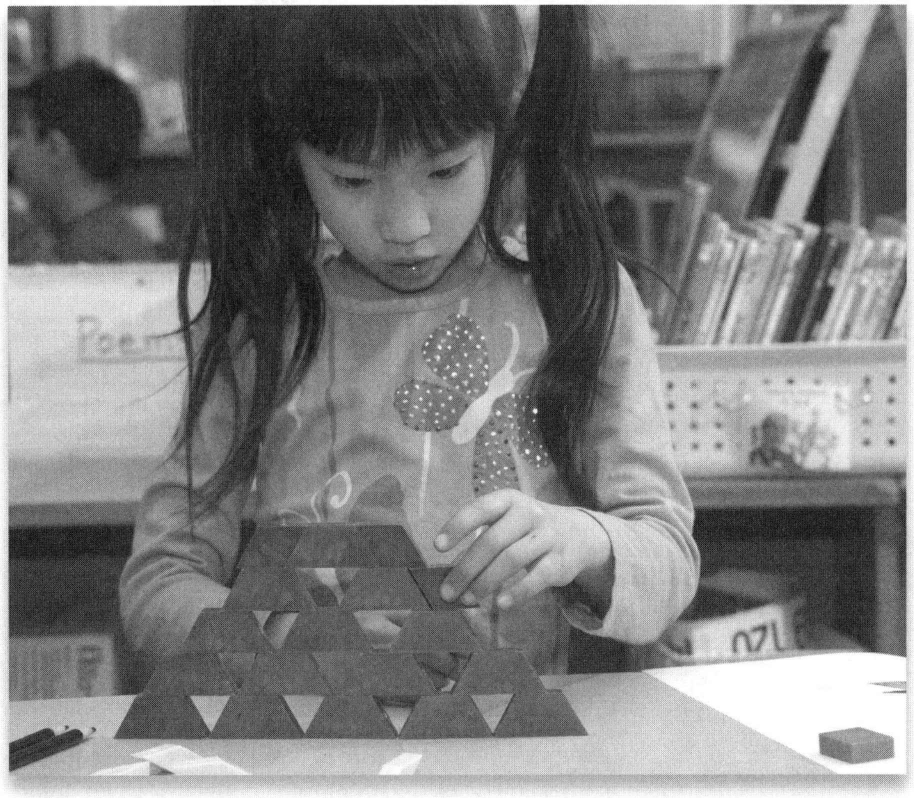

Geometry

Critical areas for instruction in the primary grades are

- **Grade 1**—Reasoning about attributes of, and composing and decomposing, geometric shapes
- **Grade 2**—Describing and analyzing shapes
- **Grade 3**—Describing and analyzing two-dimensional shapes (National Governors Association Center for Best Practice & Council of Chief State School Officers 2010b, 13, 17, 21)

There are a number of materials, apps, websites, and activities that can promote children's interest in geometry and help them meet standards. Several ideas and resources are described below.

Shapes. Many students like to manipulate shapes and create unique designs with them. Offer materials for students to use simple shapes to create more complex shapes, designs, objects, or animals. Ask questions that allow students to describe the characteristics of different shapes: "How do you know this is a triangle? What makes it different from a square? Will it still be a triangle if I turn it in different directions? How do you know?" Students can create shapes on geoboards or on an app such as *Geoboard*. They can draw their own shapes with drawing programs or with drawing tools on computers or tablets, which helps them understand the key characteristics of the shapes. Encourage them to rotate, flip, and slide their shapes to strengthening their understanding that the position of the shape does not change the basic characteristics of the shape. Children can manipulate, compose, and decompose shapes at two NCTM Illuminations web pages; there is a shape tool at http://illuminations.nctm.org/ActivityDetail.aspx?ID=35 and a patch tool at http://illuminations.nctm.org/ActivityDetail.aspx?ID=27. The patch tool can be used to create patchwork quilt shapes or other designs. PBS LearningMedia has many short videos and interactive activities related to geometry and shapes as well as videos related to other mathematics and additional subject areas (visit www.pbslearningmedia.org).

Try This!

Take a shape walk around the neighborhood or school, providing students with clipboards or another writing surface. Challenge the students to find as many shapes as they can. Ask them to draw a picture of each different shape as they see it, putting the shapes in a row on the bottom of their paper. They can then create a line plot (which shows frequency of data) by marking an *x* above the picture of the shape each time they see that shape. Challenge students to find objects composed of multiple shapes and draw those shapes as well. Students can try to create these objects using pattern blocks when they return to the classroom.

Tangrams. Tangrams offer a unique way to learn about shapes. To introduce students to tangrams, read *Grandfather Tang's Story* by Ann Tompert. Offer tangram pieces so students can create their own pictures. Provide tangram puzzles that have each of the inner shapes outlined and then provide puzzles that have only the overall picture outlined, not the individual shapes needed to complete the puzzle. Eventually, challenge students to create a square using all seven tangram pieces. The PBS Kids Cyberchase site has an interactive tangram activity at www.pbskids.org/cyberchase/math-games/tanagram-game/ along with a number of other games, activities, and videos. There are a number of websites with free traceable tangram pieces and puzzle outlines. Students can also create printable pattern blocks at http://illuminations.nctm.org/ActivityDetail.aspx?ID=205.

Engaging Math Centers

Every kindergarten through grade 3 classroom needs a math area with manipulatives, games, puzzles, and computer applications. Some teachers provide CGI or a lesson to the whole class and then have the students work in math centers for the rest of their math time to practice the skills they are learning. Math centers provide an effective way to differentiate the curriculum; provide a variety of activities at different levels and add more complex activities over time.

In writing how to help primary grade students meet the expectations of the CCSS, Evenson and colleagues (2013) explain that NCTM

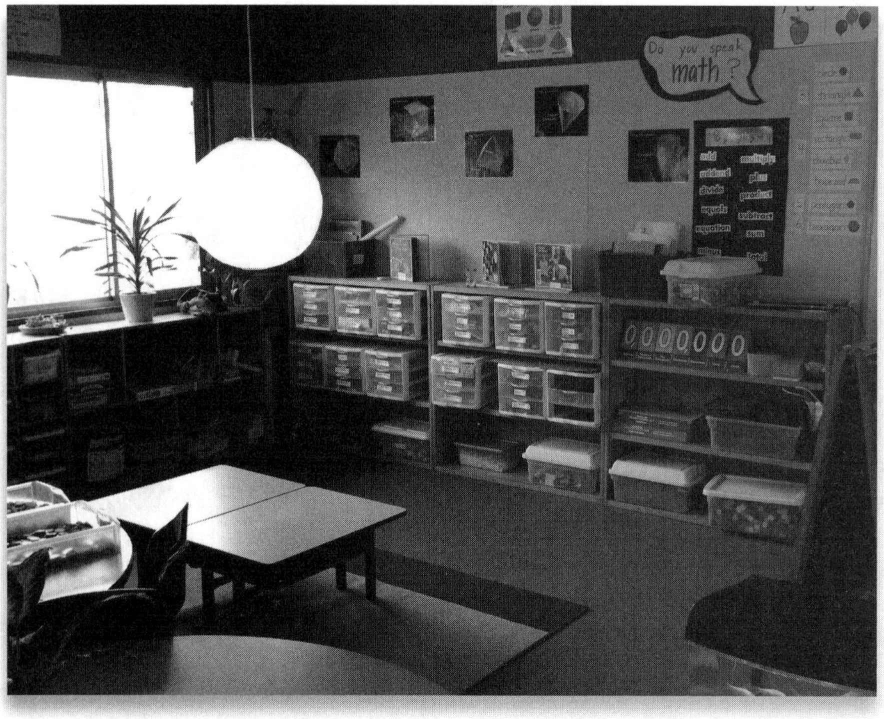

> recommends that teachers support students' ability to make sense of numbers by creating classroom environments that promote the exploration of numbers, the development of conjectures, and dialogue about the thinking process. Early childhood researchers recommend play-based activities as a way to help younger students develop their abilities to make sense of problems and persevere in solving them. (88)

Math centers are a key part of a play-based, learning-rich environment where students can be actively engaged in mathematical problem solving.

There are number of websites, such as www.k-5mathteachingresources.com, with activities to help students meet the CCSS for math. Many of the activities are designed for use at math centers and are searchable by grade level. If workbook pages are a required part of your curriculum, students can work on these pages using math center manipulatives that help them visualize the concepts. Changing manipulatives with the seasons and units of study will help to keep interest high. Some primary teachers have one math center with a variety of manipulatives and children's books on math-related topics; others offer several math centers during math time or other times during the day. Following are ideas for a variety of math centers.

Math Bulletin Board Center

Each day post a special problem of the day for the children to solve on a math bulletin board. Also include math anchor charts that you have made with students, such as one showing new math terminology along with graphics and definitions that describe the words. This helps build the academic vocabulary that will serve students in all areas of the curriculum.

Menu Math Center

Stock this center with restaurant menus collected from restaurants in your community or download them from restaurant websites. There are also several teacher websites that have menus specifically designed for menu math. Students can make their own menus as well, listing food items and prices. After looking at a menu, students can write down an order for a meal and find the total cost for the items they chose. Keep the center fresh by changing the menus and the activities students are asked to do. Students might choose different meals, work within a certain budget, or calculate the amount of money left over from the budgeted amount. Students might also go on virtual shopping trips, using store ads to plan a menu and calculate costs to feed a certain number of people or the class.

Geometry Center

The geometry area is a great place for working on math standards with pattern blocks, tangram puzzles, and other materials. Some primary teachers include a variety of blocks in this area for students to use to explore geometric concepts in depth. This area could include LEGOs, parquetry blocks, a set of hardwood unit blocks, or other types of blocks. Students can compose, decompose, and build with shapes. To promote geometry and thinking skills, as well as speaking and listening skills, ask students to work in pairs and have one child make a design with a set of shapes hidden behind a book or folder. Without showing the design, the student describes to his partner how to make it with an identical set of shapes. The second student attempts to create the design following these instructions. Students then switch roles.

Measuring Center

Supply this area with rulers, tape measures, measuring cups, balance scales, and a variety of other kinds of measuring tools. Students can use both standard and nonstandard

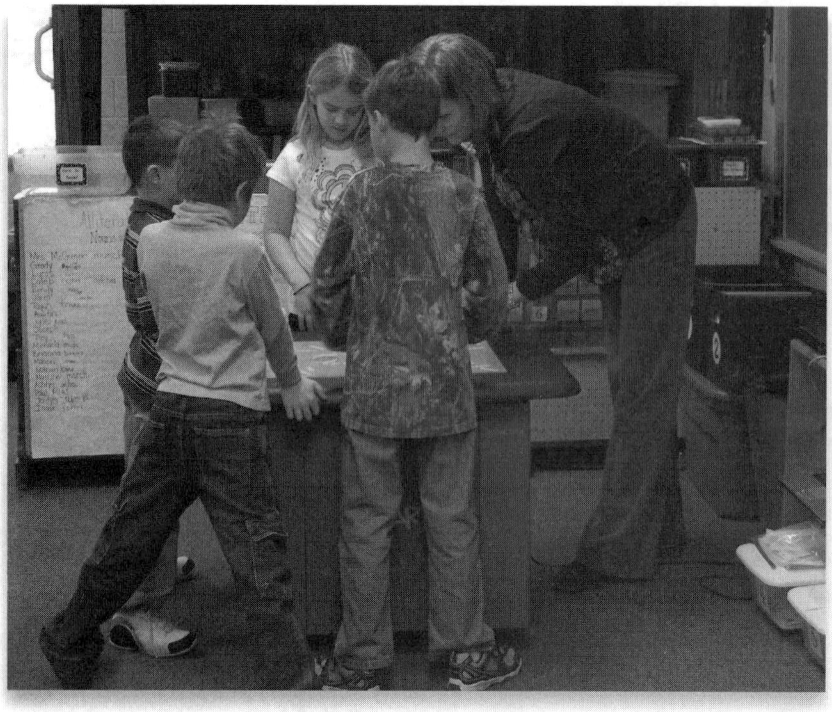

measurements to work on measuring problems, including estimating. Measurements can be done individually, in pairs, or small groups.

Math Game Center

Stock this center with math-related games and puzzles you already have in your classroom or that come from teacher supply stores or sites such as www.marcycookmath.com/. Make your own simple games with purchased clear spinners and individualize the games for topics the class is studying.

Digital Learning Center

A number of math-related games are available for digital devices, including computers, tablets, interactive whiteboards, and multitouch interactive tables, such as SMART tables. In addition to the NCTM Illuminations games and other websites mentioned in this chapter, the American Library Association has recommended websites for children at http://gws.ala.org geared to math and other subjects. The PowerMyLearning website (www.powermylearning.org/) has thousands of games, apps, and interactive activities aligned to the CCSS that teachers can differentiate for individual children. Some teachers also like to use an overhead projector as a center where students work with magnetic or foam numbers and letters or write and solve problems on clear acetate sheets.

Authentic Assessments at Centers and Throughout the Math Curriculum

Learning centers are an ideal setting for authentic assessment of students' math skills and understandings. As students are engaged in center activities, ask them to describe their problem-solving strategies. When assessing, keep in mind that you need to discover if students not only know the concepts but also understand how to apply those concepts and use them in their everyday lives. This provides insight into their progress on both the mathematical practices and standards. Use individual discussions with students to help them learn to evaluate their own work and judge whether their answers make sense in light of the data given in problems. Informing students of the learning target and actual standard you are working on can help them be more active participants in the learning standards process.

Assessment happens in other settings as well, through a variety of means, and goes hand-in-hand with instruction—for example, evaluate students' performance on class work, projects and problem-solving activities, and homework assignments. Assessments provide a window into students' understanding as well as their misconceptions. This allows teachers to adjust their instruction, clarify concepts, and move forward when students have a firm grasp of the topic. Make assessment a positive experience, showing students what they have mastered and what you will continue to work on together. Use ongoing assessment and feedback. This will enable you to implement a spiral curriculum in which you present new material, check students' comprehension, and then revisit concepts frequently at a slightly higher level.

The ultimate goal of assessment is to improve student learning. Assessing children before teaching concepts tells teachers what students already know and identifies what they still need to learn. Quick assessments at the end of lessons provide useful information about how much students comprehend and where they need more help. Leinwand (2012) suggests that our classrooms be "active environments—often noisy, but clearly productive and purposeful—as students converse mathematically and wrestle with ideas in the course of solving interesting problems" (63). He recommends that teachers do quick reviews to help students keep their skills sharp by practicing and revisiting concepts previously taught. He suggests including a

- Fact of the day
- Measurement of the day
- Place value problem of the day
- Word problem of the day
- Problem related to a skill that needs reinforcing

These could be used both as quick transition activities and informal assessments and can be done in a variety of ways to keep the activities fresh. Students can record their answers on small whiteboards, tablets, or paper. These activities could also be done as an informal discussion or in math journals. They could also be done on small file cards or slips of paper and used as *exit tickets*, which are short questions or problems answered at the end of a class period or end of the day. Display several sentence starters and ask students to complete one for their exit ticket, such as

- Today I learned that . . .
- The way this connects to what we already learned is . . .
- The way I can use this in the future is . . .
- What I liked best about math class today was . . .
- I still don't understand . . . (Evenson et al. 2013; Sousa 2008)

Exit tickets can also occasionally ask other questions that will help individualize instruction:

What do you like best about math class?

What are you good at doing in math?

What would you like to know more about?

How do you use math outside of math class?

Home<->School Connections

Children's attitudes toward math are greatly influenced by their family members. Communicate frequently to build reciprocal relationships with families and share ideas that will nurture positive attitudes about school and math. Let families know your goal of helping children feel competent in applying their math skills throughout life. Help families see the usefulness of math by designing engaging homework assignments that involve family members and allow students to gain additional experience in applying the mathematical practices. For example, you might ask younger students to choose two different items in their home to count, write down the numbers and label them. They might choose to count the number of pillows, doors, or doorknobs in their home. Then ask that they add the numbers together. They could also collect data on family members' interests, which can promote conversations. Have students graph the information they collect. Students can also write and solve problems based on their families and interests. To help students see the usefulness of math, invite family members to share how they use math in their everyday lives. They could share this information with the students by writing how they use math and sending this information to the class or posting the information on a classroom blog or website.

In addition to finding out how families would most like for you to contact them, provide several ways that they can contact you that match their preferences. Ask families to contact you if their children are having difficulties in math or in any area, as well as letting you know children's current interests and needs so you can incorporate them into your plans. Encourage families to share their ideas on a classroom blog or website regarding ways their children have learned math at home. You could provide some prompts or examples, such as "At dinner time my child and I like to multiply the number of people eating dinner by the number of ears of corn on the table."

Consider sending home or posting on your class website a weekly or monthly list of suggestions to help families support their children's mathematics development. Encourage families to look for opportunities to talk about the math they encounter at the store, bank, restaurant, and at home. Suggest questions for them to ask their children, such as "How much cornmeal will we need if we double the recipe?" "How many pens do you think will fit in this container?" "What can we order that would cost less than ten dollars?" Recommend playing card and board games that involve numbers. Families could also contribute items such as old keys, shells, and buttons to be used as manipulatives in the classroom. The national PTA has helpful family guides to the CCSS in math and English language arts at http://pta.org/parents/content.cfm?ItemNumber=2583.

Meeting Standards—and More!

Many children are intrigued by numbers and counting but begin to lose confidence in their ability to solve problems when they encounter more advanced mathematical concepts. Some students experience great frustration in doing mathematics, which can turn into math anxiety. Help students feel more confident by presenting tasks at a level that is appropriate for them. Make sure both girls and boys feel capable and confident. Promote their curiosity and interest in doing mathematics with relevant, meaningful examples and assignments, emphasizing learning strategies and understanding *how* to use them rather than just on getting the correct answer. Encourage students to ask questions and take risks without fear of losing face because their answer is wrong. Help them learn to value reflecting, thinking, and analyzing rather than simply speed. Remember that your attitudes about math greatly influence students' attitudes. Demonstrating your interest in and appreciation of math, and how it helps you in your daily activities, can help reduce students' anxiety (Sousa 2008).

Help students view math as a set of tools that can help them solve problems they encounter in their daily lives. Use questions that naturally arise in day-to-day activities as a way for children to see that math is something they need and can use successfully: "How many students are here today? How many boys? How many girls? How many snacks will we need?" Ask visitors to the class to share ways they use math in their daily lives.

Help students become proficient problem solvers who persevere in their efforts. This will help them not only in mathematics but in all areas of their lives. Students can apply their problem-solving skills to science, decoding, spelling, and even social situations. As students feel more confident in their ability to solve problems, they will be more willing to attempt new challenges in a variety of areas.

In a Nutshell

The CCSS outline mathematical practices that cut across all grade levels and standards and include making sense of problems and persevering in solving them; reasoning abstractly and quantitatively; constructing viable arguments; modeling with mathematics; using appropriate tools strategically; attending to precision; looking for and making use of structure; and looking for and expressing regularity in repeated reasoning. Students can meet the standards in the domains of Operations and Algebraic Thinking, Number and Operations in Base Ten, Number and Operations—Fractions (for grade 3 and above), Measurement and Data, and Geometry through engaging, hands-on activities, including CGI, the use of manipulatives, number lines, and math centers. Using everyday events in the problems you give to students provides motivation and helps them see the practicality and need for what they are learning. Authentic assessment enables teachers to know what students understand and to differentiate their teaching so that all children become capable, confident problem solvers who persist in thinking, reasoning, and providing evidence for their answers.

Fostering Involved Citizens Through **Social Studies**

5

The National Council for the Social Studies (NCSS) describes the purpose of social studies as helping "young people make informed and reasoned decisions for the public good as citizens of a culturally diverse democratic society in an interdependent world" (2010, 3). Carla Rinaldi suggests that the primary aim of education in general, including social studies, is "to educate *citizens of the world* who are conscious of their roots but open to cultural and geographic horizons with no boundaries" (2001, 28).

It is a privilege to be part of this lofty mission for students. Because of all the demands teachers face, however, social studies sometimes receives less attention in the classroom than reading, writing, and math. It is important not to bypass the rich social studies content. Studying history, geography, civics, and economics fosters skills, dispositions, and knowledge that will help students in both their current and future lives. Social studies learning also enhances students' skills in other areas, particularly English language arts. Students need the rich background knowledge and in-depth vocabulary gained from studying social studies concepts to comprehend texts and build the strong vocabulary that the Common Core State Standards (CCSS) and other standards expect. Students also need opportunities to use their language and literacy skills in other subject areas and to learn how to apply these skills when needed in the future. The CCSS expect that informational text will make up about half of the reading students do; social studies topics are ideal for this reading.

The National Curriculum Standards for Social Studies

In 2010 NCSS published *National Curriculum Standards for Social Studies: A Framework for Teaching, Learning, and Assessment.* This document outlined 10 themes of social studies to guide states in identifying content that should be included in their standards:

1. Culture
2. Time, Continuity, and Change

3. People, Places, and Environments
4. Individual Development and Identity
5. Individuals, Groups, and Institutions
6. Power, Authority, and Governance
7. Production, Distribution, and Consumption
8. Science, Technology, and Society
9. Global Connections
10. Civic Ideals and Practices

Students encounter many of these themes naturally through daily activities as they develop classroom rules, take turns doing classroom jobs, vote on which book they would like the teacher to read aloud, and work with classmates from various backgrounds, cultures, and abilities. Teachers need to intentionally incorporate opportunities for students to learn meaningful concepts and positive attitudes in these areas. This chapter provides ideas for integrating these concepts throughout the curriculum.

College, Career, and Civic Life (C3) Framework and Inquiry Arc

The book *Social Studies for the Next Generation: Purposes, Practices, and Implications of the College, Career, and Civic Life (C3) Framework for Social Studies State Standards* (NCSS 2013b) emphasizes the importance of social studies for students as national and world citizens. It outlines ways to meet the CCSS for reading, writing, language, speaking, and listening through social studies inquiries; it also describes the College, Career, and Civic Life (C3) Framework for Social Studies State Standards, which was designed to help states develop their standards. The book also includes indicators that students should be able to meet at the end of grades 2, 5, 8, and 12.

The C3 Framework emphasizes inquiry as the heart of social studies, which means that students will be seeking information about social studies concepts by asking compelling questions that lead to some answers along with more questions and discoveries. Questions are key to student learning, and both teacher- and student-initiated questions are a central element of teaching and learning. The framework suggests that primary teachers guide students in constructing a *compelling,* important question and in developing *supporting* questions as a way of arriving at answers to the overarching, compelling question. With guidance, students may come up with a compelling question such as, "What makes a community work well?" Their supporting questions could include "How do people support our community? Who makes the laws in our town? Why do we need laws? Where does our school get money? Why do we have parks? Who pays for parks? What stores help our community? What jobs are needed in our town?" Two of the C3 Framework indicators are that by the end of grade 2, students are able to "explain why a compelling question is important to the student" and "make connections between supporting questions and a compelling question" (NCSS 2013a, 24–25).

NCSS (2013a) recommends using an Inquiry Arc to learn social studies, featuring four dimensions of informed inquiry:

1. Developing questions and planning inquiries
2. Applying disciplinary concepts and tools (in the areas of civics, economics, geography, and history)

3. Evaluating sources and using evidence
4. Communicating conclusions and taking informed action (12)

By using the Inquiry Arc, students will discover answers that help them learn social studies concepts in civics, economics, geography, and history.

Using Long-Term Studies and the Inquiry Arc to Meet Standards

The Inquiry Arc fits very well with project-based or problem-based learning. Decades ago John Dewey recommended organizing the curriculum around real-world problems and student interests as a way to make learning relevant and enable students to be successful. Although there are many ways to help children acquire the skills designated in the Inquiry Arc, conducting a study of a problem or topic in depth over time is an effective way to learn and practice these skills and to meet standards in social studies and other areas of the curriculum. In *Social Studies Worksheets Don't Grow Dendrites*, Tate (2012) recommends using project- or problem-based learning to engage students in more meaningful learning and to improve retention of concepts.

Conducting a Long-Term Study Following the Inquiry Arc

With a long-term inquiry study, the whole class might be involved, or small groups of students can pursue subtopics related to the problem or study that are of particular interest to them. Studies last a few weeks, a month, or longer depending on student interest, the sources available for study, and the continued potential for learning and meeting standards. Studies offer opportunities in each phase to involve families in meaningful ways.

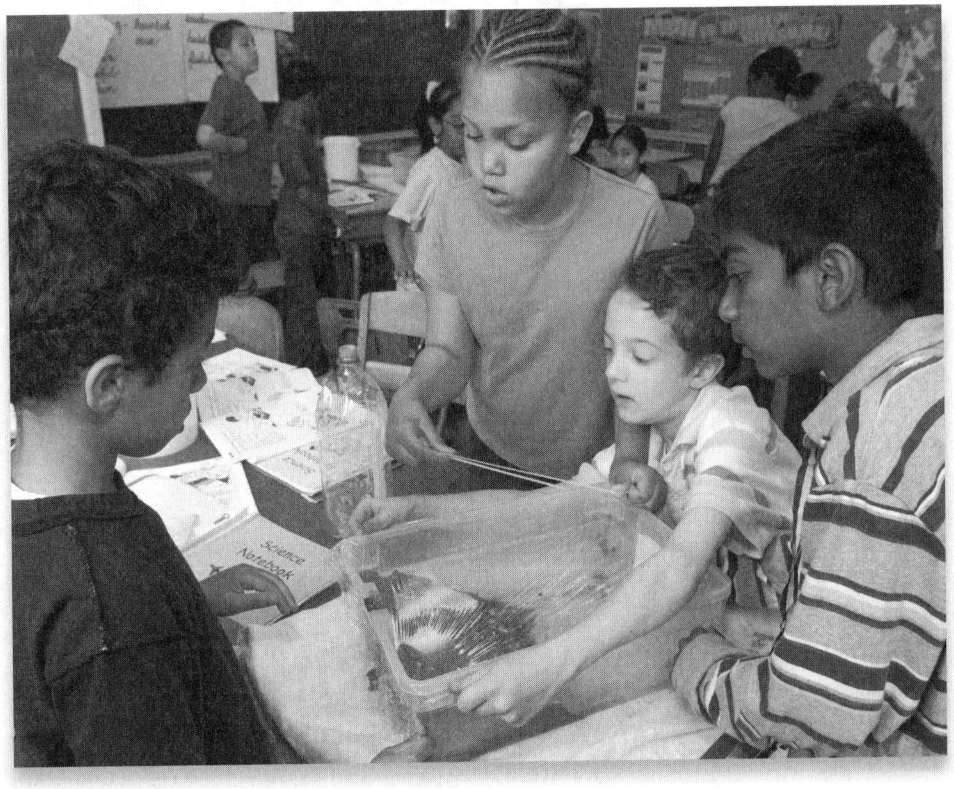

The first phase of a long-term study, **beginning the study,** starts with finding a compelling question to answer, problem to be solved, or topic to investigate as suggested in the first dimension of the Inquiry Arc. Help students identify a problem in their community that is relevant to them, such as how to make street crossings safer for students or how to make the school (or another building) more accessible. Talk with students about their interests and help them identify topics that are meaningful to them. The unit themes in your social studies text offer additional topic possibilities, such as families and communities. Many study topics have the potential to incorporate multiple disciplines, such as an "under construction" study that brings together economics with discussions of products and services needed to build new constructions, literacy in reading and writing about different types of construction and communicating plans, math involving measurements, and the arts as students build models of buildings.

Topics, problems, and compelling questions should

1. Be important and significant for student learning
2. Be meaningful and relevant to the students
3. Offer abundant opportunities for students to meet standards in multiple areas
4. Have the potential for a rich investigation with many sources and materials that students can access

The introductory phase continues by identifying and listing all the standards that exploring this topic could address. Then make a KWL chart with the students, listing the compelling question at the top as the title of the chart. Record what they already know (K) about the question or topic and supporting questions that reflect what else they want (W) to know and that will help answer the question or learn more about the topic. Keep this chart posted and revisit it frequently during the study to remind students of the questions they are pursuing and to add what they are learning (L) throughout the study.

Phases of a Long-Term Study

Begin the study: Find a compelling question to answer, problem to be solved, or topic to investigate

Investigate and represent: Learn more about the topic and investigate possible answers and solutions

Conclude the study: Communicate conclusions and take informed action

In the second phase of a long-term study, **investigating and representing,** students learn more about the topic and investigate possible answers and solutions to problems and questions they have posed. They also learn about and apply disciplinary concepts and tools (Dimension 2 of the Inquiry Arc) by reading information about their topic and completing activities that will help them understand and use concepts and tools from geography, history, civics, or economics. This might include listening to guest speakers, taking field trips, or simply exploring their own environment. As students seek out sources of information, help them evaluate the sources and use evidence to find answers to their questions, as outlined in Dimension 3 of the Inquiry Arc.

After investigating the topic for some time, students can generate a list of possible solutions to the problem or answers to the compelling question. This may lead to additional investigation and reading. Students will demonstrate what they know, meeting standards in multiple areas as they explore and record their investigations.

The final phase, **concluding the study,** typically ends with a culminating event. During this time students complete the last dimension of the Inquiry Arc, communicating conclusions and taking informed action. They might communicate their conclusions by writing a report, creating multimedia presentations such as PowerPoint, writing and performing a play, or completing another type of project. Inviting family members, school administrators, or other classes to the culminating event provides an audience and additional motivation for students to put effort into their work. The culminating event provides an opportunity to share the work students have done throughout the study and review the KWL chart with the compelling and supporting questions and the answers students have discovered.

Students might take informed action by developing an informational document to give to community leaders, starting a petition, or bringing items to a soup kitchen. Their daily work and concluding writing or presentations will help you document their learning not only in social studies but also in reading, writing, language, speaking, listening, and the arts. If available, smartphones, tablets, and digital cameras make documenting students' work much easier. Students' actual work, or photos of their work, provide authentic documentation and are an excellent way to share student progress with families (Parnell & Bartlett 2012).

More information on conducting a study or project can be found in the second edition of *Young Investigators: The Project Approach in the Early Years* (Helm & Katz 2011), and at the following websites: www.projectapproach.org/, www.bie.org/, and www.edutopia.org/teachingmodules/PBL/index.php.

Maps and Globes: A Long-Term Study Example

The topic of maps and globes offers possibilities for an engaging study in the primary grades. Many students find maps and globes fascinating and may have read about them or seen them used in the media and by their families. Students are expected to learn map and globe skills as part of the geography standards.

In the **first phase** of a study of maps and globes, look at your state standards for social studies and identify all those that students might meet while exploring this topic. Then look through the language arts and mathematics standards and jot down those you would like to focus on. The chart shown here indicates a few of the many standards that could be met in a study of maps and globes.

Examples of Standards Addressed in a Study of Maps and Globes

Content Area	Standard	Possible Activity
Social Studies: C3 Framework: Geography	D2.Geography.1.Kindergarten-Grade 2 Construct maps, graphs, and other representations of familiar places.	Make maps of the playground and community.
Social Studies: C3 Framework: Geography	D2.Geography.3.Kindergarten-Grade 2 Use maps, globes, and other simple geographic models to identify cultural and environmental characteristics of places.	Explore maps of the community, visit nearby sites, and then create a 3-D map showing cultural or environmental characteristics in the community.
CCSS for Mathematics: Measurement and Data	Grade 2.Measurement and Data.3. Estimate lengths using units of inches, feet, centimeters, and meters.	Make a map of the playground by first estimating the feet or meters from one part of the playground to another and then measuring the playground to make the map to scale as much as possible.
CCSS for Speaking and Listening: Comprehension and Collaboration	Grade 2.Speaking and Listening.2. Recount or describe key ideas or details from a text read aloud or information presented orally or through other media.	Listen to a guest speaker from the community talk about how maps of the community are made and used (such as maps of the water and telecommunications systems) and then recount what was learned in a celebration at the end of the study.

Next, sit down with students and make a KWL chart together. As outlined in Dimension 1 of the Inquiry Arc, encourage students to think about a compelling question to guide the study. Depending on the grade you teach, students' interests and needs, and the characteristics of the surrounding community, a question to explore might be, "How would more accurate maps and globes have changed the history of our country?" or "How can learning more about people across the globe help us be better neighbors in our community?" Together generate a list of supporting questions, such as the following:

- How do we read maps and globes?
- How can we make a map of our classroom, school, playground, or community?
- What kinds of maps and globes have been available throughout history?
- What might have happened if Columbus had had better maps and had been able to reach Asia as he had originally planned?
- What might have happened if pioneers had had better maps?
- What cultures are represented in our school?

In the **second phase** of investigating and representing, students would learn about and apply disciplinary concepts and tools, especially in the area of geography but also in history and potentially civics and economics (Dimension 2 of the Inquiry Arc). Talk with students about how they could learn more about maps and answer the questions they have generated. Students can read about maps and how they have influenced history, as well as about cultures around the globe, and record what they discover. Have students explore maps at www.worldatlas.com. They can calculate distances between their community and other places they have read and learned about at https://maps.google.com or locate satellite images of their school, community, and other locations around the country and globe on Google Earth (www.google.com/earth) and at National Geographic at (http://education.nationalgeographic.com/education/mapping/interactive-map/?ar_a=1).

Students can explore the features of a map or globe and how they are displayed by creating their own representations on paper, on a computer or tablet, or out of sand, papier-mâché, or other materials. Invite guest speakers, including family and community members, to share their knowledge of map making or related topics. If possible, take a field trip or walk around the school neighborhood to measure and explore geographic features. Since these activities span a wide range of standards and subject areas, they could occur at different times in your schedule during the course of the study, including during social studies time. Students can also read about maps and globes as part of the language arts block, make distance calculations as part of the math block, create maps during art time, or do these activities at a variety of learning centers or interest areas. You can block out additional time for studies or project work each week to integrate all these activities, knowing that you can scaffold students' learning and help them meet standards in many areas of the curriculum.

The **final phase,** concluding the study, might culminate with a display of student-made maps, globes, writing, and posters that document their learning. Have students use the display to share information about cultures around the globe they have learned about. Invite families to bring in artifacts or foods from their home cultures and view the display. Students might decide that inviting other students and

Try This!

To pique students' interest when you introduce a new unit or topic of study, bring an object related to the topic in a wrapped box or other mysterious packaging. Play 20 Questions with the students as they try to guess what the object is. This could become a tradition to start each major social studies unit. For example, before studying maps bring in a copy of an old map or a treasure map rolled up and tied with a ribbon or rope.

community members to this event would promote an understanding of diversity in the community and be a way of taking informed action. They could use their letter-writing skills to write invitations to the event. If students have developed multimedia presentations, show them at this event as well. Throughout the year reinforce the skills acquired through this study.

Integrated Approach

Studies provide an engaging way for students to meet standards in social studies and all areas of the curriculum, and they are a natural means of integrating the curriculum. Studies might follow the phases discussed previously or be carried out more informally while teaching social studies units by simply adding a few topic-related activities, such as those mentioned in this chapter.

Another way to integrate the curriculum is by reading books with social studies themes that integrate social studies and literacy. Visit websites with recommended books in specific social studies areas, such as www.carolhurst.com. Many books and ebooks are available in your school and local libraries. Social studies is an excellent way to enrich children's vocabulary development by introducing and using social studies-related words throughout the curriculum. Using visuals and hands-on materials will help students learn concepts and vocabulary more effectively, especially children who have learning challenges. For example, children can strengthen literacy skills and meet standards as they watch a video on a social studies subject and jot down key details. Asking children to be responsible for writing a few key details will also help to keep them focused.

With so many expectations to meet during the school day, integrating the curriculum makes sense. It also fits with what is known about how the brain works: "The purpose of integrating content is not only to make school more enjoyable and interesting, which promotes enthusiasm and a love of learning; it also is to support children's ability to connect new learning to prior knowledge, which has the effect of expanding children's memory and reasoning capacity" (Tomlinson 2014, 8).

Engaging Activities for Meeting Standards in Social Studies

There are many additional activities and experiences that will help students achieve skills and meet standards in the core disciplines of social studies—geography, history, economics, and civics—and in the 10 theme areas designated by NCSS. The ideas and activities that follow will help students meet the indicators set out in the C3 Framework of the NCSS (2013a) and standards in many other areas of the curriculum. Many of the activities are appropriate for students in any of the primary grades, while others can be simplified for younger students and those who need additional help or made more complex for those who are ready for more challenging studies.

Geography and Cultural Understanding

Children enjoy learning about fascinating people, cultures, and countries as they explore the social studies theme of People, Places, and Environments. Stock the library area with books about students' community, state, and country and countries around

Try This!

Interest students in learning about other countries by having them choose a country they would like to "visit." Working in small groups, with a partner, or individually, they can study the geographical features of the country using books and websites (such as www.timeforkids.com/around-the-world) and plan a trip. Depending on students' abilities, their plans might include how they would get to the country, how far they would need to travel, what the weather and climate would be like and how it affects the people there, what clothes and other items they would need to pack, what type of money they would use, what language is spoken there, a description of the people and their culture, what places they would like to visit there, foods they could try, the type of terrain, and other characteristics you think would be useful.

Provide a simple rubric for students to follow as they research, write, and share their findings with their classmates through reports, multimedia presentations, maps, postcards, posters, or brochures. Differentiate the rubrics to challenge students at their individual levels. By creating and presenting the information they have learned, students will meet a variety of standards in reading, writing, speaking, listening, language, and several areas of social studies.

Rubric for Country Visit

Inquiry Arc Dimension	3 Points	2 Points	1 Point
1. Developing Questions and Planning Inquiries	I wrote three or more questions to research about the country. I wrote clearly how I would get my information and talked with the teacher about my plans.	I wrote two questions to research about the country and talked with the teacher about my plans.	I wrote one question to research about the country I chose.
2. Applying Disciplinary Concepts	I wrote a good description of the weather and climate and how it affects people there. I wrote a good description about the distance from here to there and how I would get there. I wrote a good description of the country's culture, money, food, and language.	I described the weather and how it affects the people there. I wrote about how I would get there. I described the country's money, food, and language.	I described the weather. I wrote about how I would get there. I listed their money and food.
3. Evaluating Sources and Using Evidence	I used three or more sources from the class list of good resources.	I used two sources from the class list of good resources.	I used one source.
4. Communicating Conclusions and Taking Informed Action	My presentation is easy to read and understand. I listed two ways to apply what I learned (e.g., bring sunscreen/appropriate clothing).	My presentation is easy to read. I listed one way to apply what I learned.	My presentation is fairly easy to read.

A variation of this activity is for the students to choose a state or national park and describe its location, its geographic and other interesting features, how to get there, plants that grow there, animals that live in the park, and what jobs in the park they might like to do.

the world, as well as the people who live in these areas. Make story maps of books you are reading that have interesting settings. Include the geographical setting and time period and discuss ways the setting may have influenced the event or story. Use websites such as www.education.nationalgeographic.com/education/ to view videos and photos, and find lesson plans and other resources.

Geography. To make social studies come alive and help students learn more about geography, take walks around your school neighborhood or go on field trips. Virtual field trips, too, can broaden students' experiences (Kirchen 2011). Making maps—including keys—of their school, playground, neighborhood, and community will help children develop spatial skills and learn to make geographical representations.

Culture. Culture is a significant social studies theme. To help students feel a sense of pride in their own cultures and a healthy curiosity about others', start by learning about the backgrounds and cultural traditions of students and their families. Use books, posters, materials, fabrics, and other objects in the classroom environment that reflect the students' cultures. For example, post a welcome sign that includes the word *welcome* in each of the home languages spoken by the children (Wien 2004). Ask dual language learners to teach the class a few basic words in their language. Invite family members to share with the class aspects of their cultures, including holidays or festivals they celebrate, artwork, currency, and famous people. Display and read books that portray contemporary children from a variety of cultures to avoid stereotypes and misunderstandings about modern clothing, homes, or jobs Consider books such as *My Librarian Is a Camel: How Books Are Brought to Children Around the World* by Margriet Ruurs and *What Can You Do With a Paleta?* by Carmen Tafolla. Students can also learn about other countries by exploring websites such as www.exploreandmore.org/world/default.htm.

The CCSS expect primary children to retell folktales from a variety of cultures and compare different cultural variations of stories. Comparing and contrasting stories from various cultures may help students understand the cultures better. A few possibilities are *Jingle Dancer* by Cynthia Leitich Smith, *The Good Luck Cat* by Joy Harjo, and *Eagle Song* by Joseph Bruchac, all of which describe contemporary Native American children in a variety of settings.

When you read a story or folktale, locate the setting of the story on a world map that you hang in the classroom or keep on your computer. Use a pin or adhesive note to indicate the title of the book. Talk about the geographical features and cultural traditions of each place. If possible, identify and talk about the countries where the students' ancestors lived as well. Throughout the year, select stories or folktales that are set in a variety of places.

Similarities and differences. To help children learn more about the social studies theme of Individual Development and Identity, explore and celebrate a variety of similarities and differences between students. Ask students to pair with another classmate, or with an older "big buddy" student, to find out more about each other, including likes and dislikes. Then have them divide a paper in thirds vertically and list similarities they share in the middle column. They can each list their unique characteristics and preferences in one of the other columns. Provide time for students to share their lists with the class. Read books such as *The Great Big Book of Families* by Mary Hoffman and discuss different types of family structures, emphasizing respect for each type. The book *Anti-Bias Education for Young Children and Ourselves* (Derman-Sparks & Edwards 2010) and the website www.teachersagainstprejudice.org are good resources for teachers.

History

Students can explore the theme of Time, Continuity, and Change as they read books about people and events throughout history. There are many wonderful biographies and autobiographies of historical figures. Include both literature and informational text accounts of historical periods in students' reading. Scholastic has free *Listen and Read* nonfiction books on a variety of social studies topics that students can read or listen to each page of the story read aloud (see http://teacher.scholastic.com/commclub/index.htm). This is especially helpful for dual language learners and children who have difficulty reading. The *Reading Rainbow* app also has a variety of interactive books along with short videos to accompany some of the books.

Writing. Primary students should be able to generate questions about individuals and groups who have shaped history (NCSS 2013b). Students could work individually or in pairs to write letters to historical figures they are studying, asking them questions. Afterward, they could switch letters with another individual or pair to write a response from the perspective of that person. You might also ask students to imagine they are living in the time period you are currently discussing and write diary entries that include questions about why events are happening.

Literature circles or book clubs. Literature circles or book clubs motivate children to read, incorporate informational text, and help students meet social studies and language arts standards. To launch book clubs, gather multiple copies of several different books related to the topic you are studying. Ask students to sign up for the book they would enjoy reading. Allowing students to choose the book they would like to read demonstrates respect for their individual interests and provides increased incentive for participation. Depending on the students, you can appoint a different discussion leader each week and suggest some general discussion questions. The whole class could participate in small group literature circles at the same time, or a single circle could meet while others are engaged in centers or other activities. Third grade teacher Angie Bickett occasionally leads book club discussions with a small group over lunch, calling them *lunch bunches.* Her students enjoy being able to spend this special time with her and their classmates. They have also grown in their ability to pick out main ideas, form opinions, and understand others' perspectives.

Historical stories. To help students compare life in the past to life today, provide books about events in the past, such as *Araminta's Paint Box* by Karen Ackerman. This book is about a young girl's adventure traveling across the United States in a covered wagon. After reading the book, have students make a Venn diagram comparing clothing, transportation, and so on from the time period of the book and the current time. Children who need more challenging activities can write short skits that they and other classmates dramatize. Students can also take part in Readers Theater (see p. 44) to help make past events and people more real. Repeatedly rehearsing lines may be especially helpful in increasing dual language learners' fluency and self-confidence.

Family interviews. Primary teacher Katharine Walmsley asks families to send in photos of family members when they were their child's age, if available. She asks students to interview their parents or guardians to learn about what they enjoyed playing and studying at a young age, so students can compare and contrast these activities with their own lives today. Students could also interview grandparents and other relatives.

Timelines. Making timelines allows students to meet the social studies indicator of creating chronological sequences of multiple events (NCSS 2013b). Students could begin by making personal timelines using photos or drawings of themselves at different ages and describing special events in their lives. Children might work on their timelines with their families. You can make another timeline of class events, adding to it over the course of the year with photos and descriptions so it serves as a history of the school year. One additional timeline is a historical timeline spanning the years the class discusses as part of the curriculum throughout the year. Begin by adding pictures from the Internet to the appropriate place on the timeline, showing items from the past and their contemporary counterparts, such as a covered wagon, the invention of the Model T, and a picture of a car in use today. As you discuss historical events, have a student add a note to the timeline with the event and its date. Add titles of books you read to the timeline as well, corresponding with their setting. The timeline will help the students have a better understanding of how one event may have led to or influenced another.

Economics

Exploring economics and the theme of Production, Distribution, and Consumption can help children become more informed consumers. Ask students to make a list of their *wants* alongside a list of their *needs*. Discuss the differences between the two and why it is important to distinguish them. Brainstorm ways to meet both needs and wants. Discuss choices individuals and families make and how one decision will impact future decisions. Provide scenarios that students could discuss and act out, such as wanting to buy a bike but being tempted to purchase a game instead of saving up for the bike.

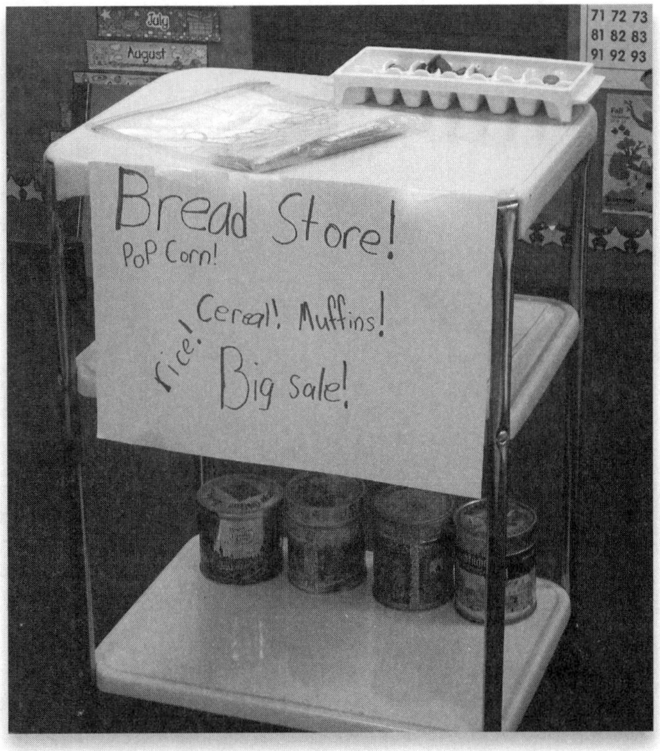

Money. Consider setting up an economic system in your room. After reading several sources about the purpose of money and visiting www.usmint.gov/kids/, ask students to design their own currency. Have them decide what denominations would be most useful, and provide materials for them to manufacture the currency. Talk about what the students might purchase with their currency. Students could set up a store with items they have made, perhaps rubber band bracelets or homemade cards. (Shops that sell greeting cards may donate envelopes from cards that are out of season to schools that request them.) Students can create advertisements and posters to promote the products they make.

Consumers and producers. Students could do a study of consumers and producers and grow their own garden outside or indoors in containers. Shirley Rosenbaum helps her primary students plant a garden in a child's wagon that they wheel in and out of doors. Family members who are interested in gardening or who are part of a gardening cooperative may be willing to come in and talk about the benefits of growing one's own food and being part of a cooperative that shares produce.

Jobs. A study of jobs in the community will familiarize students with products made locally and those brought in from other communities. Brainstorm a list of jobs that help the community function, and have students search the Internet and the business section of newspapers and phone books to discover additional jobs. Visit local shops and businesses or do virtual visits. Invite family members in to talk about their jobs and how they contribute to the community. Broaden your study to talk about the jobs that contribute to making the country operate well. Invite students to visit websites such as www.kids.usa.gov/jobs/index.shtml, which links jobs with a description and video of someone actually doing that job. The jobs and occupations game at www.turtlediary.com/grade-1-games/esl-efl-games/jobs-and-occupations.html is especially helpful in expanding vocabulary for dual language learners, providing support through pictures, explanations, and spoken words. The *Matching Jobs* app will also help students learn about different jobs and increase their vocabulary.

Broaden students' horizons one more step by exploring jobs around the world as you help students learn about the theme of Global Connections. NCSS (2010) recommends becoming e-pals with a class of students in another part of the world. Use sites such as People to People International at www.ptpi.org/community/SCP.aspx to search for classroom global pen pals. As a class compose an email to send to your e-pals once a week or so, letting them know the types of projects you have been doing. View video clips of food production across the globe and discuss ways to promote more equal distribution of food. Students might explore the Internet for different types of bread made throughout the world and read books such as *Bread, Bread, Bread* by Ann Morris. After reading the book, invite dual language learners to describe or perhaps bring in bread that is a part of their culture. Invite family members to help students make different types of bread they have read about.

Vehicles and transportation. Students can investigate the theme of Science, Technology, and Society in a study of vehicles and transportation throughout history and across the globe. Have them research the topic on the Internet and with books such as *Transportation in Many Cultures* by Martha E.H. Rustad. As part of this study they might investigate public versus private transportation and the impact both have on global resources. This will also help them meet the social studies indicator of being able to explain how and why people, goods, and ideas move from place to place (NCSS 2013b).

Civics

One of the best ways for students to learn about the theme of Civic Ideals and Practices is to experience civics in the classroom. Discussions about how to be a good citizen in the classroom so everyone feels respected and has opportunities to learn are a good

Try This!

As an alternative to simply listing classroom rules at the beginning of the year, cut a large piece of poster board or chart paper into puzzle pieces equal to half the number of students in your room. To make reassembling easier, trace the outline of the pieces on another large sheet of chart paper as a template and mark a T (for top) at the top of each puzzle piece.

As a class, discuss the characteristics of having a community of learners' environment where everyone can learn and feels safe and valued. Write student suggestions on the board, such as *respect each other* and *listen when others are talking*. Ask pairs of students to choose one of the characteristics to write and illustrate on one of the puzzle pieces. As pairs finish illustrating, they can find where their puzzle piece fits on the template. When everyone has added their pieces, glue them in place and put a title on the poster, such as "Our Classroom Community" or "Our Classroom Promises." Talk about the fact that if all the pieces are in place, the class will have a complete community where everyone can do their best. Students could sign their names at the bottom as their agreement to follow the group's expectations (if they have studied the Declaration of Independence, note the similarities to the process of signing that famous document).

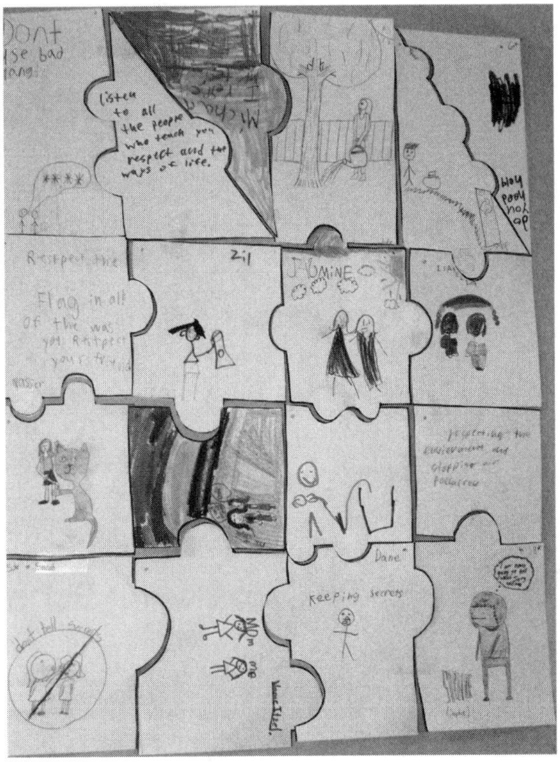

place to start. Indicators for civics in the primary grades include applying civic virtues in school settings; comparing one's point of view with others; describing democratic principles of equality, fairness, and respect for legitimate authority and rules; following agreed-upon rules for discussion and responding attentively to others; and explaining the purpose of roles in and outside of school (NCSS 2013b). Encourage students to reflect on ways they have demonstrated good citizenship and how they might do even more in the future.

Power and its responsibilities. Students can explore the theme of Power, Authority, and Governance as they experience fairness and order in the classroom and learn how to solve conflicts. Discuss what a government is and the roles and responsibilities of those in power. Read books, such as *I Grew Up to Be President* by Laurie Calkhoven, that describe the early lives of US presidents. Ask students to write about what they would accomplish if they had the power and authority of the president. Discuss other important positions, such as advocates for various causes and groups of people. Provide books about such advocates as Malala Yousafzai, Eleanor Roosevelt, Martin Luther King Jr., and Nelson Mandela, all of whom worked to gain rights for people.

Try This!

As part of a study on the community, ask students to write a letter of application for a job they would like in their neighborhood community, stating why they would be a good candidate for the job and how they would make a difference to the community in that role.

Communities. Studying the community can help children explore the theme of Individuals, Groups, and Institutions and meet indicators of explaining how all people play an important role in a community and how communities work together to accomplish common goals. Ask students to interview family members or other friends and relatives who live in the community to learn about their jobs and how they contribute to the community. Invite each student to create a page for a class book titled *People Who Contribute to Our Community.*

Contributions to society. Students can also read about individuals who contributed to society, such as Clara Barton, who founded the Red Cross, Maya Angelou, poet and civil rights activist, and Mario Carpino, a young boy with cancer who has been raising money to help find a cure that will help other children with cancer. Create a list of diverse individuals who have made contributions to society and include a sentence for each person describing his or her contributions. Ask students to choose a person from the list and research and write a short biography, including what the individual did to make a difference. As a culminating activity and authentic assessment, Jayne Taylor likes to have the class share what they have learned in a "wax museum" format. Students attach the biographies they wrote to cardstock and wear them as nametag labels as they pose like wax museum figures around the room. Students write invitations to families and other classes to view their "museum."

Home<->School Connections

Invite families into the classroom to work with children, attend special events and field trips, and share information about their home cultures and jobs. Family members may enjoy coming in and working with the students on setting up a classroom store and helping them choose and then make items to sell. Dantong Song invites the families of her students to join her for a school lunch once a month in her classroom. She shares projects and standards that students are working on and provides suggestions of what they can do to help their children at home. Dantong also describes upcoming study topics and asks for their input on possible field trips, activities, and how they might like to be involved. She encourages family members to discuss their questions, concerns, and suggestions with each other, encouraging them to view themselves as equal partners in their children's education. Dantong finds that the number of families who join her increases over the course of the year, as she works to build mutual trust and respect. Josh Chasing Hawk invites family members once a quarter to breakfast picnics before school to accommodate working parents' schedules. Some mornings students read to families as they eat a breakfast picnic. Other mornings they have quick 15-minute workshops on the importance of reading to children daily at home and other topics. Family members and teachers co-present these workshops.

Send home notes or emails asking families to talk with their children about the topics you are covering. This is a good way to increase vocabulary and concepts and to include families in their children's learning. One of students' daily activities could be to write and illustrate in a family connection journal something they learned about a topic they are studying. Each night they can bring their journal home to share with their families along with a question of the day. For example, a question might ask what other states or countries family members have visited. The next day, children could locate the places on a world map in the classroom; older children could calculate the distance from those states or countries to your town. If the class is studying transportation, students might ask their families about the different types of transportation parents, grandparents, and great-grandparents have used over the years. Children can write the answers to the questions in their journals, and parents could add a sentence as well (which would also verify that they have seen it each night).

Meeting Standards—and More!

Social studies provides ideal opportunities for students to learn ways to be contributing members of a classroom and community. They can build on their individual strengths and grow in their appreciation of the similarities and differences among their classmates. Read stories about historical figures from a variety of cultures whose characteristics and actions students could emulate, such as Martin Luther King Jr., Sacajawea, Cesar Chavez, Helen Keller, and Ruby Bridges, a first-grader who persevered as the first black child in her New Orleans school despite the daily racism and hatred she had to face. Help students understand the value of cooperation for the common good, the importance of caring for each other, and the responsibilities of each member of a community. Social justice issues make excellent *compelling questions* to explore with students. They also offer opportunities for students to take *informed action*, both now and in the future. Students might write letters to support a cause, make no-sew, fleece tied-blankets for hurricane victims from kits available in fabric stores, plant trees that have been donated, or perform other service projects.

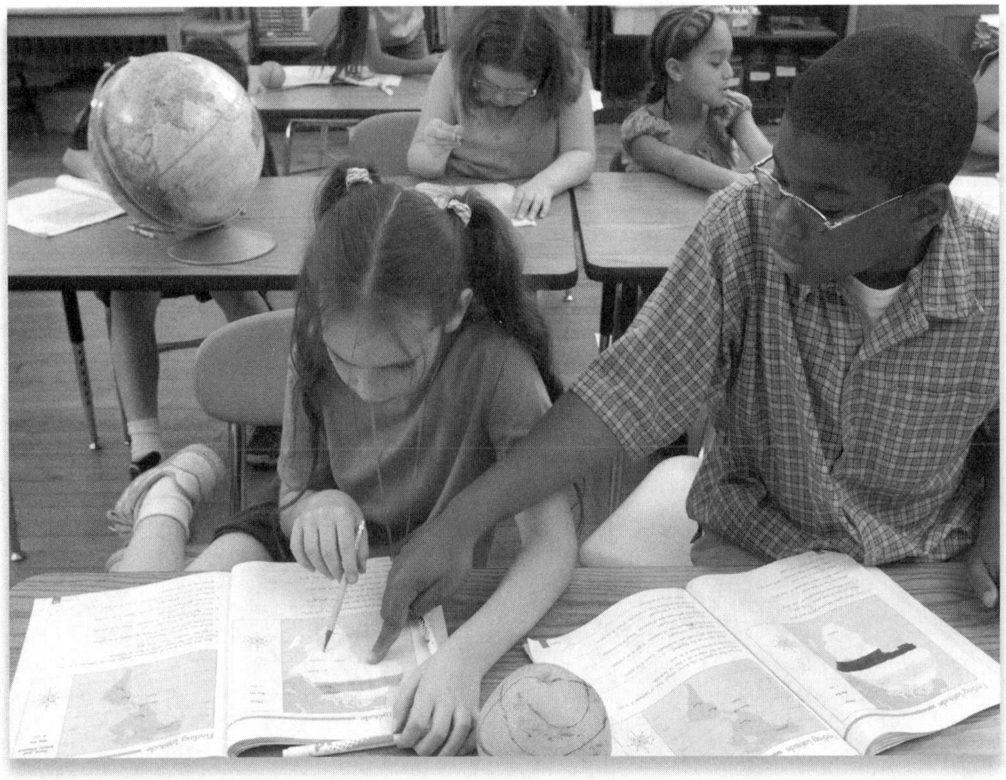

Calkins, Tolan, and Ehrenworth (2010) recommend encouraging students to contribute to the "grand conversation" about topics students are reading and researching. Grand conversations are interactive communications where students share ideas in a back-and-forth conversational style. Teachers are involved as one of the participants in the conversation. Calkins, Tolan, and Ehrenworth suggest celebrating the end of a literacy study about nonfiction texts by asking groups to plan and lead discussions with the class on nonfiction books they have been reading. The books students read can focus on important social topics, including democratic principles, such as equality and fairness as outlined in the C3 Framework for Social Studies State Standards. Students can then plan talking points on the importance of the topic, the main idea from their reading, and supporting points. They can also suggest ideas about how individuals can demonstrate or put into action the principles they are discussing.

In a Nutshell

NCSS (2013b) suggests that social studies be based on inquiries with compelling questions that focus on enduring issues and concerns. The NCSS Inquiry Arc indicates that students learn social studies by 1) developing questions and planning inquiries; 2) applying disciplinary concepts and tools in the areas of civics, economics, history, and geography; 3) evaluating sources and using evidence; and 4) communicating their conclusions and taking informed action. Investigations of social studies topics, such as maps and globes, families, communities, and transportation, fit this Inquiry Arc well, as does the integrated model of learning recommended by NCSS. There are many other inquiry-based activities that follow this model and encompass the ten content themes outlined by NCSS, such as reading and discussing literature on social studies topics, doing research projects, writing and performing skits and Readers Theater scripts, exploring cultures, taking on-site and virtual field trips, making timelines, developing class rules, using technology, and studying influential people from a variety of cultures.

Meeting the Next Generation Science Standards

6

Children are curious about the world and how things work. They love to explore and investigate, and science encourages them to do this. There is a "substantial body of research that supports the close connection between the development of concepts and skills in science and engineering and such factors as interest, engagement, motivation, persistence, and self-identity" (NGSS Lead States 2013, 6). Use students' curiosity and inquisitiveness to help them learn concepts in science and extend their enthusiasm for learning to all areas of the curriculum.

Science knowledge is critical to navigating our complex world and required for students to be the innovators of the future. Therefore, a solid science education is necessary to prepare them for the future.

The Next Generation Science Standards

The National Research Council (NRC) (2012) developed *A Framework for K–12 Science Education: Practices, Crosscutting Concepts, and Core Ideas* (www.nap.edu/openbook.php?record_id=13165&page=7), which outlines a broad set of expectations for students' science learning. The framework is based on current research in science and scientific learning and identifies the content and sequence of learning expected for all students in grades K–12.

> The overarching goal of our framework for K–12 science education is to ensure that by the end of 12th grade, *all* students have some appreciation of the beauty and wonder of science; possess sufficient knowledge of science and engineering to engage in public discussions on related issues; are careful consumers of scientific and technological information related to their everyday lives; are able to continue to learn about science outside school; and have the skills to enter careers of their choice, including (but not limited to) careers in science, engineering, and technology. (NRC 2012, 1)

The framework does not detail standards grade by grade; rather it provided a vision for science education and laid the groundwork for the development of a new set of science standards to guide students' learning. State-led teams, along with science educators, industry experts, and other stakeholders, used the framework to develop the Next Generation Science Standards (NGSS) (NGSS Lead States 2013).

Each standard has three dimensions, taken from the NRC framework: 1) scientific and engineering practices; 2) crosscutting concepts; and 3) core disciplinary ideas in physical sciences; life sciences; earth and space sciences; and engineering, technology, and applications of science. To support meaningful science learning, teachers need to integrate all three of these dimensions (NGSS Lead States 2013).

Scientific and Engineering Practices

The NRC framework and the NGSS outline the following as scientific and engineering practices (NRC 2012, 3):

- Asking questions (for science) and defining problems (for engineering)
- Developing and using models
- Planning and carrying out investigations
- Analyzing and interpreting data
- Using mathematics and computational thinking
- Constructing explanations (for science) and designing solutions (for engineering)
- Engaging in argument from evidence
- Obtaining, evaluating, and communicating information

These practices are similar to the mathematical practices outlined in the Common Core State Standards (CCSS). As you help students gain proficiency in these practices—which involve acquiring knowledge as well as building specific skills—you also reinforce the skills students need in mathematics and other areas. For example, students develop models, make representations of what they observe, use technological tools, apply thinking skills, and ask and explore meaningful questions in math and social studies as well as in science. As students learn to ask questions, formulate possible answers or theories, collect data to investigate their theories, display their data in posters, electronic presentations, or other formats, and explain their findings to others, they follow the scientific method, which mirrors the steps involved in problem solving outlined on page 21 in Chapter 2. Children will follow these steps as they explore science, solve math problems, decode words, engage in social interactions with peers, and grow in other areas of their lives. Students could try out these steps with simple ice experiments beginning with deciding on a question they would like to investigate. One idea might be to investigate how to prevent an ice cube from melting as long as possible in the classroom or outside or how to make it melt as quickly as possible. Once students have their questions, they can formulate possible solutions to solve their problem, choose a solution to try out, and then record data—how many minutes did it take to melt in multiple trials? Students can record their data in graphs and write a short description of their findings to share with their classmates.

Language and literacy skills, too—such as asking questions, constructing explanations, engaging in argument from evidence, and obtaining, evaluating, and communicating information—are strengthened by engaging in scientific and engineering practices. Science offers dual language learners many opportunities to increase their language skills because discussions focus on shared experiences with hands-on materials (Michaels, Shouse, & Schweingruber 2007). Students will learn new vocabulary, especially when teachers intentionally point out new words and use them multiple times in meaningful contexts. Science experiences also help students, including dual language learners, learn to identify parts of words, such as prefixes and suffixes, that provide clues to the overall meaning of a word; for example, *ovi* means "egg," *micro* means "very small," *saurus* means "lizard," and *tri* means "three."

To help students sharpen their thinking, deepen their scientific understanding, and express their thoughts, the NRC publication *Ready, Set, Science! Putting Research to Work in K–8 Science Classrooms* (Michaels, Shouse, & Schweingruber 2007) recommends that they engage in rigorous and active discussions—questioning, examining, and sharing their ideas, and sometimes changing their position based on ideas presented by others and on new evidence. Work with students to establish parameters for such discussions, such as listening carefully, expressing their ideas clearly, and respectfully questioning ideas by presenting evidence.

In *Ready, Set, Science!*, the authors suggest that when students work in groups on an investigation, each group member be assigned a role, similar to the approach used in reciprocal teaching (see p. 35 in Chapter 3). For example, one student might lead the discussion about the groups' predictions, and others could take charge of planning, testing, or forming conclusions.

Science notebooks. As students engage in science experiments and investigations, recording their observations in a science notebook will improve their science and writing skills. They record the **problem** or question being explored, make **predictions** about what will happen, develop **plans** for testing their predictions, perform their experiments or investigations, analyze results of their **testing** and any data collected during the investigation, and draw **conclusions,** including what they learned and what it might mean. They can use drawings and sketches as the NGSS recommend to help describe any of these steps, adding more words as they are able. The Foss website has suggestions for using science notebooks as well as many other resources (see the links at www.fossweb.com/science-notebooks).

Graphs and tables. Representations that students create in mathematics will also help them in science. Creating graphs and tables helps them better understand representation and how to construct models. They can create physical models, diagrams, drawings, and electronic versions of models. Students who are just learning about graphs might use strips of green paper to measure the growth of a narcissus stem spouting from a bulb in the classroom until it begins to flower or students notice there has been no increase in height for several weeks. They could take turns measuring each week, cutting the paper strip to the exact height of the stem. Each week they glue the measured strip onto a sheet of paper alongside the others to make a graph and track the plant's growth. After charting this growth for a few weeks and discussing how the graph represents the growth, students could take turns measuring the plant with both the green strips and a ruler. With teacher guidance, the student who is measuring can begin charting the ruler measurements on another bar graph without the physical representation of the green paper stem. This graph requires more symbolic thinking; make sure all children understand the relationship between the actual ruler measurement and what they see on the graph. This type of scaffolding will help students be able to create and understand more complex science and math models.

Crosscutting Concepts

The NRC framework and the NGSS describe the following crosscutting concepts (NRC 2012, 3):

- Patterns
- Cause and effect: Mechanism and explanation
- Scale, proportion, and quantity
- Systems and system models
- Energy and matter: Flows, cycles, and conservation
- Structure and function
- Stability and change

These concepts cut across all the major topic areas of the science curriculum. For example, students observe patterns in nature: Baby animals and young plants look similar to their parents, but not exactly. The sun rises and sets each day, summer follows spring. Understanding these patterns allows us to predict growth and future events. With guidance, meaningful experiences, and repetition in various contexts, students gain increasingly deeper understanding of these concepts as they progress though the grades.

Many captivating experiences can help students explore these crosscutting concepts, including these:

- Students investigate *cause and effect* and *energy* by placing a small amount of water in a plastic film canister, adding a seltzer tablet, snapping on the lid, and observing the effect created. They can experiment with varying amounts of water and tablets.
- Students explore *energy and matter: Flows, cycles, and conservation* by experimenting with batteries and hobby motors, which can be obtained inexpensively online and at electronics stores. Students love the challenge of using batteries and wires to complete electrical circuits, providing energy for the motors to run, and then attaching card stock circles and other shapes to make fans. Students can predict the *effect* of touching markers to the card stock fans while they are spinning. Additional explorations, such as trying to light small hobby light bulbs and designing small beepers that make noise using the energy of a battery, will add to their understanding of *energy.*
- Students learn about scale, proportion, and quantity by building scale models of their classroom with blocks, LEGOs, or drawings.

Disciplinary Core Ideas

Science standards are divided into core disciplines. In the NGSS these disciplines are physical sciences, life sciences, earth and space sciences, and engineering, technology, and applications of science (see the box). The NGSS are written as *performance expectations*, describing what students should be able to do in order to demonstrate that they have met the standards. As with the Common Core State Standards for Mathematics, the NGSS focus on fewer concepts, with the goal of students attaining a deeper understanding and application of these concepts. There are only 12 performance expectations at the first grade level across the four core disciplines, 14 for second grade, and 18 for third grade. If students are sufficiently prepared with core knowledge and know how to seek additional information, they can continue their learning and development into adulthood (NGSS Lead States 2013). Engaging activities to help students meet standards in each of the disciplinary core ideas will be presented later in this chapter.

All children can become capable, competent participants in science. Appendix D of *Next Generation Science Standards* (NGSS Lead States 2013) provides case studies of teachers supporting diverse groups of learners. The authors suggest using language-rich, hands-on activities that engage students and project-based science learning that focuses on authentic questions and activities that have meaning for students (see www.nextgenscience.org/appendix-d-case-studies).

Disciplinary Core Ideas in the Next Generation Science Standards

Physical Sciences

PS1: Matter and its interactions

PS2: Motion and stability: Forces and interactions

PS3: Energy

PS4: Waves and their applications in technologies for information transfer

Life Sciences

LS1: From molecules to organisms: Structures and processes

LS2: Ecosystems: Interactions, energy, and dynamics

LS3: Heredity: Inheritance and variation of traits

LS4: Biological evolution: Unity and diversity

Earth and Space Sciences

ESS1: Earth's place in the universe

ESS2: Earth's systems

ESS3: Earth and human activity

Engineering, Technology, and Applications of Science

ETS1: Engineering design

ETS2: Links among engineering, technology, science, and society

From National Research Council (NRC), *A Framework for K–12 Science Education: Practices, Crosscutting Concepts, and Core Ideas* (Washington, DC: National Academies Press, 2012), 3.

Supporting Learners in Meeting Science Standards

As with other standards, the science standards outline *what* to teach, not *how* to teach. *Next Generation Science Standards* (NGSS Lead States 2013) advises that for students to meet the standards at an optimal level, they must *do* explorations and experiences, not simply listen to how they are done or watch the teacher demonstrate them. In its position statement on the NGSS (www.nsta.org/about/positions/ngss.aspx), the National Science Teachers Association (NSTA) recommends that students be actively engaged in diverse investigations that integrate the practices, core ideas, and crosscutting concepts; such engagement in the practices will strengthen students' understanding of the core ideas. NSTA also suggests striving to maintain an atmosphere that promotes reflection, respect for logical thinking, and openness to alternate explanations that are based on research.

Whether you use the NGSS or other science standards, provide a number of materials that encourage hands-on investigations, such as balance scales, magnifiers, and microscopes. Many schools have science textbooks that teachers are required to use. These texts contain helpful background material for students that can be used in a variety of ways, depending on the topic and the students. For some units you may choose to read the background material together. For other topics you might decide that students would gain more by reading the text in small groups or individually and then reading other informational text on the topic. This is also a good opportunity for supporting literacy standards.

Many other resources are available, depending on the topic. The NGSS document itself is a good resource. To support students as they begin to demonstrate proficiency in the performance expectations, provide experiences that will scaffold their progress. The NGSS document presents the standards in grade-level charts that include a detailed explanation of the disciplinary core idea, the scientific and engineering practices, and the crosscutting concepts that were combined to develop each performance expectation. The three concepts are presented together to demonstrate the interconnectedness of the knowledge and practice of science. For each science standard the chart also lists connections to specific Common Core State Standards for English Language Arts and Mathematics.

The table shown here provides an abbreviated version of a first grade physical sciences performance expectation. For students to meet this standard—"plan and conduct investigations to provide evidence that vibrating materials can make sound and that sound can make materials vibrate"—(NGSS Lead States 2013), they will need multiple opportunities to actually plan and carry it out. Students might work in small groups to plan an investigation to design and make a musical instrument that would vibrate and make sound. Grouping students with a range of abilities will allow them to learn from each other's thinking. Provide a variety of materials, such as shoeboxes, rubber bands, water bottles, beads, and pie pans for them to use. As the groups discuss possibilities, ask clarifying questions that will help to scaffold their understanding and promote further thought and problem solving: "What materials do you think might be able to vibrate

<table>
<tr><th colspan="3">Sample Next Generation Science Standard, First Grade Physical Sciences</th></tr>
<tr><td colspan="3">1-PS4 Waves and Their Applications in Technologies for Information Transfer
Students who demonstrate understanding can:
1-PS4-1 Plan and conduct investigations to provide evidence that vibrating materials can make sound and that sound can make materials vibrate. (performance expectation)</td></tr>
<tr><td>Science and Engineering Practices</td><td>Disciplinary Core Ideas (DCI)</td><td>Crosscutting Concepts</td></tr>
<tr><td>Planning and Carrying Out Investigations
Constructing Explanations and Designing Solutions</td><td>PS4.A: Wave Properties
• Sound can make matter vibrate, and vibrating matter can make sound.</td><td>Cause and Effect
• Simple tests can be designed to gather evidence to support or refute student ideas about causes.</td></tr>
<tr><td colspan="3">Connections to other DCIs in first grade: N/A</td></tr>
<tr><td colspan="3">Common Core State Standards Connections:
CCSS Writing. 1.7. Participate in shared research and writing projects
CCSS Mathematical Practices 5. Use appropriate tools strategically

Source: Next Generation Science Standards: For States, By States, NGSS Lead States (Achieve, Inc. 2013). www.nextgenscience.org/1ps4-waves-applications-technologies-information-transfer. © 2013 Achieve, Inc.</td></tr>
</table>

the most? What could you add that would make even more sound or a different sound? How could you test your ideas? What else could you try?"

Next, provide books and websites for students to research and gain additional ideas on ways they might design their instruments. Support students as they create posters showing their designs. Groups could share their ideas and posters with each other and hear suggestions for improvements from their peers. Students could revise their designs based on these suggestions, then create their instruments. Afterward, groups could demonstrate their instruments and reflect on how they were able to make the sounds, tying in the crosscutting concept of cause and effect. Students might design other investigations to further test their ideas about the cause of the sound. This type of investigation could take place over a few days or could extend much longer as you provide additional opportunities for students to further explore sound and light waves.

Name	Date
My Science Log	
Problem/Question	
Predict	
Plan (include sketch)	
Test	
Conclude	

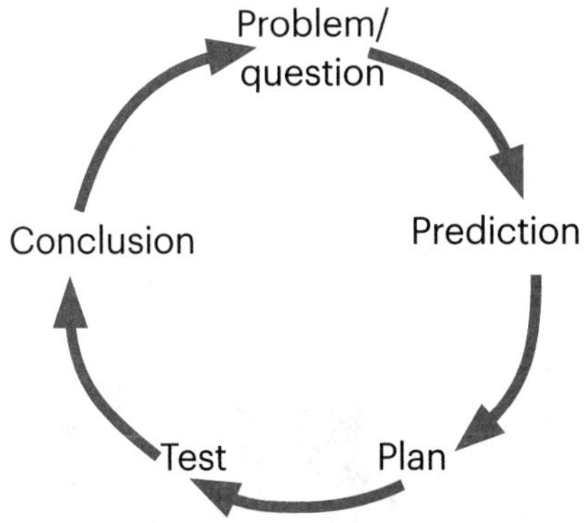

Students' designs and constructed instruments provide documentation for assessing their ability to plan and carry out investigations of vibrating materials and sounds. For further documentation and to assess their understanding, ask them to fill out a simple investigation form as they go through the process and include the following information: 1) their **problem,** question, or goal; 2) their **prediction** of how they can solve the problem; 3) their **plan** to test their prediction (which could include their sketches); 4) a description of their **testing process** (perhaps including a digital photo, video or sound recording of their completed instrument); and 5) their **conclusions** about the effectiveness of their plan, what they learned, and what they might do differently next time.

Engaging Activities to Explore Science and Integrate the Curriculum

The NGSS authors recommend that teachers plan and implement units that address groups of the science standards, rather than addressing them in isolation, to help students understand the interconnectedness of concepts. Many schools find that an integrated approach and problem-based learning, described on page 97 in Chapter 5, are effective ways to help students meet multiple science standards as well as standards in all areas of the curriculum. Integrating the curriculum makes efficient use of the limited time teachers have with students. Also, the NRC notes,

> Students need to work with scientific concepts presented through challenging, well-designed problems—problems that are meaningful from both a scientific standpoint and a personal standpoint. They need to be challenged to think about the natural world in new and different ways. They need guidance in adopting the practices of the scientific community, with its particular ways of seeing, building explanations, and supporting claims about knowledge. (Michaels, Shouse, & Schweingruber 2007, 149)

The NGSS authors suggest looking at the disciplinary core ideas as sources for meaningful questions and problems to explore, such as biodiversity, which is emphasized in both second and third grades. A study on this type of topic addresses a wide variety of science standards related to plants, animals, habitats, and diversity of life, as well as standards in other subject areas.

An integrated example: biodiversity. You might begin a study of biodiversity by asking students to each list or draw all the living things they can think of in five minutes. Then ask students to share their lists and help you put them into categories as you record them on the whiteboard. Point out the number of plants, insects, mammals, fish, and other categories they were able to come up with in that short amount of time and note that this is only a tiny amount of all the diverse plants and animals around us. You might project photos of a desert, forest, and jungle and ask students to count or notice the diverse plants and animals. Introduce the prefix "bio" and let students know that when they see "bio" in front of a word it refers to life and living things and that the word *biodiversity* refers to the amazing amount of different living things on earth. Then make KWL charts with students. Have them create their own charts by listing what they already know (K) about the topic of biodiversity and what (W) questions they have about it. (They will fill in what they learn [L] as they study the topic.) This promotes individual engagement and helps you learn each student's current level of understanding; it also activates previous learning, helping the brain to connect and process the new information. After collecting students' individual charts, create a class KWL chart that will focus the direction of the study by exploring the questions students have generated.

Students could study the diversity of living things nearby. Go to the playground or a nearby park together and have students write down all the living things they see in the area. On another day, use Hula-Hoops or string to rope off small areas that pairs of students investigate with magnifying glasses, recording all the life they find.

Later, students could work to identify as many different plants and animals as possible in the playground, woods, park, or other area you have chosen; these might include grasses, flowers, trees, birds, squirrels, and insects. They can draw what they see, adding distinguishing characteristics, or take photos to compare with information in field guides or on websites such as www.bugfacts.net/ and www.allaboutbirds.org/guide/browse. There are paper and electronic field guides to an amazing number of living things. Topics covered by the National Audubon Society First Field Guides include various animals, trees, night sky, rocks, weather, and shells. Consider field guides that are available as books and smartphone or tablet apps, such as *The Sibley Guide to Birds*.

Students will gain math skills as they gather data on the numbers of plants and animals they see and graph their findings. Incorporate social studies and civic engagement by helping students enter their information into databases such as www.ebird.org, which maps birds worldwide in an effort to understand their habits and protect them. Similarly, you could participate in the Great Backyard Bird Count each year in February, which collects data from people all over the world on the number and type of birds they see in a four-day period (visit http://gbbc.birdcount.org for more information).

Extend the study by exploring questions such as how species in another area compare with those in the area the class originally studied. The class can also read about and investigate how changes in an environment, such as temperature extremes and excess or lack of water, can affect the plants and animals there as outlined in the performance expectations. Such studies help students realize that nature is interconnected and that what happens to one species can affect others, including people. It can also increase their appreciation for the amazing diversity of living things around them and how they can help to protect them.

As a culminating project, create a class field guide to the area, using students' drawings and/or photographs of plants and animals along with written descriptions of their distinguishing characteristics, habitats, and other information. Students could work individually, in pairs, or in small groups to research plants or animals they are particularly interested in, which will strengthen their language and literacy skills. Some students might want to research small animals, such as squirrels, in the area; others may be more interested larger animals, such as deer. Post the field guide on your class website and let families and other classes know about it so they can use it to identify local species.

The field guide can serve as an informal performance assessment, providing a picture of what students are able to do. Reeves (2002) contends that performance-based assessment that takes place as students are involved in meaningful activities is more rigorous in many ways than the high-stakes paper-and-pencil tests in which students can simply guess at the correct answer. In performance assessment students need to actually perform and show their work. Provide rubrics on what needs to be included on their pages. At the end of the project, have students fill in the last section of their individual KWL charts, which will provide another informal assessment of their learning. After collecting the charts, fill in the last column of the class chart together, helping the students to reflect on the concepts they have learned and applied throughout the study.

Books about science. Providing science-related books in the classroom library and using them in the literacy curriculum is another way to integrate science into your busy schedule. Review the science standards to help you choose books. Include biographies of scientists, astronauts, and inventors, such as Jane Goodall, Sally Ride, Neil Armstrong, George Washington Carver, the Wright brothers, Louis Pasteur, Thomas Edison, Neil deGrasse Tyson, and Mario Molina, who won the Nobel Prize for his work studying the ozone layer. For times when students read on their own, promote comprehension by including a card in the book with a few questions for them to think about as they read. Encourage the development of writing skills by having students write about science-related topics, using their science notebooks to record observations or creating posters and electronic presentations on science experiments.

Science/discovery area. Another way to integrate the curriculum is to set up a science/discovery area that you change for different units of study. This area might contain magnifying glasses, binoculars, and a student microscope for close observations; a balance scale for comparing balanced and unbalanced forces; a variety of plants, seeds, tadpoles, and fish for learning about living things; and a variety of other materials to explore science concepts outlined in the standards, such as tuning forks, flashlights, mirrors, and magnets. It can also be the place to store other science equipment. It should offer opportunities to learn through multiple senses to promote more in-depth understanding. Adding books related to the topics makes the science/discovery area another place for students to do research as part of integrated units of study, boosting reading and writing skills as well. Students will learn new vocabulary as they read and talk about the science materials and gain math skills as they sort, collect data, and graph.

The next section of this chapter describes ways to help children explore and discover in the disciplinary core ideas of physical sciences; life sciences; earth and space sciences; and engineering, technology, and applications of science.

Investigations in Physical Sciences

The physical sciences—topics such as sound, light, magnetism, matter, energy, force, and motion—intrigue primary students. Through engaging cooking experiences, you and the students can explore states of matter as well as the effects of heating and cooling and whether those effects can be reversed. Incorporate books, recipe charts, and writing to boost language and literacy skills. Read books such as *If You Give a Pig a Pancake* (Laura Numeroff) and look at a pancake recipe written on a chart or projected on the whiteboard. Ask students to write the ingredients in their science notebooks or tablets, dividing them into lists of liquids and solids. Have them write their predictions of what will happen when the ingredients are mixed. Will the resulting mixture be a solid or liquid? Then have them test their predictions, either in small groups with each student having her own set of ingredients, or as a class using one bowl. Before you heat the pancake on an electric griddle, ask students to predict whether cooking the batter will result in a solid, liquid, or gas. As students enjoy the results of their experiment, discuss whether this process can be reversed. What conclusions can they draw from their investigation? Continue with similar explorations to further their understanding of the effects of heating and cooling. For example, supply ingredients for students to make individual bags of ice cream and explore the effects of cooling.

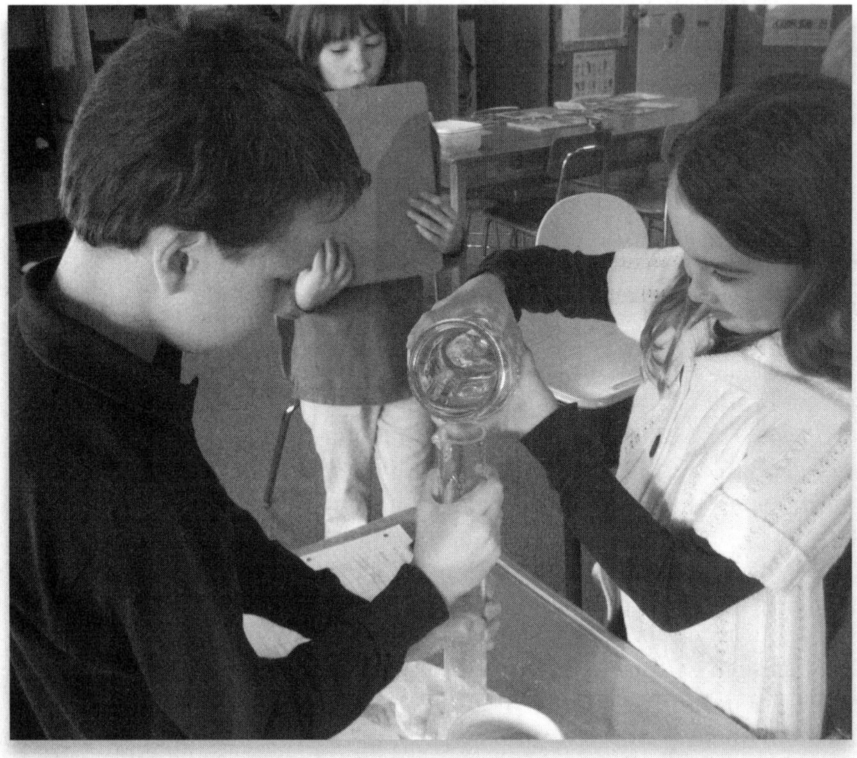

Comparing mixtures. Search the Internet to find a variety of mixtures for students to create and explore. Look for some recipes that require heating and others that require cooling. Here are a few ideas to try.

◆ **Playdough recipes:** Try mixing one part hair conditioner and two parts cornstarch, or two parts shaving cream and one part cornstarch. En-

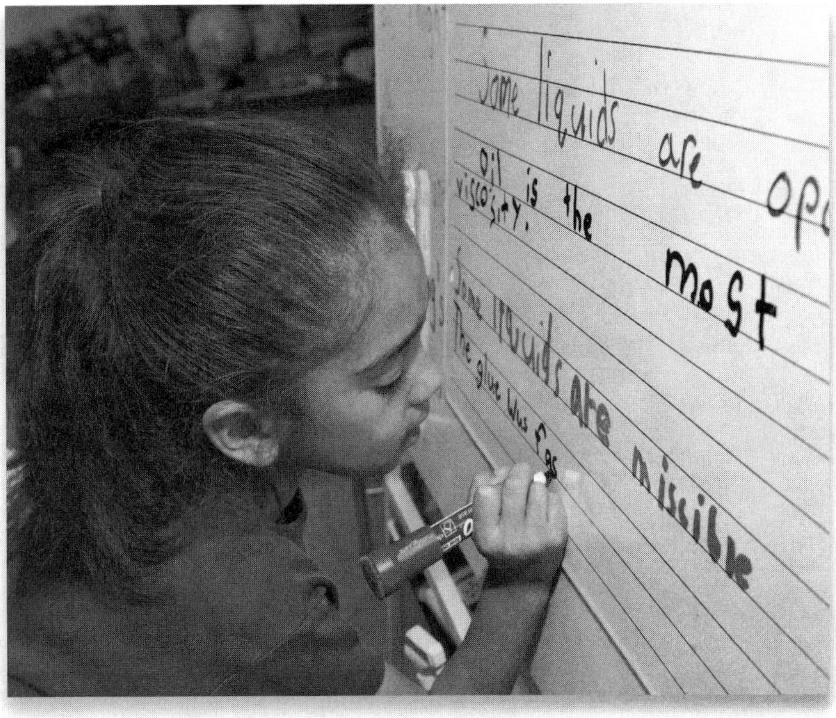

courage students to experiment with different amounts of the ingredients to alter the consistency of the mixture. Add washable liquid watercolors for color if desired.

- **Cornstarch and water:** Have students experiment by pouring cornstarch into a bowl or small plastic container, slowly adding water, and mixing until the cornstarch is dissolved. Is the result a liquid? a solid? How does it show properties of each? What happens if you add more water or more cornstarch? This mixture should be disposed of in a garbage can to avoid drain problems.
- **Glue:** Have students design and carry out experiments to test substances that can be mixed with glue, such as liquid starch, cornstarch, and flour to find out which glue mixtures can stretch the farthest, mold into a shape, or show other characteristics students would like to examine. This supports them as they meet standards such as the NGSS second grade standard of analyzing data from testing to determine which materials have properties best suited for a certain purpose.

Playing thinking games. A weekly game of 20 Questions can help students expand their thinking and questioning skills as well as deepen their understanding of matter. Place an object (or the name of an object written on a piece of paper) in a bag and ask students to guess what it is by asking questions about its properties—the types of material it is made of, whether it is solid or liquid, and so on. Although it may be difficult at first, encourage them to only ask questions that can be answered with a *yes* or *no*. After you have modeled this several times, students can take turns bringing or choosing an object for their peers to guess. Occasionally illustrate their process of narrowing the possibilities on the whiteboard as students guess, and encourage students to illustrate the process as well. There are many ways you could do this, but the process might look like the example on the following page.

Exploring light. To help students explore light, enlist their ideas about how to build a light table or light box for the classroom. There are a number of suggestions on the Internet (see, for example, www.pinterest.com) that include making a basic wooden frame or using a plastic tote box, topped by translucent Plexiglass, with a light source underneath. Children can experiment with placing different materials on the Plexiglass. They can also explore shadows and flashlights. Working with these materials will help prepare students to meet a variety of science standards, including these NGSS first grade standards: "plan and conduct investigations to determine the effect of placing objects made with different materials in the path of a beam of light" (1-PS4-3) and "design and build a device that uses light or sound to solve the problem of communicating over a

An Example of Mapping the Thinking Process for 20 Questions

1. Living? NO ↘	
2. Non-Living? YES ↘	Non-Living
3. Liquid? NO ↘	
4. Gas? NO ↘	
5. Solid? YES ↘	Solid
6. Made of wood? NO ↘	
7. Made of glass? NO ↘	
8. Made of metal? YES (mostly) ↘	Made of metal mostly
9. Longer than a yardstick? NO ↘	
10. Longer than a ruler? NO ↘	
11. Longer than my thumb? YES ↘	Longer than my thumb but shorter than a ruler
12. Is it a tool? NO ↘	
13. Do we need it for our schoolwork? NO ↘	
14. Is it a toy? YES ↘	Toy
15. Does it come in many colors? YES ↘	Comes in many colors
16. Is it a Slinky? NO ↘	
17. Is it a Transformer? NO ↘	
18. Is it a toy car? YES!!	IT IS A TOY CAR!!

distance" (1-PS4-4). Students who are ready for additional challenges may enjoy exploring apps such as Exploratorium's Sound Uncovered and Color Uncovered.

Investigations in Life Sciences

The developmentally appropriate practice of using students' interests as a basis for learning is an effective way to help students meet standards. Subjects such as animals—of great interest to many primary students—will entice students to read informational texts and motivate them to create posters, reports, and other presentations to demonstrate what they learn. National Geographic's online magazine *Young Explorer* (http://ngexplorer.cengage.com/ngyoungexplorer/) is equipped with an audio button that students can press to listen to a story being read. Each word is highlighted as it is read. This is especially helpful for dual language learners or other students who find reading challenging.

Classroom pets and other animals. Classroom pets, such as guinea pigs or fish, can provide firsthand experiences for meeting many of the life sciences standards—animal adaptations, life cycles, survival needs, habitats, and similarities between parents and offspring. Before bringing a pet into the classroom, check local health department and school policies about live animals in the classroom and make sure none of your students have allergies that could be aggravated by animals. If a pet is allowable, have students design a classroom habitat for it—an excellent learning experience. Discuss what animals need to thrive and what types of animals are best suited to classrooms. If you can offer students a choice of pets, asking them to write a persuasive essay on the animal of their choice could be very motivating. Students can research the animal they would most like to have as a class pet, including its food, water, and habitat needs and its suitability for the classroom, and write their essays based on this research. Have them design a presentation and give it to the class. After the presentations students can vote on which animal they would like to have in the classroom based on the information presented. Discuss how students will share the responsibilities of caring for the pet. Once you have a pet, integrate its care into other learning activities, such as measuring and graphing the pet's growth over time.

Even if you do not have a pet, you may be able to occasionally bring in an animal or have visits from a zoo mobile or other animal organizations. Purchase or make a butterfly garden with netting and have students record their observations about metamorphosis in their journals. Students can also watch the life cycle of mealworms. There are kits commercially available for growing ladybugs, tadpoles, and other animals, or you and the students may be able to find insects, tadpoles, worms, or other animals to observe. Look for websites with animal cams positioned so students can see nesting birds and other animals. The Cornell Lab of Ornithology has links to a variety of nesting and feeding bird cams, along with activity guides for bird cams, kits, and free resources at www.birdsleuth.org/kits-and-resources/. The eagle cam in Decorah, Iowa (www.ustream.tv/decoraheagles), will encourage students to watch throughout the year to see a life cycle in action. The website www.eagles4kids.com has additional cams and resources for the classroom.

Try This!

Use students' observations of animal cams, classroom pets, or videos to discuss animal adaptations. For example, students will enjoy making blubber gloves to learn how blubber helps whales adapt to cold water. Have students fill a resealable plastic bag with shortening and seal it shut. Working in teams, students take turns wrapping this sealed bag around their partner's hand. Next, they put their partner's wrapped hand into a larger (empty) resealable bag and secure it around the wrist. The student places both his wrapped and unwrapped hands into a large bucket of ice water to experience the protection the "blubber" provides (Brenneman 2009; McDonald & Hershman 2010). After all students have had a chance to experience this, challenge students to work in pairs to discuss why blubber is useful to whales. Show short videos and read books about survival mechanisms of plants and animals. Then ask students to use ideas from what they have learned to generate solutions to a problem humans face that could include protecting our bodies from cold, heat, and injury.

The life cycle of plants. Understanding the life cycle of plants, what they need to live, and adaptations that help them survive can deepen children's knowledge and appreciation of the natural world as well as help them meet science standards. Growing a variety of plants and observing them both indoors and outdoors are some of the best ways for students to learn about plants. A small space, such as a few planters on the playground, or a larger space, such as a park in easy walking distance with plants and trees, are ideal settings for learning about plants. Students can observe plant life and record any changes they see in the trees and plants over time.

Students might use two-liter plastic bottles or rotisserie chicken containers to make their own terrariums to learn more about plants and what they need to survive. For even more ideal conditions in which to learn and experiment, consider creating an indoor or outdoor greenhouse; search the Internet for suggestions on how to do this. There are also a number of virtual experiences that can help students learn about plants. TeacherTube.com and YouTube.com have several informative videos demonstrating the life cycle of plants. After viewing a video such as "Pollination Rock" at www.youtube.com/watch?v=V5yya4elRLw, challenge children to create their own model of pollination or seed dispersal; they might choose to share it through a song, a skit, or drawings on a

Try This!

Try planting bean seeds in an empty CD case. First talk about what plants need to grow successfully. Discuss how you might be able to test these conditions using bean seeds and individual, clear CD cases. Together make a grid showing a combination of growing conditions to try, such as light/no light, soil/no soil, soil/cotton ball, water/no water, and so on. Have students work in small groups to test one of the conditions. Those using potting soil can put it in the bottom quarter of the case and add a couple of bean seeds. The hinge side should be at the top so students have a little watering hole. They can tape the bottom shut so the soil stays in and use an eyedropper to add water. Students can record and measure the growth and then discuss which combination of conditions seemed to work best. When the beans have sprouted and grown a bit, use a permanent marker to label the parts of the plant right on the CD case. There are directions and teaching suggestions to accompany this project at www.mrsprinceandco.com/2013/05/we-grew-plants-in-what.html.

tablet or other device. The Urban Programs Resource Network has a number of helpful interactive videos available in both English and Spanish, such as *Dr. Arbor Talks Trees* at www.urbanext.illinois.edu/kids/.

As part of students' study of plant needs, demonstrate how plants take up water by asking students to hypothesize what will happen if they put a white carnation in water with a generous quantity of food coloring or washable watercolor. Ask students to think about what the colored water helps them to see that they may not be able to notice otherwise. Bring in flowers with multicolored petals and invite students to explain how florists are able to produce the different colors. Have them draw a model of how this might occur and then test out their ideas. Show them that one way to accomplish this effect is by cutting a stem several inches lengthwise into three sections and placing the sections into three florist vials with concentrated red, yellow, and blue coloring. Try this again using a celery stalk with leaves. Students will be able to clearly see the tubes that help to transport water to the leaves. Then discuss the importance of water to the growth of plants.

Investigations in Earth and Space Sciences

NGSS in Earth and Space Sciences (NGSS Lead States 2013) include the following:

- **First grade:** observing and describing patterns in the sun, moon, and stars and describing the amount of daylight at different times of the year
- **Second grade:** providing evidence from various sources that earth events can occur quickly (for example, hurricanes) or slowly (for example, erosion) and identifying where water is found on Earth
- **Third grade:** making claims about solutions that reduce the impact of weather-related hazards and making tables to display typical seasonal weather conditions and climates

Amount of daylight. Students can gather data by keeping track of when sunrise and sunset occur and various weather conditions each day. Place an indoor/outdoor thermometer where students can view it to assist in this process. Have them record the data on individual and class charts—on paper or in a computer file that can be projected on the whiteboard—and then graph the data each month to help them see trends. Discussing the data their charts display will help them to represent data in graphs and tables and be able to talk about weather that is typical at certain times of the year, as the NGSS expect by third grade.

Erosion. Discuss erosion with the students and brainstorm experiments for testing the effects of erosion on soil and sand. Check websites, such as www.teacher.scholastic.com/dirt/index.htm, for experiment suggestions. After students have carried out several experiments, discuss ways to help prevent erosion from wind and rain. Ask students to choose two possible erosion solutions and make a poster or digital presentation showing the benefits and drawbacks of each solution; have them share their presentations with the class.

Earth science resources. NASA's Space Place at www.spaceplace.nasa.gov has games, apps, facts, activities, videos, and more on a variety of topics related to earth and space science, in English and Spanish. Search the Internet for other helpful sites, such as www.kids.nationalgeographic.com/kids/ and www.scholastic.com/magicschoolbus/games/sciencenews/index.htm. Sites such as www.weatherwizkids.com and www.crh.noaa.gov/gid/?n=weatherforkids, provide background knowledge students can use to help them meet standards, such as being able to discuss the merits of solutions for lessening the effect of weather-related hazards, such as tornados.

Try This!

Making and using homemade weather instruments will deepen students' understanding of weather concepts. Students can make a simple rain gauge by placing a funnel into a cylinder-shaped jar, such as an olive jar. Tape a clear ruler to the outside or use the ruler to mark measurements on the jar with a permanent marker and cover the marks with clear packing tape. A web search will reveal a number of sites with directions for other homemade instruments, including anemometers, sundials, and even creative snow rulers. Students can work together to design their own instruments; www.ciese.org/curriculum/weatherproj/engineering_windsock/ has a good example of an engineering design project for making a windsock.

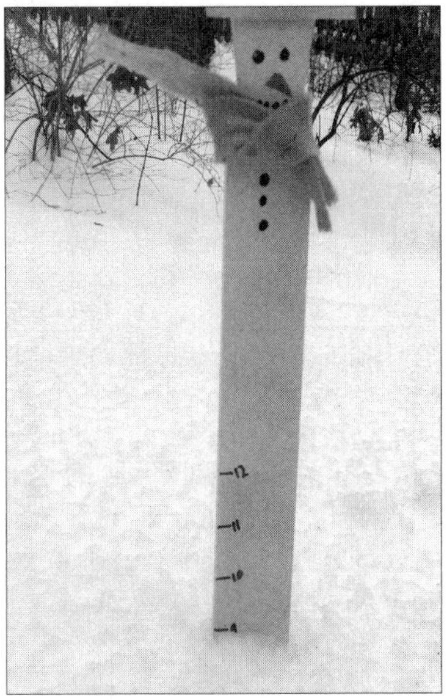

Investigations in Engineering, Technology, and Applications of Science

Science, engineering, and technology have been combined in the NGSS, enabling students to put science and math skills into practice. STEM (science, technology, engineering, and mathematics) has received a great deal of attention nationally and is seen as an important field for future jobs and opportunities. It is vital to support both girls and boys in these fields by providing hands-on activities and enjoyable experiences with technology that will support their interests and enhance their self-confidence—for example, they might explore Jim Henson's *Sid's Science Fair* app.

The developers of the NGSS hoped that by combining engineering design with the science standards, students would be better prepared to develop models and solutions to environmental and other challenges society faces today. The Boston Science Museum has an excellent description and graphic of the design process at www.eie.org/overview/engineering-design-process.

NGSS in Engineering, Technology, and Applications of Science. There are several standards (NGSS Lead States 2013) in this area for primary students:

- **First and second grades:** define a simple problem that can be solved with a new tool or object by asking questions, making observations, and gathering data on a situation people would like to change; develop a drawing or physical model to show how an object's shape helps it to solve a problem; compare data from tests of two objects designed to solve a problem to see how each performs

- **Third grade:** define a design problem related to a need or want, including criteria for success; generate and compare possible solutions; plan and carry out tests to find aspects that can be improved in a model or prototype

Define a problem; find a solution. You might introduce the idea of design problems by asking students to work in small groups to design a marble maze. The class could discuss parameters, problems they might encounter, and materials they might employ for a solution, such as LEGOs, pool noodles, cardboard tubes, or rain gutters. Students can sketch their solutions and then construct their models. Students could share their mazes, discussing benefits and problems, and then draw and construct changes to their mazes to make them more effective. This type of project is well suited to differentiation, as it allows students to work at their own pace and advance as far as they are able and interested. Visit www.ciese.org/engineeringproj.html to view a variety of design problems and ideas for supporting students' efforts.

Discussions about societal problems, such as pollution, could lead to comparing various solutions, such as recycling. Students can work in small groups to discuss possible solutions and research the web, children's magazines, and informational text to learn more about solutions. For example, students might explore ways to recycle paper by looking at sites such as www.pbskids.org/zoom/activities/sci/recyclingpaper.html. Small groups could discuss alternate designs for straining the water from the paper pulp, sketch, and test out their ideas. This would make an appropriate Earth Day project.

Students could also work together in groups to design a solution for reducing noise pollution in their environment. After students have spent time brainstorming ideas, you might narrow their focus by suggesting they design something they might wear. Once they have a list of ideas, ask them to evaluate their designs for effectiveness, safety, and practicality.

Discuss items that could be recycled in the classroom, such as old crayons. Students could talk about shapes that might be best for new crayons and how to make those shapes with melted crayons. Have students peel and sort the crayons by color. Melt the used crayons in recycled tin cans in a water bath in a skillet on low heat, letting the students know that this is one part of the design process that you need to conduct by yourself for safety reasons. Pour the melted crayons into molds students have suggested, such as recycled yogurt containers.

Try This!

Create a class book titled *How To Build a Better . . .* by asking each student to research a topic of choice and create a design for a new, improved version of their selected object. They can use digital drawing programs, such as those featured at www.cooltoolsforschools.wikispaces.com and www.freetech4teachers.com. Students might choose to write about a better bus, robot, boat, subway, windmill, or any number of creative ideas, enhancing their engineering, science, and literacy skills.

Home↔School Connections

Involve families in your science program. Provide copies of the standards you are helping the children to meet and ask family members if they have any expertise they could share. If you are able to take field trips, you could ask for suggestions of places to visit that would enhance children's science learning. Some family members may be interested in accompanying the class and leading a small group. Families are often happy to contribute materials or supplies. Some teachers make a wish list that they pass out at an open house or post on their website with items they would like donated. The list includes items that would be used throughout the year, such as measuring cups, batteries, cornstarch, flour, food coloring, and other ingredients for mixtures.

Send home suggestions of simple explorations families can do at home, along with a form for jotting down their process and conclusions. Knowing the students' families and their resources is essential. You might find it most beneficial to send home simple science kits that include a book and the materials needed for an activity. For example, one kit might include directions for an engineering challenge of designing and building a boat of aluminum foil that can stay afloat. Another challenge might be to add pennies to the boat and refine the design to accommodate the additional weight. Pair this activity with a few poems you provide about water from a book such as *Water Music: Poems for Children* by Jane Yolen. This type of activity can help students learn about engineering, science, and literacy and promote family engagement. Encourage families to experience the beauty of nature together if possible and to talk about their appreciation for plants, animals, and the world around them.

Consider hosting a STEM or STEAM (science, technology, engineering, arts, and mathematics) evening and invite families to help plan and assist. You could set up several stations inside or outdoors that children and adults could participate in together, including each of the STEM or STEAM areas. This could include building and testing ramps made from a variety of PVC tubing, rain gutters, and other materials for rolling ping pong balls, marbles, or miniature cars. Explore forces, interactions, and gravity by creating art made by filling a knee high stocking with a cup of aquarium or pea gravel, tying it closed, dipping in several colors of paint in a pie tin, and then dropping on a large sheet of paper. Families could explore painting with magnets by placing a piece of paper in a shoebox, adding drops of paint, paperclips, and other metal objects on the paper, and then moving a magnet under the shoebox to create a painting. You could also offer pendulum painting, by providing a tripod or materials such as PVC pipes that families and children can use to make a small stand, suspend a plastic cup with a small hole in the bottom from the stand, and add tempera paint, salt, sand, or another material to the plastic cup. Set the pendulum in motion over a large piece of paper and watch the pattern it creates. A simplified version of this can simply be a marker or paintbrush attached to a string that the child starts moving back and forth. Families could visit a technology station with laptops and tablets that have developmentally appropriate, interactive apps and programs. At another station students and families could sketch or create a scale model of a space station with recycled materials.

Meeting Standards—and More!

One of the goals in the primary grades is to nurture children's sense of wonder and appreciation for the world. Rachel Carson's (1965) words express this hope beautifully, "If I had influence with the good fairy who is supposed to preside over the christening of all children I should ask that her gift to each child in the world be a sense of wonder so indestructible that it would last throughout life" (45). She continues, "If a child is to keep alive his inborn sense of wonder . . . he needs the companionship of at least one adult who can share it, rediscovering with him the joy, excitement, and mystery of the world we live in" (55). Teachers have the privilege of being one of the adults who can keep children's sense of wonder alive. For some children you may need to rekindle their wonder. You may be the only adult who will. Science can be a magnificent window into the world of wonder, and connecting students to nature is one important way to provide this. Research shows important benefits to putting children in touch with nature, including improved cognitive and observational skills and an increased sense of health and well-being (Rivkin 2014). Connecting with nature can create a buffer for stress and has even been shown to help lessen symptoms of attention deficit disorder (www.childrenandnature.org/research).

Deepen children's appreciation for the natural world by providing opportunities to walk through a park or woods or even simply notice flowers, trees, or other living things nearby. Add a few flowerpots or a raised planter box to your school's outside area where students can plant seeds and bulbs. Add items from nature to the classroom, such as pinecones, seashells, rocks, and plants. Students' families may enjoy contributing nature items to the classrooms. Look for further resources and nature information at www.nature-explore.org.

It may also be beneficial for students to feel that they can be part of the scientific and global community that is working to improve the environment. Taking part in recycling and cleanup efforts are some of the ways they can contribute. There are also several sites where the class can contribute data to worldwide efforts, such as eBird mentioned previously in this chapter on page 119. In the GLOBE program (www.globe.gov/documents/10157/380993/tg_intro.pdf), students can enter data such as when they see the first spring buds open in your neighborhood. Choosing games and websites that promote environmental awareness and positive values, such as www.meetthegreens.org/, can also help students make connections to the world around them.

The science, engineering, and technology topics you introduce may tap into students' interests, unlocking a passion for learning and a desire to learn more about an area they want to pursue. Engineering design challenges and discussions may spur an interest that could lead to students pursuing solutions to global needs, such as wind or solar power.

Through the experiences you provide, students can grow into concerned, knowledgeable citizens who want to be good stewards of their environment and preserve it for future generations. Helping students discover and explore the world beyond them can aid in their social and emotional development as well, assisting them in understanding their interconnectedness with nature.

In a Nutshell

Having a strong foundation in science will help prepare students for future success: There is increasing demand for people who are competent in the STEM areas. The NGSS were developed to help students prepare for future college, career, and civic engagement. The standards outline scientific and engineering practices; disciplinary core ideas of physical sciences, life sciences, earth and space sciences, and engineering, technology, and applications of science; and crosscutting concepts. To meet the standards students need to plan and carry out investigations, test out their ideas, and draw conclusions and clearly communicate their thoughts, plans, processes, and results.

There is considerable crossover in the expectations listed in the Common Core State Standards, the C3 Framework for Social Studies Standards, and the NGSS. Actively involving students in scientific inquiry, investigations of topics of interest and worth, and engineering design challenges can help them meet standards in all areas of the curriculum. Science is an excellent way for students to gain and practice skills in literacy, mathematics, social studies, and the arts, as they read science-related books, plan and write up investigations, draw design plans, and prepare and share their conclusions in a variety of presentations and discussions. Through science, students can also deepen their sense of wonder, appreciation for the natural world, and desire to preserve their environment.

Reaching Beyond the Standards

7

This final chapter addresses ways to support students in the creative arts and physical development and health. The chapter closes with final thoughts on how teachers can support students in meeting standards while promoting their love of learning and discovery.

Promoting Learning Through the Arts

The arts contribute to learning in all areas of the curriculum. In addition to the value of studying the arts for their own sake, engaging in the arts promotes creativity and imagination, which facilitate students' ability to consider all types of problems from new perspectives. It can even be critical to scientific breakthroughs, as this excerpt shows:

> In the area of the visual arts, the human brain has the incredible ability to form images and representations of the real world or sheer fantasy within its mind's eye. Solving the mystery of DNA's structure, for example, required James Watson and Francis Crick in the early 1950s to imagine numerous three-dimensional models until they hit on the only image that explained the molecule's peculiar behavior—the spiral helix. This was an incredible marriage of visual art and biology that changed the scientific world forever. (Sousa 2006)

The creative arts promote brain development, problem solving, and emotional well-being and help children develop skills that are necessary to all learning, such as focus and persistence (President's Committee on the Arts and the Humanities 2011; Sousa 2006). They also provide a means of expressing thoughts and feelings. The creative arts are one of the easiest avenues for children to understand that one thing can represent another—for example, when they draw a square with a triangle on top and call it a house. Symbolic thought is critical to understanding how letters and numbers function and how they are used to represent thoughts.

To be maintained, however, creativity needs to be nurtured. One study found that although 95 percent of first-graders considered themselves to be creative, that percentage dropped as students got older (Rosenow 2012). Only 50 percent of fourth-graders and 5 percent of high school seniors viewed themselves as creative. In one of the most watched TED Talks, Ken Robinson (2006) makes the case that schools kill creativity. He suggests that creativity is as important in education as literacy and that children have an enormous capacity for innovation. He believes that one reason children are creative is that they are willing to take risks, until the educational system convinces them that mistakes are a sign of failure to be avoided. He makes a plea for educating the whole child in an atmosphere where it is safe to take risks, valuing creativity and the arts.

Developed by the Consortium of National Arts Education Associations (1994), national standards for the arts include the areas of visual arts, music, dance, and theater (visit https://artsedge.kennedy-center.org/educators/standards/full-text/K-4-standards). The following section provides ideas for meeting arts standards, as well as using the arts to meet standards in other areas of the curriculum.

The Visual Arts

Surround students with art in your classroom. Hang prints of artists—Monet's gardens, Mondrian's simple lines and colors, Oscar Howe's Native American children at play, Jeff Wambugu's portrayals of life in Africa, and Mary Cassatt's portraits of children—to inspire you and the students. Many libraries and museums will loan art and art books and have collections that you can view with students online, such as www.bostonchildrens-museum.org/exhibits-programs/collections. Local artists may be honored to share their art in your classroom. Look for artists that reflect diverse genres and cultures, including those of the children in the class. Display student art on the walls, bulletin boards, and shelves as well, conveying the message that you value what they create.

Art and illustration area. Set up an area where students can try some of the techniques used by artists and create their own original art. Students can also use this area during literacy center time to add illustrations to the writing they have done, and to do a variety of art activities at other times of the day, depending on your schedule. Vary the materials throughout the year, and include an assortment of paints and brushes, paper, markers, clay, glue, yarn, twigs, and other natural materials to encourage students' creativity. Students love painting at an easel; if one is not available permanently, perhaps you can borrow one for short periods of

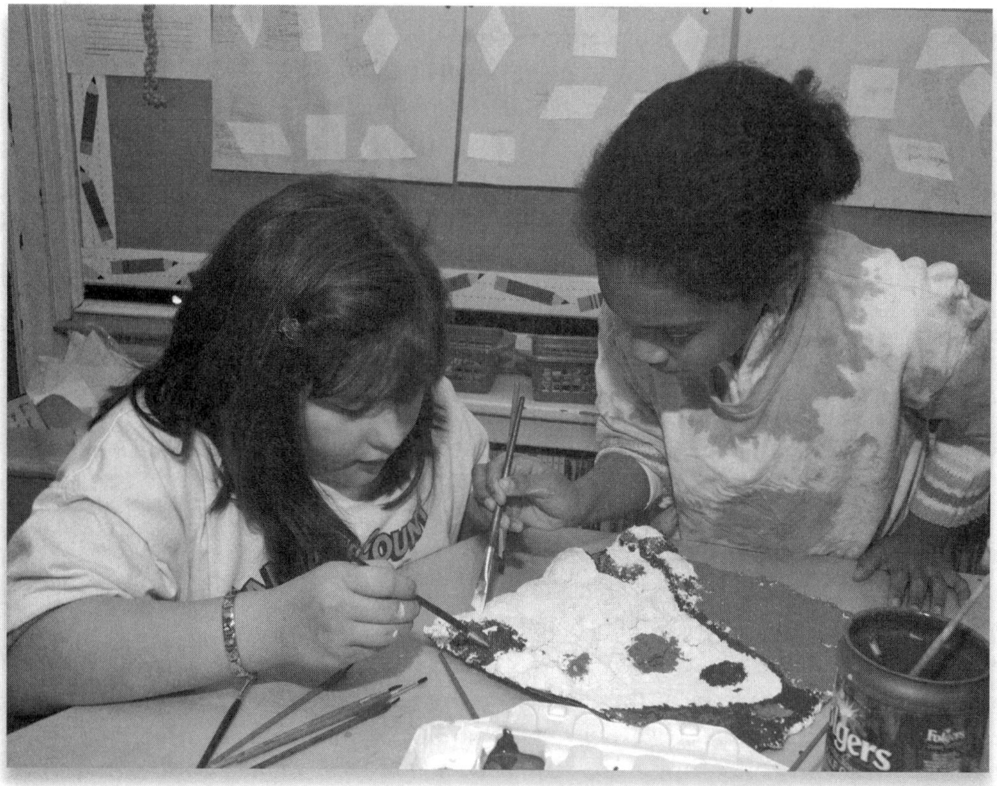

time. From time to time or as part of a study or during a change of season, have children paint on windows with tempera paint, a few children at a time. Provide opportunities for students to work both on projects you suggest and their own creations.

Creating greeting cards, invitations, posters, murals, mobiles, advertisements, menus, presentations, or illustrations for poems, books, and science activities can enhance students' art, literacy, and other skills. Talk about the role of illustrators and how illustrations help to tell a story. Each week designate a student to create an award for a children's book illustrator and affix the award to the book.

Try This!

Provide time, materials, and space so students can create covers for their favorite books, designing them as if they were the illustrator. Assemble all the covers created by the students together into a book, make a cover for it, and place it in the art and illustration center or the classroom library for all to enjoy.

Electronic drawing tools. Many computer programs and tablet apps provide drawing tools that enable students to illustrate their writing. These tools, such as Tux Paint (www.tuxpaint.org) and the *Doodle Buddy* app, may stimulate children's interest in writing. Before they read a story, students could draw pictures depicting what they think the story will be about, and then draw pictures after reading the story as well (Hutchison, Beschorner, & Schmidt-Crawford 2012). Students can create cartoons and comic strips to retell or create stories with the *Toontastic* app and at the ReadWriteThink website (www.readwritethink.org/files/resources/interactives/comic). These tools are especially helpful for dual language learners and students who might benefit from using pictures to support their writing.

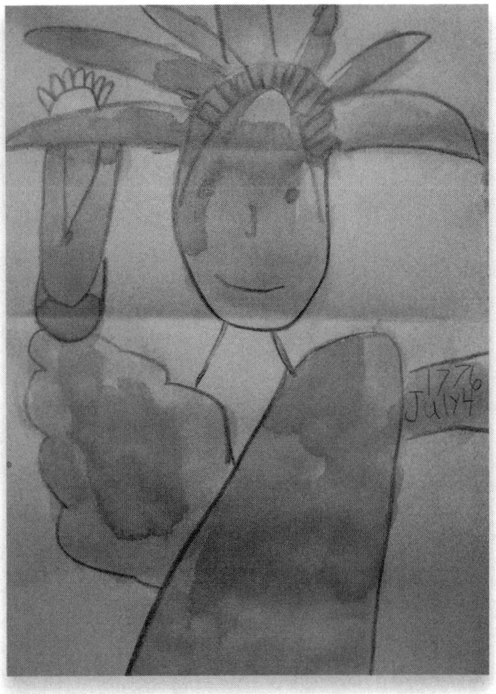

Teaching basic drawing techniques may help children better express their thoughts and creativity. Websites such as www.edemberley.com provide step-by-step instructions to help develop drawing skills. Images at www.charleyharperprints.com demonstrate how simple images can communicate beauty and may inspire students' drawings. Teach students the basics of proportion by having them study a variety of portraits and observe the placement of features in relationship to each other. Provide mirrors so students can observe their own features. Dual language learners may find illustrating a satisfying, successful way to express themselves. As their English skills grow and they become more confident, they can add words in their home language and in English to their illustrations.

Photography. Many students enjoy taking digital photos. Photography can focus their observational skills and enable them to see things and reflect on them with a new perspective—through the eyes of an artist. Their writing skills will develop as they describe people, scenes, and objects with the perspective of seeing them through the camera lens.

Students can use photography to learn more about science by taking pictures of clouds, weather events, plants, and animals. Have them document the stages of their experiments and engineering designs with photos and enrich their understanding of social studies by photographing the community and its geological features. They can use photos to enhance their presentations, reports, or other works related to the current topics of study.

Try This!

Share with students the alphabet photos from nature at www.dnr.state.mn.us/young_naturalists/natures_alphabet/index.html and other sites. Then go outside. Challenge students to find letters or numbers in nature, and take digital photos of what they find. Assemble the photos into a class book.

Music

Music has many benefits for children. Playing music while students are working, such as inspiring classical selections (for example, Vivaldi's "Four Seasons") and other pieces that you and the students find uplifting, may add to the positive climate of the room. Instrumental, background music helps many students stay focused while writing, working in centers, or at other quiet activities. Research shows that music can stimulate spatial thinking, memory, and visual imagery and that music instruction has positive effects on both math and reading achievement (President's Committee on the Arts and the Humanities 2011; Sousa 2006). Singing rhyming songs while pointing to the words on chart paper may support children's phonemic awareness, fluency, and word recognition. Providing books with words to songs is especially helpful for emerging readers. Singing with students can also foster an atmosphere that supports a community of learners. Use charts and books with songs that promote this concept, such as *We All Sing With the Same Voice* by J. Phillip Miller and Sheppard M. Greene.

Repetition helps the brain learn (Saville 2011), and singing is an engaging way to provide repetition. Search the Internet for suggestions on setting concepts to rap and other forms of music. Although helpful for all students, learning concepts through singing may be especially helpful for children who need additional support, such as those who need extra repetition to practice math facts and other skills. Students with autism may respond well to directions set to music. Singing songs is also an appealing, low-pressure way for dual language learners to practice English skills. Students may also enjoy exploring music with apps such as *Singing Fingers*, *Noteimals*, and *Magic Piano*, which will even allow them to play virtual pianos!

Dance

Dance can support the development of spatial awareness, timing, and rhythm (Sousa 2006). Encourage students to compose their own songs about topics you are studying and to choreograph simple movements to the songs. In his TED Talk mentioned earlier in this chapter, Robinson also discusses the importance of dance, along with the other creative arts. He recounts the story of Gillian Lynne, one of the most renowned choreographers, whose work includes "Cats" and "Phantom of the Opera." As a child Gillian had difficulty sitting still and focusing. At the age of 8 she was taken to a specialist to see if she had a learning disorder. Fortunately, after spending time with her and seeing her body respond to the music playing on the radio, the specialist suggested that what Gillian needed was the opportunity to dance, so her parents enrolled her in a dance school. Robinson suggests that others may have put her on medication and stifled her amazing talent.

The Kennedy Center ArtsEdge website has suggestions for teaching dance, including helping children in grades K–4 explore questions about what dance is, how it works, and why it is important. They recommend providing support as children discover similarities and differences between dance and other subject areas, learning about dance elements of space, time, force, and energy. The website has a number of lesson plans for teaching dance, such as the Chinese Lion Dance, and other resources at https://artsedge.kennedy-center.org/educators.

Theater

Theater is another area of the arts that promotes learning. As with the other arts, it can also promote imagination, self-expression, and aesthetic appreciation, and serve as an emotional outlet. Students who have the opportunity to participate in drama can increase their self-confidence, collaboration, empathy, and communication skills. Acting out fiction and nonfiction texts they are reading supports students' comprehension skills, and Readers Theater productions help students work on fluency. Record their dramatizations with a tablet and play them on an interactive whiteboard for additional practice and an opportunity to share with classmates. Students can also write, act out, and record a scene from the biography of an important figure to strengthen their writing, reading, oral communication, and social studies skills.

Authentic Assessment Through the Arts

The creative arts provide a wealth of authentic ways for students to demonstrate what they are learning. Authentic or performance assessments that allow children to demonstrate their understanding through meaningful tasks can be highly motivating and promote further pursuit of learning. Through the arts, students can represent new concepts and make their learning visible. For example, they can

- Use drawings to illustrate science and social studies concepts
- Compose songs and raps or use creative movements to convey new knowledge
- Write and perform a skit about a historical event or other concept
- Digitally record their compositions and skits to create a permanent product you can watch and critique together

Gaining Appreciation for Cultures Through the Arts

The creative arts provide a beautiful way for students to develop an appreciation for other cultures. Playing music from a variety of cultures and learning simple cultural dances together can help children learn to appreciate other cultures as well as their own.

Read books about a variety of cultures and countries, including *Nasreddine*, a Turkish tale by Odile Weulersse. Visit websites that expand learning about that culture or country, such as http://kids.nationalgeographic.com/explore/countries/turkey.html. Search the Internet to explore the arts of cultures and countries, using them and books you read to inspire students' writing and art. *Colors! ¡Colores!* by Jorge Luján offers a beautiful way for students to explore colors, poetry, and strengthen English and Spanish language skills. After reading this type of book, students could write their own short poetry books, illustrating them with watercolors. Read Tomie dePaola's *The Legend of the Indian Paintbrush,* a legend about a young Native American boy who paints the sunset, and talk about the appreciation native cultures have for nature. Encourage students to try their hand at painting a sunrise or sunset. Watch short videos of Navajo sand painting and provide materials so students can try that art form.

Supporting Children's Physical Well-Being and Health

Just as art and music can help the brain focus, so can movement (Galinsky 2010). In an attempt to provide more time for addressing standards, some schools have reduced or eliminated recess. Yet physical activity may be just what students need to persist at academic learning the rest of the day. Studies show that regular physical activity increases the amount of oxygen in the blood, significantly enhancing cognitive performance. Activity actually increases the number of capillaries in the brain, facilitating the transportation of blood and the oxygen it carries to the brain (Sousa 2006). "At some point in every lesson, students should be moving about, talking about their new learning. Not only does the movement increase cognitive function, but it uses up some kinesthetic energy so students can settle down and concentrate better later. Mild exercise before a test also makes sense" (Sousa 2006).

Movement Throughout the Day

Use creative ways of incorporating movement into your curriculum. For example, ask students to stand and, imagining their bodies to be a balance scale, show what would happen if they held a cup of water in their left hand and a cup of ice in their right. While they remain in their poses, ask them to explain their reasoning and reflect on the responses of their classmates. Ask them to shift their pose if the reasoning presented by their peers causes them to change their minds. Students can then weigh the cups on a scale and continue with further predictions, discussions, and testing of their hypotheses.

Make sure to add physical activity throughout the day when students need a break. Try quick jumping jacks, running in place, or stretching and touching opposite toes. Play music and encourage students to dance or move with the music. You might even try moving together with videos of children doing Zumba. Here are a few good options: *Waka, Waka, This Time for Africa* at www.youtube.com/watch?v=0uzJ8NDtKAg, *Roar* at www.youtube.com/watch?v=mCnml4Mr9cQ, and *Hamster Dance* at www.youtube.com/watch?v=brj9NX4rPaA. Each time students do the movements, they will improve, making the activity more enjoyable and beneficial. Some schools have found that sitting on stability balls allows for quiet movement and helps improve focus and concentration, especially for children with attention-deficit/hyperactivity disorder (Spalding & Kelly 2010).

Try This!

Play games in which students are physically active, such as Fact or Fiction. Designate and label one spot of the room, or a space outside, for facts and another spot for statements that are not true. Make statements related to a topic the class is currently studying, such as "Water can be found as both a liquid and a solid on Earth—fact or fiction?" Students run, walk, or move in some other way to the spot that shows whether they believe the statement to be true or not. Ask students in each area to offer evidence for their answer, then proceed to the next question.

Oertwig and Holland (2014) discuss the interconnectedness of movement and learning, suggesting that physical activity is one of the best ways to stimulate learning. They note research demonstrating that movement helps students concentrate, focus, reduce stress, and lift their mood. "Brain research also suggests that physical activity prior to class and during class increases students' ability to process and retain new material" (111). They recommend that teachers integrate regular movement into their curriculum through daily recess, stretching, walking, dancing, physical education, drama, and hands-on learning activities. Go outdoors when possible, taking a walk with students to look for something related to a topic of study, creating a chalk map on the playground, or acting out a skit. If possible, to extend learning outside the classroom, collaborate with physical education teachers to share topics and concepts you are working on that might be incorporated into games and activities they offer.

Focus on Health Concepts

One way to incorporate health concepts into the curriculum is through a study on healthy lifestyles that you might refer to as "Livin' the Really Good Life!" Challenge students to create a video for other students their age that illustrates how to live a healthy life. Students could work in groups, with each group learning about and reflecting on one aspect of health: healthy food choices, exercise and movement, rest and relaxation, and ways to deal with stress and express emotions. After writing and revising their scripts, students could use a tablet or other device to shoot video scenes, such as making homemade vegetable soup or popcorn, planting a vegetable garden, playing basketball, exercising, singing, and curling up with a good book.

Try This!

To stimulate brain productivity, provide opportunities for students to move and practice skills at the same time. With a small group or the whole class in a large indoor space or outside, have students practice spelling words, math facts, or other key information as they jump rope, dribble a ball, or even use a Hula-Hoop. Students could also do this in pairs or individually in a corner of the classroom. The rhythmic pace and repetition of such activities make learning enjoyable. Suggest that families do this at home as a fun way to reinforce concepts their children are learning at school.

Home⟷School Connections

Use newsletters, conferences, and classroom websites to share resources with families, such as www.fit4theclassroom.com, that are designed to empower children and families to make healthy lifestyle choices. This website, a collaborative project sponsored by Discovery Education, WebMD, and Sanford Health, is based on the four pillars of their *fit* initiative: mood, move, food, and recharge. The website contains free resources for families, videos, interactive activities, lesson plans, and other resources that can be tied to math, science, and other subjects.

Some family members may be interested in helping you plan a health fair for students and families. Students could join in planning, gaining experience in doing "informed action" as the National Council for the Social Studies recommends. They could write letters to invite health-related services and programs from the community to set up information booths at the fair. Health care providers could offer screenings and brochures on health issues and services available in the community. Dentists and hygienists might demonstrate proper dental care and provide free toothbrushes. Local fitness instructors could offer short demo classes or activities. Invite students and family members to come early to help prepare healthy snacks for the event. Ask restaurants or health food stores to donate healthy foods for taste testing.

Consider collaborating with family and consumer sciences departments at the high school or college level to offer healthy cooking classes where family members could learn and share skills, plan menus, and prepare meals to take home for dinner. Local food banks or other organizations may be willing to help supply food for these classes. Talk with families about whether they might like to help start a school or community garden that would allow students and families to grow fresh produce.

Send home information about the value of the arts and encourage families to visit museums, and sing and dance together. Post or send home material on the importance of creativity and the benefits of providing opportunities for children to freely create art, sing, dance, and move. Request donations of paper that is clean on one side and offer to share it with families. Family members may enjoy helping set up a school or classroom art show where student artwork could be displayed and celebrated. They might also like to share their cultural art forms in a family cultural arts evening or simply come to the classroom to share music, dance, drama, or works of art.

A Call to Action

Standards alone will not change the quality of education or the future for most students. There are still many inequalities and issues, such as overwhelming poverty and lack of equity in resources, that need to be addressed to improve student outcomes. Teacher education programs need to prepare teachers to actively engage students in problem solving, finding solutions, providing evidence for their conclusions, and clearly communicating in multiple formats. Teachers need meaningful professional development to help students truly achieve the twenty-first century skills outlined in the standards. A first step to addressing the achievement gap that prevents many children from reaching their potential is a commitment to ensuring that all students receive a high-quality education. Standards, when addressed using best practices, provide research-based benchmarks to guide us in achieving this goal.

Join the Conversation

As concerned educators, we need to be active in the collective conversation about standards, including the Common Core. Let's advocate for teaching in developmentally appropriate ways that support learning in all areas, including social and emotional, cognitive, language, physical, and the arts. We must inform parents, administrators, and colleagues about the engaging activities we are using to help students meet standards in ways that respect their stage of development and that promote active learning, problem solving, and communicating. We can describe what has worked well for students and suggest how the standards might be revised.

Engage Students in Meaningful Learning

Let's commit to teaching in developmentally appropriate ways that cultivate students' interests, ignite their passion for pursuing knowledge, and expand their horizons. The standards challenge us to adopt new ways of teaching. In a TED talk, award-winning teacher Ramsey Musallam (2013) described this new role by saying, "But if we as educators leave behind this simple role as disseminators of content and embrace a new paradigm as cultivators of curiosity and inquiry, we just might bring a little bit more meaning to their school day, and spark their imagination."

Collaborate

Amid the challenges we face in our efforts to meet standards and provide a high-quality education that engages students in learning, we are not alone. One of the most effective ways of finding solutions is to exchange ideas with colleagues and others who share our passion and understand the tremendous task before us. There is power in collaboration. You can also find like-minded individuals, and support for advocating for best practices, from professional organizations such as NAEYC (www.naeyc.org), the National Science Teachers Association (www.nsta.org), the National Council of Teachers of Mathematics (www.nctm.org), and the International Reading Association (www.reading.org). These sites offer an increasing number of resources. You will also find support at a number of other sites, such as Pinterest and teacher blogs.

Commit to Helping All Students Succeed

Students need and deserve outstanding teachers who will inspire and support them in meeting standards. Communicating our unconditional positive regard and belief that all students are capable of learning will help them recognize and honor their own strengths. As teachers we accept a sacred trust to be dedicated to helping all students acquire the tools they need to be self-directed, compassionate learners who can make a real contribution to their families and communities. "Seeing our children joyfully, physically, and intellectually engaged in meaningful learning about their world and everyone and everything in it is the truest measure of our success as educators" (Copple et al. 2014, xi).

Using Both the Art and Science of Teaching to Support Students

As scientists we use research-based practices and keep up with the latest research in the field to provide high-quality experience for students. We also conduct our own teacher research, keeping data on what is working well and how we might improve our instruction. As artists we participate in the "dance" between teacher and student, becoming more fluid and graceful as the partners get to know each other's strengths and interests. We help students see themselves and the world with a new lens, full of opportunities for discovery. Through the thoughtful experiences and support we provide, we can help students not only meet standards but also expand their sense of wonder and joy in learning that will last a lifetime.

Frequently Asked Questions

Why do primary teachers need to address students' social and emotional development? There are no standards for this. Isn't that area more important for younger children?

Social and emotional development is a critical part of children's development in the primary grades. Students who exhibit a healthy sense of self-esteem, empathy, self-regulation, cooperation, social competence, understanding of their emotions, and respect and appreciation for others will be more successful in both school and life. They are more willing to take on challenges and persist when problems arise. Taking time to nurture children's social and emotional development will help them make progress in all areas of the curriculum.

Does it help students to know what standards we are working on?

It is always easier to achieve a goal when you know what you are aiming for. Let students know the standards you are trying to help them achieve. Clearly communicate the standards in words they will understand. Choose a few key standards, written in student-friendly terms, to post on the board each week.

How do you make centers work in a primary schedule?

There are many ways to actively involve students in learning. Many teachers find centers or interest areas to be a useful way to do this. Some offer literacy centers to be used as part of the literacy block, others provide math centers available to children during a portion of the time scheduled for math, and a number of teachers use both. In other classrooms, the schedule includes a center time during which students work in a variety of centers, such as reading, writing, math, science, and technology. This center time can be a key component of your program or used as enrichment, depending on your curriculum. Centers provide a way to differentiate instruction by offering activities and materials that support students at varied skill levels, freeing you to work with individuals and small groups while other students are engaged in center work.

Q There are children with challenging behaviors in my classroom. What are some strategies for helping them learn to use positive behaviors while helping all students meet standards?

The strategies teachers use to prevent and respond to children's challenging behaviors depend in part on the reasons behind the behaviors. Nevertheless, the following developmentally appropriate strategies will help most children succeed.

Strive to create a community of learners in which students are actively engaged in meaningful activities that are challenging but achievable. Predictable but flexible routines provide a sense of security. Think about the day's schedule. Which times seem to elicit more challenging behaviors? Students may be more successful if they have at least some time during the day to move around and talk with each other; this will also support language and speaking standards. Students can work on standards as with partners or in small groups on collaborative problem solving, centers, and other motivating activities that relate to their interests. Encourage students to speak at a volume that is easy for their partners or group members to hear but is not loud enough to disturb others. Make learning more meaningful by talking about what they will be learning when you give assignments and why that learning will be important.

Transition times present challenges for some students. Let students know when a transition is about to occur by giving five-, two-, and one-minute notices. Minimize the amount of time students are simply waiting—this is difficult for most people, even adults. Always have something they can do.

Work at strengthening relationships with students and among the students themselves. Students are less likely to be disruptive when they feel like successful, competent members of a group that is interested in supporting their success. Read books in which characters serve as positive role models and help students gain respect for themselves and each other. Brainstorm how to create a community of learners and make a class book with a title such as *How to Be a Successful Second-Grader.* Ask each child to write and illustrate a page depicting a different subject, part of the day, routine, or positive habit to display. Encourage students to talk to themselves and each other in supportive ways. Operation Respect, founded by Peter Yarrow, offers a free curriculum guide at www.operationrespect.org/curricula as well as a number of songs that can help students develop a deeper respect for each other and prevent teasing and bullying behaviors.

Help students develop self-regulation. Visit websites and read books about how the brain learns, such as *Your Fantastic, Elastic Brain: Stretch It, Shape It* by JoAnn Deak. Let students know that they are in control of their thoughts and behaviors; challenge them to think of themselves as being in mission control and to choose the best actions to achieve their mission and goals. Discuss and role-play ways to make good choices and how to act in a variety of situations. Children need practice, as well as adult support and patience, to develop self-regulation.

Develop a few positive classroom guidelines together, and help students understand how and why the guidelines will help them have a better classroom experience. When students do have difficulties, try using the *FLIP IT!* approach to help them "flip" their behavior around.

FLIP IT

F—Acknowledge the student's **feelings** and help her identify the feelings causing her behavior.

L—Remind the child of positive **limits**, surrounding her with a sense of consistency, safety, and trust.

I—Inquiries: Encourage the student to problem solve and think about possible solutions.

P—Prompts: Provide hints, suggestions, and cues to support the child's problem-solving process.

(Sperry 2011)

Look at what might prompt students' challenging behaviors and think about ways you could change those situations. Greet students who have challenging behaviors (as well as all students) each day as they arrive and provide encouraging words to get them off to a good start. It may also be helpful to pair students with challenging behaviors with students who have good self-regulation skills. If you need additional support, consult with the children's families or specialists in your school for additional resources. School counselors, psychologists, the principal, and special educators may have suggestions.

Q What kinds of assessments can tell me whether students are making progress toward meeting standards?

Assessment should be used to determine and document progress, improve student learning, and inform your teaching. *Authentic performance assessment* that uses meaningful tasks, demonstrating student competence in action, is most appropriate for primary grade students. This might be having students write a letter, write and perform a skit, or design and carry out a science investigation to solve a problem. The task can be evaluated by means of a rubric, also referred to as a scoring guide. Making rubrics with the students can help give them a deeper understanding of the expected requirements. Make sure students understand any rubrics you use and can explain them in their own words. Once you have a rubric that works well, modify it as needed to match the skills students are working on. Seek out online tools to help in developing rubrics, such as at http://rubistar.4teachers.org/. Collecting portfolios of students' work provides another form of authentic assessment by demonstrating progress over time. This is especially true of student writing, which is dated and collected over the year. These authentic assessments can provide evidence of meeting standards by themselves, but can also be combined with other assessments if mandated by the school.

Many school districts use standards achievement reports to supplement or replace the traditional report card. The reports can be used as a checklist to guide teacher observation and assessment. They provide information about which standards are being met and which require more attention for individual children, classrooms, schools, and districts. Reeves (2002) recommends using a file folder for each student's reports, with literacy, math, science, and social studies standards printed on each of the four sides. He suggests listing standards the district believes are most important and indicating student proficiency in each standard. Teachers and administrators can collaborate to determine which standards are most important and what scale would be most beneficial for evaluating student progress and motivating students (for example, *not introduced, beginning level, making progress, proficient*). The scale can match the terminology used in your rubrics (such as *beginning level, making progress, proficient*), providing authentic evidence for scoring the achievement reports. Teachers and students can choose student work samples and rubrics to keep inside the folder to demonstrate progress and share with parents. Choose standards to focus on each quarter, knowing that some standards will remain as "not introduced" on the report until later in the year.

Share assessment information with families, and seek information from them about their child's growing skills. Provide information about applicable standards on your school or class website, in newsletters, and in conferences. Partner with families to help their children make progress. When carried out appropriately, assessment can motivate and inspire students to work harder to accomplish goals because they can see the progress they are making (Ferguson, Green, & Marchel 2013).

Are there any advantages to teaching a new language to students, such as Spanish or French? How can I go about doing this?

There are many advantages to speaking more than one language, not only in the United States but also in today's global society where we can be connected to others around the world in a heartbeat. Preparing students for the future includes supporting them in gaining the skills they need to be able to communicate with potential future employers, clients, patients, colleagues, or those in need worldwide. Children who can speak multiple languages show cognitive benefits over children who speak only one language. Bilingual children tend to have increased creative and divergent thinking, greater working memory capacity, and better control of their attention, and they are better able to think and talk about language (Adesope et al. 2010). Switching between the sounds, grammar, and words of both languages appears to promote brain development. Children who hear the sounds of other languages before the age of 10 form connections in the brain that make learning those new languages much easier (Black 2000).

In Wheeling, West Virginia, students in the Ohio County schools who participated in foreign language instruction—primarily Spanish, with limited exposure to several other languages—for several years not only learned the new language but also scored at the top in the state in both reading and mathematics. (To learn more, visit www.asbj.com/MainMenuCategory/Supplements/MagnaAwards/MagnaNominations/Magna-Search.html?Magna=yes&ID=920.)

Although not as effective as a focused program, consider these resources for helping students learn another language:

- Use apps such as *Spanish Word Wizard* and websites such as http://pbskids.org/noah/index.html and www.chillola.com/index.html to help students learn new words and phrases in the new language.
- Use sites that translate and audibly pronounce simple greetings and phrases for students to learn, such as www.translate.google.com and Google's *Translate* app.
- Play CDs with simple songs in the new language, especially songs students already know in English, or bilingual songs as students are working or during transitions.

- Have students listen to bilingual books on tape at a listening center.
- Label one item in your room each day in both English and Spanish (or another language you are studying), using a different color for each language.
- Invite interested dual language learners to teach the class some simple words and phrases in their home languages. This boosts their self-confidence and aids their own language acquisition as they use both of their languages to help their peers learn. Families might also enjoy sharing useful words and phrases with the class.

Q How can I find appropriate educational websites, apps, and other technology? How do I protect students from inappropriate sites and apps?

Several websites rate children's apps and other technology. For example, Children's Technology Review (www.childrenstech.com) provides trusted reviews of children's interactive media products. Zoodles (zoodles.com) allows you to select students' age range and then provides apps, games, videos, storybooks, and an art studio; inappropriate sites and advertisements are blocked. Common Sense Media (www.commonsensemedia.org) rates children's media and provides resources for families and educators, including a searchable database of recommended technology products for supporting the Common Core State Standards.

Q Isn't play important just for younger children? Does it really have any value in the primary grades?

Play can be defined as an activity that the individual *wants* to do, one that provides choice, intrinsic motivation, self-direction, enjoyment, and value to the person. Vygotsky describes play as the preeminent educational activity of childhood writing that it allows a child to develop self-control and act "as though he were a head taller than himself" (Vygotsky 1978, 102). When students play, they perform at the peak of their abilities, above their typical daily behavior because they are motivated and interested. Provide opportunities for students to choose activities that are motivating and enjoyable to them, such as using educational apps, investigating batteries and motors, exploring ramps and pulleys, engineering LEGO structures, writing and performing a skit, choosing from a variety of centers, playing educational board games, or engaging in outdoor play. Supporting students through these types of activities will help them meet standards and deepen their interest in pursuing further learning.

Q I know that engaging with families is important. How can I partner with families so we both can make genuine contributions to students' education?

Family engagement does make a difference to students' educational success. Striving to build true *reciprocal* relationships with parents, where both sides feel equally valued, respected, and capable, will go a long way toward encouraging engagement. Let parents know that you honor their role as parents and co-educators; when they know you truly care about *their* child, they are more likely to want to work with you.

A class website provides information families can access when it is convenient for them; the site might include a welcome letter, photos of class activities, schedules, homework, a calendar with upcoming events, and links to your newsletters. Sites such as www.shutterfly.com, www.schoolrack.com, and www.classjump.com can host your site if you do not have access to one through your school. Upload short videos of students' skits, Readers Theater, and other activities so families can see how and what their children are learning. Make sure you have signed parental permission to post photos and video of children. Use your website and newsletters to provide links to helpful family resources, such as www.pbs.org/parents and www.bblocks.samhsa.gov/family. Have students put together a monthly classroom newspaper to keep families up to date on what's happening. They could take turns being reporters and editors and switch roles the following month.

At the beginning of the year, create a welcome packet with information on classroom procedures, supplies, your guidance philosophy, the curriculum, contact information, and volunteer opportunities. Include a note that communicates your excitement about the opportunity to work with the children and your willingness to hear what they think is important for their children. Hand out the packets at an open house. When new students arrive during the year, give the packet to families to ease the transition (McDonald & Hershman 2010). Think about other events you might host for families, such as a special reading or math night with activities families can enjoy doing together, including reading and making multiples or halves of recipes to make their own snack.

Calling each family at the beginning of the year gets the relationship off to a good beginning. You could also send an email greeting, welcome letter, or postcard that shares a bit about yourself, your teaching philosophy, and your goals for the class. Find out how families would prefer you to contact them. In addition to conferences, set up a schedule to communicate with a few families each week so you can keep in touch with all of them throughout the year. Whenever you talk with parents, start with something positive about their children and perhaps include a suggestion of an enjoyable activity they can do at home. Make sure to send communications in families' home languages. There are online sites that allow you to translate, but have someone familiar with the language read it over as a safeguard. At www.colorincolorado.org there are reading tip sheets for parents available in 11 languages as well as many other resources for working with dual language learners. Welcome all families so that each child feels equally valued and respected.

Find out what families feel they need and pursue ways the school community may be able to meet those needs. Some school districts offer evening English classes for family members of dual language learners. Becoming more proficient in English can help both the children and the adults. Consider establishing a family mentor program for those who are interested by asking parents and guardians of children you have already had in your class to mentor current family members. Mentors can share their experiences, helping new families with information about the school, schedule, what to expect, and advice from another family perspective. This could be especially helpful in pairing families of dual language learners who have the same first language and could become a school-wide initiative. You could also pair families in the same class to support each other.

Update families about opportunities to volunteer and contribute during the school day or at home. Grandparents might appreciate a special invitation to spend a day each month helping with activities, such as working with students to write stories on the computer or working one-on-one with students who need assistance. Develop an information sheet or packet for volunteers that clearly outlines what to do while they are there; this will increase their effectiveness and help them feel more useful and at ease. Make a similar packet with information on tasks that volunteers can complete at home.

Use your newsletters and website to share information with families about what students are learning. Let parents know that the standards require advanced skills such as problem solving, looking for and providing evidence, and recording and communicating findings. Explain what you are doing to help students to achieve these skills. At the end of the year, send home a calendar with simple suggestions families can do daily or weekly to sustain and advance learning, focusing on enjoyable activities that will also foster positive family relationships. Helping parents in their role as their children's first and most important teachers will benefit students for the rest of their lifetime.

References

Adesope, O., T. Lavin, T. Thompson, & C. Ungerleider. 2010. "A Systematic Review and Meta-Analysis of the Cognitive Correlates of Bilingualism." *Review of Educational Research* 80 (2): 207–45.

Alanis, I. 2013. "Where's Your Partner? Pairing Bilingual Learners in Preschool and Primary Grade Dual Language Classrooms." *Young Children* 68 (1): 42–46.

Anderson, L.W., & D.R. Krathwohl, eds. 2001. *A Taxonomy for Learning, Teaching, and Assessing: A Revision of Bloom's Taxonomy of Educational Objectives*. New York: Longman.

Anderson, R., E. Hiebert, J. Scott, & I. Wilkinson, with contributions from members of the Commission on Reading. 1985. *Becoming a Nation of Readers: The Report of the Commission on Reading.* Washington, DC: US Department of Education, National Institute of Education.

Annie E. Casey Foundation. 2010. *Early Warning! Why Reading by the End of Third Grade Matters: A KIDS COUNT Special Report From the Annie E. Casey Foundation, Summary.* Baltimore, MD: Annie E. Casey Foundation. http://floridakidscount.fmhi.usf.edu/_assets/docs/pubs/Reading%20Report%20Executive%20Summary.pdf.

Bear, D.R., M. Invernizzi, S. Templeton, & F. Johnston. 2012. *Words Their Way: Word Study for Phonics, Vocabulary, and Spelling Instruction.* 5th ed. Boston: Pearson/Allyn & Bacon.

Benjamin, A., & J.T. Crow. 2013. *Vocabulary at the Core: Teaching the Common Core Standards.* Larchmont, NY: Eye On Education.

Black, S. 2000. "Neuron to Neuron." *American School Board Journal* 187 (1): 42–45.

Bodrova, E., & D.J. Leong. 2007. *Tools of the Mind: The Vygotskian Approach to Early Childhood Education.* 2nd ed. Upper Saddle River, NJ: Pearson/Merrill Prentice Hall.

Boushey, G., & J. Moser. 2014. *The Daily 5: Fostering Literacy Independence in the Elementary Grades.* 2nd ed. Portland, ME: Stenhouse.

Brenneman, K. 2009. "Let's Find Out! Preschoolers as Scientific Explorers." *Young Children* 64 (6): 54–60.

Caine, R.N. 2008. "How Neuroscience Informs Our Teaching of Elementary Students." In *Comprehension Instruction: Research-Based Best Practices*, 2nd ed., eds. C.C. Block & S.R. Parris, 127–41. New York: Guilford.

Calkins, L., M. Ehrenworth, & C. Lehman. 2012. *Pathways to the Common Core: Accelerating Achievement.* Portsmouth, NH: Heinemann.

Calkins, L., K. Tolan, & M. Ehrenworth. 2010. *Units of Study for Teaching Reading, Grades 3–5: A Curriculum for the Reading Workshop.* Portsmouth, NH: Heinemann.

Carpenter, T.P., E. Fennema, M.L. Franke, L. Levi, & S.B. Empson. 1999. *Children's Mathematics: Cognitively Guided Instruction.* Portsmouth, NH. Heinemann.

Carson, R. 1965. *The Sense of Wonder.* New York: Harper Row.

Combs, W.E. 2012. *Writer's Workshop for the Common Core: A Step-by-Step Guide.* Larchmont, NY: Eye On Education.

Comer, J.P. 2005. *Leave No Child Behind: Preparing Today's Youth for Tomorrow's* World. New Haven, CT: Yale University Press.

Common Core State Standards Initiative. 2014. "About the Standards." Accessed May 1. www.corestandards.org/about-the-standards/.

Consortium of National Arts Education Associations. 1994. "K-4 Standards in Dance, Music, Theater and Visual Arts." https://artsedge.kennedy-center.org/educators/standards/full-text/K-4-standards.

Copley, J.V. 2010. *The Young Child and Mathematics.* 2nd ed. Washington, DC: NAEYC; Reston, VA: NCTM.

Copple, C., & S. Bredekamp, eds. 2009. *Developmentally Appropriate Practice in Early Childhood Programs Serving Children From Birth Through Age Eight.* 3rd ed. Washington, DC: NAEYC.

Copple, C., S. Bredekamp, D. Koralek, & K. Charner, eds. 2014. *Developmentally Appropriate Practice: Focus on Children in First, Second, and Third Grades.* Washington, DC: NAEYC.

Crawford, G.M., C.T. Cobb, R.M. Clifford, & S. Ritchie. 2014. "The Groundswell for Transforming Prekindergarten through 3rd Grade." Chap. 1 in *FirstSchool: Transforming PreK-3rd Grade for African American, Latino, and Low-Income Children,* eds. S. Ritchie & L. Gutmann, 9–28. New York: Teachers College Press.

Danielson, C. 2007. *Enhancing Professional Practice: A Framework for Teaching.* 2nd ed. Alexandria, VA: ASCD.

Danielson, C. 2010. *Implementing the Framework for Teaching in Enhancing Professional Practice.* Alexandria, VA: ASCD.

DEC (Division for Early Childhood of the Council for Exceptional Children), NAEYC (National Association for the Education of Young Children), & NHSA (National Head Start Association). 2013. "Frameworks for Response to Intervention in Early Childhood: Description and Implications." www.naeyc.org/content/frameworks-response-intervention-paper.

Denton, K., & J. West. 2002. *Children's Reading and Mathematics Achievement in Kindergarten and First Grade.* Washington, DC: National Center for Education Statistics.

Derman-Sparks, L., & J.O. Edwards. 2010. *Anti-Bias Education for Young Children and Ourselves.* Washington, DC: NAEYC.

Dodge, J. 2009. *25 Quick Formative Assessments for a Differentiated Classroom: Easy, Low-Prep Assessments That Help You Pinpoint Students' Needs and Reach All Learners.* New York: Scholastic.

Dweck, C.S. 2008. *Mindset: The New Psychology of Success—How We Can Learn to Fulfill Our Potential.* New York: Ballantine.

Epstein, A.S. 2014. *The Intentional Teacher: Choosing the Best Strategies for Young Children's Learning.* Rev. ed. Washington, DC: NAEYC; Ypsilanti, MI: HighScope Press.

Evenson, A., M. McIver, S. Ryan, & A. Schwols. 2013. *Common Core Standards for Elementary Grades K-2 Math & English Language Arts.* Alexandria, VA: ASCD; Denver, CO: McRel.

Ferguson, C.J., S.K. Green, & C.A. Marchel. 2013. "Teacher-Made Assessments Show Children's Growth." *Young Children* 68 (3): 28–37.

Forum on Child and Family Statistics. 2013. "America's Children: Key National Indicators of Well-Being, 2013." www.childstats.gov/americaschildren/special1.asp.

Fountas, I., & G.S. Pinnell. 1996. *Guided Reading: Good First Teaching for All Children.* Portsmouth, NH: Heinemann.

Fountas, I.C., & G.S. Pinnell. 2001. *Guiding Readers and Writers Grades 3–6: Teaching Comprehension, Genre, and Content Literacy.* Portsmouth, NH: Heinemann.

Fountas, I.C., & G.S. Pinnell. 2006. *Teaching for Comprehending and Fluency: Thinking, Talking, and Writing About Reading, K–8.* Portsmouth, NH: Heinemann.

Galinsky, E. 2010. *Mind in the Making: The Seven Essential Life Skills Every Child Needs.* New York: HarperStudio.

Goldstein, L.S. & M. Bauml. 2012. "Supporting Children's Learning While Meeting State Standards: Strategies and Suggestions for Pre-K–Grade 3 Teachers in Public School Contexts." *Young Children* 67 (3): 96–103.

Graham, M.J. 2013. *Google Apps Meet the Common Core.* Thousand Oaks, CA: Corwin.

Graves, M.F., J.F. Baumann, C.L.Z. Blachowicz, P. Manyak, A. Bates, C. Cieply, J.R. Davis, & H. Von Gunten. 2014. "Words, Words, Everywhere, But Which Ones Do We Teach?" *The Reading Teacher* 67 (5): 333–46.

Hart, B., & T.R. Risley. 1995. *Meaningful Differences in the Everyday Experience of Young American Children.* Baltimore, MD: Paul H. Brookes.

Helm, J.H., & L. Katz. 2011. *Young Investigators: The Project Approach in the Early Years.* 2nd ed. New York: Teachers College Press; Washington, DC: NAEYC.

Holden, B. 2007. "Preparing for Problem Solving." *Teaching Children Mathematics* 14 (5): 290–95. http://edcg668-su12.wikispaces.umb.edu/file/view/11.2+Preparing+for+problem+solving.pdf.

Hutchison, A., B. Beschorner, & D. Schmidt-Crawford. 2012. "Exploring the Use of the iPad for Literacy Learning." *The Reading Teacher* 66 (1): 15–23.

Hyson, M. 2004. *The Emotional Development of Young Children: Building an Emotion-Centered Curriculum.* New York: Teachers College Press.

Hyson, M. 2008. *Enthusiastic and Engaged Learners: Approaches to Learning in the Early Childhood Classroom.* New York: Teachers College Press; Washington, DC: NAEYC.

Jacobs, J. 2011. *A Winning Formula for Mathematics Instruction: Converting Research Into Results.* Alexandria, VA: Educational Research Services.

Kaufeldt, M. 2010. *Begin With the Brain: Orchestrating the Learner-Centered Classroom.* 2nd ed. Thousand Oaks, CA: Corwin.

Kay, K., & V. Greenhill. 2013. *The Leader's Guide to 21st Century Education: 7 Steps for Schools and Districts.* Boston: Pearson.

Kenny, D. 2012. *Born to Rise: A Story of Children and Teachers Reaching Their Highest Potential.* New York: Harper Collins.

Kirchen, D.J. 2011. "Making and Taking Virtual Field Trips in Pre-K and the Primary Grades." *Young Children* 66 (6): 22–26. www.naeyc.org/files/yc/file/201111/Kirchen_Virtual_Field_Trips_Online%201111.pdf.

Lanning, L. 2013. *Designing a Concept-Based Curriculum for English Language Arts: Meeting the Common Core With Intellectual Integrity, K–12.* Thousand Oaks, CA: Corwin.

Leinwand, S. 2012. *Sensible Mathematics: A Guide for School Leaders in the Era of Common Core State Standards.* 2nd ed. Portsmouth, NH: Heinemann.

Machado, J.M. 2013. *Early Childhood Experiences in Language Arts: Early Literacy.* 10th ed. Belmont, CA: Wadsworth, Cengage Learning.

McDavid, K.A. 2007. "The Goldilocks Rule for Choosing a Book That Is 'Just Right.'" Poster. www.ourclassweb.com/center_activities/readers_workshop/rw_poster_goldilocks_rules.pdf.

McDonald, E.S., & D.M. Hershman. 2010. *Classrooms That Spark! Recharge and Revive Your Teaching.* 2nd ed. San Francisco, CA: Jossey-Bass.

Michaels, S., A.W. Shouse, & H.A. Schweingruber. 2007. *Ready, Set, Science! Putting Research to Work in K–8 Science Classrooms.* Washington, DC: The National Academies Press.

Miller, D. 2009. *The Book Whisperer: Awakening the Inner Reader in Every Child.* San Francisco, CA: Jossey-Bass.

Miller, D. 2013. *Reading With Meaning: Teaching Comprehension in the Primary Grades.* 2nd ed. Portland, ME: Stenhouse.

Musallam, R. 2013. "3 Rules to Spark Learning." Filmed Apr. 2013. TED video, 6:29. www.ted.com/talks/ramsey_musallam_3_rules_to_spark_learning.

NAEYC. 2012. "The Common Core State Standards: Caution and Opportunity for Early Childhood Education." Washington, DC: NAEYC. www.naeyc.org/files/naeyc/11_CommonCore1_2A_rv2.pdf.

National Council for the Social Studies (NCSS). 2010. *National Curriculum Standards for Social Studies: A Framework for Teaching, Learning, and Assessment.* Silver Spring. MD: NCSS.

National Council for the Social Studies (NCSS). 2013a. "The College, Career, and Civic Life (C3) Framework for Social Studies State Standards: Guidance for Enhancing the Rigor of K-12 Civics, Economics, Geography, and History." Silver Spring, MD: NCSS. www.socialstudies.org/system/files/c3/C3-Framework-for-Social-Studies.pdf.

National Council for the Social Studies (NCSS). 2013b. *Social Studies for the Next Generation: Purposes, Practices, and Implications of the College, Career, and Civic Life (C3) Framework for Social Studies State Standards.* Silver Spring, MD: NCSS.

National Governors Association Center for Best Practices (NGA) & Council of Chief State School Officers (CCSO). 2010a. *Common Core State Standards for English Language Arts and Literacy in History/Social Studies, Science, and Technical Subjects.* Washington: DC: NGA & CCSO. www.corestandards.org/wp-content/uploads/ELA_Standards.pdf.

National Governors Association Center for Best Practices (NGA) & Council of Chief State School Officers (CSSO). 2010b. *Common Core State Standards for Mathematics.* Washington: DC: NGA & CCSO. www.corestandards.org/assets/CCSSI_Math%20Standards.pdf.

National Institute of Child Health and Human Development. 2000. *Report of the National Reading Panel. Teaching Children to Read: An Evidence-Based Assessment of the Scientific Research Literature on Reading and Its Implications for Reading Instruction.* Washington, DC: US Government Printing Office. www.nichd.nih.gov/publications/pubs/nrp/pages/smallbook.aspx.

National Research Council (NRC). 2012. *A Framework for K–12 Science Education: Practices, Crosscutting Concepts, and Core Ideas.* Washington, DC: National Academies Press.

Neuman, S.B., & T.S. Wright. 2013. *All About Words: Increasing Vocabulary in the Common Core Classroom, PreK–2.* New York: Teachers College Press.

NGSS Lead States. 2013. *Next Generation Science Standards: For States, By States*. Achieve, Inc. www.nextgenscience.org/next-generation-science-standards.

Oczkus, L. 2010. *Reciprocal Teaching at Work: Powerful Strategies and Lessons for Improving Reading Comprehension*. 2nd ed. Newark, DE: International Reading Association.

Oertwig, S., C. Gillanders, & S. Ritchie. 2014. "The Promise of Curricula." Chap. 4 in *FirstSchool: Transforming PreK-3rd Grade for African American, Latino, and Low-Income Children*, eds. S. Ritchie & L. Gutmann, 81–101. New York: Teachers College Press.

Oertwig, S., & A.L. Holland, 2014. "Improving Instruction." Chap. 5 in *FirstSchool: Transforming PreK–3rd Grade for African American, Latino, and Low-Income Children*, eds. S. Ritchie & L. Gutmann, 102–24. New York: Teachers College Press.

Owocki, G. 2005. *Time for Literacy Centers: How to Organize and Differentiate Instruction*. Portsmouth, NH: Heinemann.

Pardo, L.S. 2004. "What Every Teacher Needs to Know About Comprehension." *The Reading Teacher* 58 (3): 272–80.

Parnell, W. & J. Bartlett. 2012. "iDocument: How Smartphones and Tablets are Changing Documentation in Preschool and Primary Classrooms." *Young Children* 67 (3): 50–57.

Partnership for 21st Century Skills. 2010. "Up to the Challenge: The Role of Career and Technical Education and 21st Century Skills in College and Career Readiness." www.p21.org/storage/documents/CTE_Oct2010.pdf.

Pianta, R.C., J. Belsky, N. Vandergrift, R. Houts, & F.J. Morrison. 2008. "Classroom Effects on Children's Achievement Trajectories in Elementary School." *American Educational Research Journal* 45 (2): 365–97.

Pianta, R.C., K.M. LaParo, & B.K. Hamre. 2008. *Classroom Assessment Scoring System (CLASS) Manual, K–3*. Baltimore, MD: Brookes.

Pinnell, G.S., & I.C. Fountas. 2007. *The Continuum of Literacy Learning, Grades K-2: A Guide to Teaching*. Portsmouth, NH: Heinemann.

President's Committee on the Arts and the Humanities. 2011. "Reinvesting in Arts Education: Winning America's Future Through Creative Schools." Washington, DC: President's Committee on the Arts and the Humanities. www.pcah.gov/sites/default/files/photos/PCAH_Reinvesting_4web.pdf.

Reeves, D. 2002. *Making Standards Work: How to Implement Standards-Based Assessments in the Classroom, School, and District*. 3rd ed. Denver, CO: Advanced Learning Press.

Reutzel, D.R, C.D. Jones, P.C. Fawson, & J.A. Smith. 2008. "Scaffolded Silent Reading: A Complement to Guided Repeated Oral Reading That Works!" *The Reading Teacher* 62 (3): 194–207.

Reutzel, D.R., & R.B. Cooter Jr. 2013. *The Essentials of Teaching Children to Read: The Teacher Makes the Difference*. Boston: Pearson.

Rinaldi, C. 2001. "Introductions." *Making Learning Visible: Children as Individual and Group Learners*, eds. C. Giudici, C. Rinaldi, & M. Krechevsky, 28. Reggio Emilia, Italy: Reggio Children.

Rivkin, M.S., With D. Schein. 2014. *The Great Outdoors: Advocating for Natural Spaces for Young Children*. Rev. ed. Washington, DC: NAEYC.

Robinson, K. 2006. "How Schools Kill Creativity." Filmed Feb. 2006. TED video, 19:24. www.ted.com/talks/ken_robinson_says_schools_kill_creativity.

Rosenow, N. 2012. *Heart-Centered Teaching Inspired by Nature*. Lincoln, NE: Dimensions Educational Research Foundation.

Ruday, S. 2013. *The Common Core Grammar Toolkit: Using Mentor Texts to Teach the Language Standards in Grades 3–5*. Larchmont, NY: Eye on Education.

Rushton, S., A. Juola-Rushton, & E. Larkin. 2010. "Neuroscience, Play and Early Childhood Education: Connections, Implications and Assessment." *Early Childhood Education Journal* 37 (5): 351–61.

Sarama, J., & D.H. Clements. 2009. "Teaching Math in the Primary Grades: The Learning Trajectories Approach." Beyond The Journal: *Young Children* on the Web (March). www.naeyc.org/files/yc/file/Primary_Interest_BTJ.pdf.

Saville, K. 2011. "Strategies for Using Repetition as a Powerful Teaching Tool." *Music Educators Journal* 98 (1): 69–75.

Shanahan, T. 2005. *The National Reading Panel Report: Practical Advice for Teachers.* Naperville, IL: Learning Point Associates.

Sousa, D.A. 2006. "How the Arts Develop the Young Brain." *The School Administrator* 63 (11): 26–31. www.aasa.org/SchoolAdministratorArticle.aspx?id=7378.

Sousa, D.A. 2008. *How the Brain Learns Mathematics.* Thousand Oaks, CA: Corwin.

Spalding, A. & L.E. Kelly. 2010. *Fitness on the Ball: A Core Program for Brain and Body.* Champaign, IL: Human Kinetics.

Sperry, R.W., With the Devereux Center for Resilient Children. 2011. *Flip It! Transforming Challenging Behavior.* Lewisville, NC: Kaplan.

Tate, M.L. 2012. *Social Studies Worksheets Don't Grow Dendrites: 20 Instructional Strategies That Engage the Brain.* Thousand Oaks, CA: Corwin.

Teachstone Training. 2011. *Classroom Assessment Scoring System (CLASS) Dimensions Guide, K–3.* Baltimore, MD: Brookes.

Tomlinson, H.B. 2012. "Cognitive Development in the Kindergarten Year." Chap. 3 in *Growing Minds: Building Strong Cognitive Foundations in Early Childhood*, ed. C. Copple, 25–32. Washington, DC: NAEYC.

Tomlinson, H.B. 2014. "An Overview of Development in the Primary Grades." Chap. 3 in *Developmentally Appropriate Practice: Focus on Children in First, Second, and Third Grades*, eds. C. Copple, S. Bredekamp, D. Koralek, & K. Charner, 9–38. Washington, DC: NAEYC.

Trelease, J. 2013. *The Read-Aloud Handbook.* 7th ed. New York: Penguin.

Vance, E. 2014. *Class Meetings: Young Children Solving Problems Together.* Rev. ed. Washington, DC: NAEYC.

Vasinda, S., & J. McLeod. 2011. "Extending Readers Theatre: A Powerful and Purposeful Match With Podcasting." *The Reading Teacher* 64 (7): 486–97.

Vygotsky, L.S. 1978. *Mind in Society: The Development of Higher Psychological Processes.* Cambridge, MA: Harvard University Press.

Wagner, T. 2008. *The Global Achievement Gap: Why Even Our Best Schools Don't Teach the New Survival Skills Our Children Need—and What We Can Do About It.* New York: Basic Books.

Wien, C.A. 2004. *Negotiating Standards in the Primary Classroom: The Teacher's Dilemma.* New York: Teachers College Press.

Wien, C.A. 2008. *Emergent Curriculum in the Primary Classroom: Interpreting the Reggio Emilia Approach in Schools.* New York: Teachers College Press; Washington, DC: NAEYC.

Williams, J. 2010. "Taking on the Role of Questioner: Revisiting Reciprocal Teaching." *The Reading Teacher* 64 (4): 278–81.

Willis, J. 2008. *Teaching the Brain to Read: Strategies for Improving Fluency, Vocabulary, and Comprehension.* Alexandria, VA: ASCD.

Wingate, K.O., V.C. Rutledge, & L. Johnston. 2014. "Choosing the Right Word Walls for Your Classroom." *Young Children* 69 (1): 52–57.

Zeno, S.M., S.H. Ivens, R.T. Millard, & R. Duvvuri. 1995. *The Educator's Word Frequency Guide.* Brewster, New York: Touchstone Applied Science Associates.

Children's Books

Araminta's Paint Box (1998), by Karen Ackerman, illus. by Betsy Lewin

Bread, Bread, Bread (1989), by Ann Morris, photographs by Ken Heyman

Colors! ¡Colores! (2008), by Jorge Luján, illus. by Piet Grobler

Compost Stew: An A to Z Recipe for the Earth (2010), by Mary McKenna Siddals, illus. by Ashley Wolff

Do You Know Which Ones Will Grow? (2011), by Susan A. Shea, illus. by Tom Slaughter

Eagle Song (1997), by Joseph Bruchac, illus. by Dan Andreasen

Gimme-Jimmy (2012), by Sherrill S. Cannon, illus. by Kalpart

The Good Luck Cat (2000), by Joy Harjo, illus. by Paul Lee

Grandfather Tang's Story (1990), by Ann Tompert, illus. by Robert Andrew Parker

The Great Big Book of Families (2011), by Mary Hoffman, illus. by Ros Asquith

Have You Filled a Bucket Today? A Guide to Daily Happiness for Kids (2006), by Carol McCloud, illus. by David Messing

Hey Little Ant (1998), by Phillip and Hannah Hoose, illus. by Debbie Tilley

How Many Feet in the Bed? (1991), by Diane Johnston Hamm, illus. by Kate Salley Palmer

How Many Seeds in a Pumpkin? (2007), by Margaret McNamara, illus. by Brian Karas

I Grew Up to be President (2011), by Laurie Calkhoven, illus. by Rebecca Zomchek

If You Give a Moose a Muffin (1991), by Laura Joffe Numeroff, illus. by Felicia Bond

If You Give a Pig a Pancake (1998), by Laura Joffe Numeroff, illus. by Felicia Bond

I'm in Love With a Big Blue Frog (2013), by Leslie Braunstein, illus. by Joshua S. Brunet

The Important Book (1949), by Margaret Wise Brown, illus. by Leonard Weisgard

Jingle Dancer (2000), by Cynthia Leitich Smith, illus. by Cornelius Van Wright and Ying-Hwa Hu

The Kindness Quilt (2006), by Nancy Elizabeth Wallace

The Legend of the Indian Paintbrush (2000), by Tomie dePaola

Maria Had a Little Llama/María tenía una llama pequeña (2013), by Angela Dominguez

Math for All Seasons: Mind Stretching Math Riddles (2005), by Greg Tang, illus. by Harry Briggs

Math Jokes for Mathy Folks (2012), by G. Patrick Vennebush

The Moccasins (2004), by Earl Einarson, illus. by Julie Flett

Moonshot: The Flight of Apollo 11 (2009), by Brian Floca

My Librarian Is a Camel: How Books Are Brought to Children Around the World (2005), by Margriet Ruurs

Nasreddine (2006), by Odile Weulersse, illus. by Rébecca Dautremer

One Is a Snail, Ten Is a Crab (2006), by April Pulley Sayre and Jeff Sayre, illus. by Randy Cecil

Pete the Cat and His Four Groovy Buttons (2012), by Eric Litwin, illus. by James Dean

Pete the Cat: Rocking in My School Shoes (2011), by Eric Litwin, illus. by James Dean

The Rough-Face Girl (1998), by Rafe Martin, illus. by David Shannon

Silver Seeds (2003), by Paul Paolilli and Dan Brewer, illus. by Steve Johnson and Lou Francher

Sing . . . Sing a Song (2013), by Joe Raposo, illus. by Tom Lichtenheld

Sonia Sotomayor: A Judge Grows in the Bronx/La juez que creció en el Bronx (2009), by Jonah Winter, illus. by Edel Rodriguez

Take Me Out to the Yakyu (2013), by Aaron Meshon

Transportation in Many Cultures (2009), by Martha E.H. Rustad

Water Music: Poems for Children (1995), by Jane Yolen, photographs by Jason Stemple

We All Sing With the Same Voice (2001), by J. Phillip Meyer and Sheppard M. Greene, illus. by Paul Meisel

What Can You Do With a Paleta? (2009), by Carmen Tafolla, illus. by Magaly Morales

Wild About Books (2004), by Judy Sierra, illus. by Marc Brown.
In Spanish: *¡Qué locura por la lectura!*

Wilfrid Gordon McDonald Partridge (1992), by Mem Fox, illus. by Julie Vivas

Wise Crackers: Riddles and Jokes About Numbers, Names, Letters, and Silly Words (2011), by Michael Dahl

Yeh-Shen: A Cinderella Story From China (1982), retold by Ai-Ling Louie, illus. by Ed Young

Your Fantastic, Elastic Brain (2010), by JoAnn Deak, illus. by Sarah Ackerley

About the Authors

Gera Jacobs is a professor of early childhood education at the University of South Dakota. She served as president of the National Association for the Education of Young Children (NAEYC) from 2012 to 2014. She taught children in preschool through eighth grade for many years. She has published articles in a number of national and regional journals and produced a CD-ROM on inclusion for young children with special needs. She has presented at numerous state, regional, national, and international conferences, and has conducted many in-service presentations for teachers. Gera was named the South Dakota Professor of the Year by the Carnegie Corporation, and she also received the Children's Champion Award from the South Dakota Voices for Children.

Kathy Crowley is a kindergarten teacher and has taught preschool through the primary grades for many years. Serving as a teacher-leader for a statewide mathematics initiative, she provided training to other teachers on Cognitively Guided Instruction and other innovative math strategies. She was director of an after-school program and has presented at numerous state, regional, and national conferences. Kathy served as vice president of the South Dakota Association for the Education of Young Children (SDAEYC) and received the SDAEYC state service award. Her community also named her the Teacher of the Year.

Gera and Kathy have helped to organize annual statewide primary and kindergarten academies for many years in South Dakota. They are the coauthors of *Reaching Standards and Beyond in Kindergarten: Nurturing Children's Sense of Wonder and Joy in Learning* (Corwin & NAEYC, 2010) and *Play, Projects, and Preschool Standards: Nurturing Children's Sense of Wonder and Joy in Learning* (Corwin, 2007), winner of the 2008 Teachers' Choice Award, sponsored by Learning Magazine, and the 2007 Distinguished Achievement Award from the Association of Educational Publishers. Their collaboration began many years ago as team-teachers.

Acknowledgments

The ideas for this book were generated through many conversations with teachers, principals, superintendents, and other professionals at schools around the country. We are grateful to all who contributed their time and ideas to help this book become a reality. A tremendous thank you is offered to those who patiently reviewed chapters and shared their expertise: Angie Bickett, Karen Kindle, Jayne Taylor, Linda Reetz, Susan Gapp, Judy Jablon, Kevin Reins, Lynda Venhuizen, Brittney Scherrer, Sarah Sherlock, Cathy Ezrailson, Brian Koelewyn, Rebecca Onstatt, and students in the USD Curriculum in Early Childhood course. Thank you to Linda Froschauer for providing science resources and Isabel Baker for her suggestions of quality children's literature. We express our thanks to our supportive administrators Darla Hamm, Garreth Zalud, Hee-Sok Choi, Kris Reed, Nick Shudak, and Rick Melmer.

We gratefully acknowledge the schools, teachers, and administrators who allowed us to take photographs in their classrooms: Austin, Jolley, and St. Agnes Schools, Vermillion, SD; Beresford Elementary School, Beresford, SD; Explore Knowledge Academy, Las Vegas, NV; Kennedy Elementary School, Mankato, MN; McCook Central Elementary, Salem, SD; San Diego Cooperative Charter School and Urban Discover Academy, San Diego, CA; Tracy Corcoran; Megan Fairbairn; Ann Fisher; Jenna Gilkyson; Kimmarie Johnson; Shawnya McGregor; Krystina Mendoza; Kaylani Mercado; Cindy Moser; Kevin Nelson; Wendy Ranck-Buhr; Lourdes Reeves; Brittany Scherrer; Amber Steckler; Jayne Taylor; and Bethany Teeple.

Thank you to the dedicated and talented editors and creative services staff at NAEYC, including Kathy Charner, Liz Wegner, Derry Koralek, Holly Bohart, Malini Dominey, and Eddie Malstrom, whose thoughtful work enhanced our book. Finally, we wish to thank our wonderful families for their belief in us, ideas and feedback, and incredible support and understanding. To all who helped us bring the dream of this book to life, we express our deepest gratitude.

Index

A

achievement gap, 138
Ackerman, Karen, 104
ADHD, 136
A Framework for K-12 Science Education (NRC), 111–12
Alanis, I., 24
alphabet and alphabetic principle awareness, 41
alphabet photos, 133
American Library Association, 90
anchor charts, 36, 55
Anderson, L.W., 61
arts education, 131–37
assessment, 15, 32–33, 41, 46–48, 72, 90–91, 135
Association for Library Service to Children, 40
attachment, 26
attention-deficit hyperactivity disorder, 136
author's celebration, 48
author's chair, 48
autism spectrum, 14

B

Bauml, M., 5
Becoming a Nation of Readers (Commission on Reading), 69
behavior management, 16
Benjamin, A., 61
best practices, 2, 4–7, 17–18, 138
Bickett, Angie, 9, 68, 104
biodiversity, 118–119
Bloom's Revised Taxonomy (Anderson and Krathwohl), 61
book clubs, 104
Book Whisperer (Miller), 35
brain-based learning, 7–8
brain development, 9, 20
brain-friendly activities, 60–61
brain productivity, 63, 78, 137
Brett, Jan, 43
Brewer, Dan, 51
Brown, Margaret Wise, 22
Bruchac, Joseph, 103
buddy reading center, 66–67

C

Calkhoven, Laurie, 107
Calkins, L., 58, 109
Cannon, Sherrill S., 27
Carson, Rachel, 127
CCSS. *See* Common Core State Standards
Center for Interactive Learning and Collaboration (CILC), 7
CGI (Cognitively Guided Instruction), 74–77
character building, 71
choral reading, 44
Civic Ideals and Practices theme, 106–8
civics, 106–108
Classroom Assessment Scoring System (CLASS), 15
classroom environment, 8–13
classroom materials wish lists, 10
classroom pets and other animals, 122–23
Clements, D.H., 80
Cognitively Guided Instruction (CGI), 74–77
collaboration, 139
College, Career, and Civic *Life* C3 Framework for Social Studies State Standards, 1, 96–97, 101, 109, 129
Comer, James, 13
Common Core State Standards (CCSS)
  about, 1
  English language arts, 8, 57–62
  foundational reading skills, 41
  growth mindset development and, 14
  library centers and, 64
  mathematics practices, 73–93, 112
  in primary grades skill development, 3–4, 7–8
  reading literacy goals of, 29–31, 34, 43
  research skills goal of, 54–55
  scientific knowledge standards crossover, 129
  social and emotional development and, 19
  speaking and listening goals of, 56–57
  writing skills goals of, 48–49, 52–53, 55–56
communication skills
  brain-friendly activities, 60–61
  communication standards, 56–57
  comprehension and collaboration, 56
  grammar, 57–58
  home-school connections, 69–71
  interactive experiences, 61–62
  language knowledge, 58
  listening and speaking, 56–57
  oral vocabulary, 59–60
  presentation of knowledge and ideas, 56–57, 72
  rimes and word families, 60
  spelling, 58
  standard English conventions, 57–58
  strengthening through science and engineering practices, 112–13

vocabulary acquisition and use, 59–62
See also literacy centers; reading literacy
Communities theme, 107–8
comprehension goals in reading literacy, 34–35
computer center, 68
concept development promotion, 16
conferencing, 32–33, 46–48, 72, 90–91
See also assessment
connectedness, need for, 24–25
Consortium of National Arts Education Associations, 132
Consumers and Producers theme, 106
Contributions to Society theme, 108
Copple, C., 4
Cornell Lab of Ornithology, 123
country visit rubric, 102
creative arts education
art and illustration area, 132–33
assessment through, 135
cultural appreciation through, 135
dance, 134, 136
electronic drawing tools, 133
home-school connections, 137–38
music, 134
photography, 133
promoting learning through, 131–37, 139
theater, 135
visual arts, 132–33
crosscutting concepts, 114
Crow, J.T., 61
cultural understanding, 101, 103
curriculum integration, 101

D

Dahl, Michael, 57
daily routines, reading opportunities in, 30–31
dance, 134, 136
Decorah Eagle Cam, 123
dePaola, Tomie, 135
designing classroom interest areas, 12–13
Developmentally Appropriate Practice (Copple), 4
Devereux Center for Resilient Children, 27
Dewey, John, 97
differentiation of practice, 13–14
digital learning centers, 90
disciplinary core ideas, 115
diversity, 38, 71, 135
See also social studies
Doodle Buddy app, 133
dopamine, 63
The Dreamkeeper and Other Poems (Hughes), 71
dual-language learners, 24, 30, 35, 51, 133
Dweck, Carol, 14

E

earth and space science investigations, 124–25
echo reading and choral reading, 44
Economics theme, 105–6
Ehrenworth, M., 58, 109
Einerson, Earl, 50
electronic drawing tools, 133
emotional development, 2, 25–27
emotion and attention, 74, 78
empathy, cultivation of, 24, 26
engagement, 13, 19–20, 34–41
engineering, technology, and applications of science investigations, 125–27
enthusiasm, 19–20
erosion, 124–25
Evenson, A., 88
executive function of the brain, 20

F

family interviews, 105
feedback quality, 16–17
flash cards, 74
Florida Center for Reading Research, 54
fluency development, 43–45, 72
focused attention, 9, 13, 74, 78
fostering independence, 10–11, 19
Fountas, I.C., 30, 62
friendships, importance of, 24

G

Galinsky, E., 20
genre wheel use, 40
geography, 101, 103
geometry, 87–88, 89
Gillanders, C., 6
The Global Achievement Gap (Wagner), 20
GLOBE program, 128
Goldstein, L.S., 5
Google Apps for Education, 53
Google Apps Meets Common Core (Graham), 53
Google Drive, 53
Google Earth, 100
Graham, Michael, 53
grammar skills, 57–58
graphic organizers, 38–39, 50
graphs and tables use, 86, 113–14
Great Backyard Bird Count, 119
Greene, Sheppard M., 134

Growing Minds (Tomlinson), 5
growth mindset development, 14
Guided Reading (Fountas and Pinnell), 62
Guiding Readers and Writers Grades 3-6 (Fountas and Pinnell), 62

H

hands-on activities and learning, 8, 13, 75–76, 78
Harjo, Joy, 103
Harlem Village Academies, 4
Hart, B., 59
health and well-being support, 136–37
health education, 137–38
Hello Crayon (drawing program), 81
Henson, Jim, 125
high-frequency words, 43
historical stories, 104–5
history, 104–5
Hoffman, Mary, 103
Holden, Becky, 76
Holland, L., 137
home-school connections, fostering, 11, 27–28, 69–71, 91–92, 108–9, 126–27, 137–38
Hughes, Langston, 71
Hyson, M., 19–20

I

idea organization, 52
IEPs (Individualized Education Programs), 14
The Illustrative Mathematics Project, 79
inchworm rulers, 86
independence, fostering, 10–11, 19
independent writing, 46–48
Individualized Education programs (IEPs), 14
informative/explanatory writing, 49–50
initiative, 26
Inquiry Arc use, 96–97, 97–101, 109
Inside Mathematics, 79
instructional learning formats, 16
integrated approach to learning, 33–34, 117–18
interactive experiences, 61–62
interactive whiteboard center, 68
interest area design, 12–13
International Reading Association (IRA), 34

J

Jacobs, Judith, 74
Jobs theme, 106
just right texts, 30–31

K

Kennedy Center ArtsEdge website, 134
Kenny, Deborah, 4
key ideas and details in texts, understanding, 34–37
kindness, cultivation of, 24, 26
knowledge and idea integration, 33–34, 38–39
Krathwohl, D.R., 61
KWL chart use, 98, 100

L

language knowledge, 58
language modeling, 17
learning centers and stations, 62–63
learning scaffolding. *See* primary grades skills development
Lehman, C., 58
Leinwand, S., 91
library center, 64
life sciences investigations, 122–24
Listen and Read books (Scholastic), 104
listening and speaking, 56–57
listening center, 64
literacy centers
  buddy reading center, 66–67
  comprehension center, 66
  computer center, 68
  design, 63–69
  interactive whiteboard center, 68
  learning centers and stations, 62–63
  library center, 64
  listening center, 64
  management, 68–69, 72
  poetry center, 65
  read the room center, 66
  rhyming/word family center, 66
  spelling center, 68
  word study center, 67–68
  writing center, 65
  See also communication skills; reading literacy
literature circles, 104
Loecker, Kayla, 54
Louie, Ai-Ling, 38
Luján, Jorge, 135
Lynne, Gillian, 134

M

manipulatives use, 75–76, 80
mapping the thinking process, 122
maps and globes use, 99–101
Martin, Rafe, 38
Matching Jobs app, 106
materials wish lists, 10
math bulletin board center, 89
mathematical practice standards, 73–74
mathematical symbols, 80–81
mathematics
  assessment, 90–91
  building math confidence, 92–93

cognitively guided instruction, 74–77
Common Core State Standards on, 73–74, 112
C.U.B.E. method of word problem solution, 82
digital learning center, 90
estimating, 86
flash cards, 74
geometry, 87–88, 89
graphs, 86
home-school connections, 91–92
manipulatives use, 75–76, 80
math centers, 77, 88–90
mathematical practice standards, 73–74
mathematical symbols, 80–81
math journals, 76
measurement and data, 85–87
measuring center, 89–90
measuring tools, 85–86
meeting standards for, 77–88
money, 87
number and operations-fractions, 84–85
number and operations in base ten, 82–84
number charts, 83–84
number lines, 80
number relationships, 81
operations and algebraic thinking, 79–82
problem-solving strategies, 74–75
shape manipulation, 87
shape recognition, 88
six-step CGI method, 76–77
skip counting, 79–80
small group learning, 75
tangrams, 88
ten frames use, 82
think-pair-share strategies, 75
time, 86
timed testing, 74
understanding, 83
word problems, 82
math journals, 76
McLeod, J., 44
meaningful learning, 138
measurement and data, 85–87, 89–90
meeting area establishment, 11–12
meeting standards, 92–93
Meet the Author studies, 49–50
mentor texts use, 49
menu math center, 89
Meshon, Aaron, 42
Miller, D., 33, 35
Miller, J. Phillip, 134
minds-on mental engagement, 13
mini lessons, literacy, 31–32
money, 87, 105–6
Morris, Ann, 106
movement and learning, 78
Musallam, Ramsey, 138
music, 134
My People (Hughes), 71

N

narrative writing, 50–51
National Association for the Education of Young Children (NAEYC), 4, 139
National Audubon Society First Field Guides, 118
National Center for Education Statistics, 19, 86
National Council for the Social Studies (NCSS), 95–96, 101, 137
National Council of Teachers of English (NCTE), 34
National Council of Teachers of Mathematics (NCTM), 74, 79, 88
National Curriculum Standards for Social Studies (NCSS), 95–96
National Geographic Society, 100, 122
National Reading Panel, 29–30, 35, 42, 44, 58, 59, 62, 67
National Research Council (NRC), 111–12, 113–14
National Science Teachers Association (NSTA), 115, 139
negative learning environment, 15
Neuman, S.B., 59
neuroscience research in brain-based learning, 7–8
Next Generation Science Standards (NGSS), 1, 4, 111–16, 125–27, 129
NRICH Maths Project, 77–78
number and operations-fractions, 84–85
number and operations in base ten, 82–84
number charts, 83–84
number lines, 80
number relationships, 81

O

Oczkus, L., 36
operations and algebraic thinking, 79–82
opinion writing, 49
oral vocabulary, 59–60
organization skills, 19
Ortweig, S., 6, 137
Owocki, G., 66

P

Paolilli, Paul, 51
Partnership for Assessment of Readiness for College and Careers (PARCC), 77
partner talk, 46
PBS Kids Cyberspace, 88
People to People International, 106
personal readers, 44
Peterson, Andrea, 23
phonemic awareness, 41
phonics and word recognition, 41–43

photography, 133
physical science investigations, 120–22
Piaget, Jean, 62
Pinnell, G. S., 30, 62
plant life cycle, 123–124
playing thinking games, 121
poetry writing, 51, 65
positive approaches to learning
  brain development and, 20
  framework for, 19–21
  home-school connections, fostering, 27–28
  problem solving processes and, 21
  social and emotional development, 21–27
  social skills development, 22–25
  See also primary grades skills development
positive learning environment, 15
Power, Authority, and Governance theme, 107
PowerMyLearning (website), 90
prefixes and suffixes, 43
Presidential Award for Excellence in Mathematics and Science Teaching, 76
primary grades skills development
  behavior management, 16
  best practices, 2, 4–7, 17–18
  brain-based learning in, 7–8
  Common Core State Standards in, 3–4
  concept development promotion, 16
  differentiation of practice in, 13–14
  feedback quality, 16–17
  growth mindset development in, 14
  home-school connection, 11
  instructional learning formats use, 16
  language modeling, 17
  meeting standards, 5–6
  motivation through a growth mindset, 14
  negative climate avoidance, 15
  positive climate creation, 15
  resource utilization, 6–7
  room design, 8–13
  student perspectives, regard for, 15
  teacher productivity, 16
  teacher sensitivity, 15
  teacher-student interactions, 15–17
  See also positive approaches to learning
print concepts engagement, 41–42
problem-based learning, 6, 97, 117
problem-solving strategies, 74–75
Production, Distribution, and Consumption theme, 105
production and distribution of writing, 51–54
productivity, 16
professional development, 138

R

Race to the Top competition, 7
Readers' Theater, 27, 44, 105, 110
Readers' Workshop, 31–33
reading literacy
  alphabet and alphabetic principle awareness, 41
  anchor chart use, 36
  comprehension, 34–35, 66
  conferencing and assessment, 32–33, 41
  craft and structure of, 37–38
  echo reading and choral reading, 44
  engaging learners, 34–42
  fluency development, 43–45, 72
  genre wheel use, 40
  graphic organizers, 38–39
  knowledge and idea integration, 33–34, 38–39
  language standards, 29–30
  mini lessons, 31–32
  personal readers, 44
  phonemic awareness, 41
  phonics and word recognition, 42–43
  phonological awareness, 41–42
  practice and rereading, 43
  print concepts, 41–42
  range and text complexity, 39–41
  Readers Theater, 44
  readers' workshop, 31–33
  reading log use, 40
  reading opportunities in daily routines, 30–31
  reading range and text complexity, 39–41
  reciprocal teaching, 35–37
  rhythm and rhyme awareness, 41
  singing, 43–44
  text selection, 30, 31
  understanding key ideas and details in texts, 34–37
  See also communication skills; literacy centers
reading log use, 40
reading opportunities in daily routines, 30–31
Reading Rainbow app, 104
reading range and text complexity, 39–41
read the room center, 66
ReadWriteThink (website), 34, 39, 133
Ready, Set, Science! (NRC), 113
reciprocal teaching strategies, 35–37
Reeves, D., 119
Reggio Emilia, Italy, early childhood programs, 10–11
rekenrek mathematics tool, 80
relatedness, need for, 24–25
relationships, importance of, 22–24
resilience, development of, 26–27
resource utilization, in primary grades, 6–7, 16
Response to Intervention groups (RIT), 32
Reutzel, D.R., 40

rimes and word families, 41, 60, 66
Rinaldi, Carla, 95
Risley, T.R., 59
Ritchie, S., 6
RIT (Response to Intervention) groups, 32
Robinson, Ken, 132, 134
room design, primary grades, 8–13
Rosenbaum, Shirley, 106
Ruday, S., 57
rules, following, 19
Rustad, Martha E.H., 106
Ruurs, Margaret, 103

S

Sarama, J., 80
Sayre, April Pulley, 84
Sayre, Jeff, 84
Science, Technology, and Society theme, 106
science/discovery center, 119–20
science library, 119
science notebook use, 113
scientific knowledge
  classroom pets and other animals, 122–23
  comparing mixtures, 120–21
  crosscutting concepts, 114
  disciplinary core ideas, 115
  earth and space science investigations, 124–25
  engineering, technology, and applications of science investigations, 125–27
  exploring light, 121–22
  graphs and tables use, 113–14
  home-school connections, 126–27
  integrated approach to, 117–19
  life sciences investigations, 122–24
  mapping the thinking process, 122
  next generation science standards, 111–15
  physical science investigations, 120–22
  plant life cycle, 123–24
  playing thinking games, 121
  problem-based learning, 117
  science/discovery center, 119–20
  science library, 119
  science notebook use, 113
  scientific method practice, 113, 117
  supporting learners, 115–26
  weather conditions, 124
self-regulation, 27
sensory-rich activities, 8
shape manipulation, 87
shape recognition, 88
Sid's Science Fair app, 125
Sierra, Judy, 42
sight words, 43
singing, 43–44
six-step CGI method, 76–77
skills development. *See* primary grades skills development
skip counting, 79–80
small group learning, 75
Smarter Balanced Assessment Consortium, 77
Smith, Cynthia Leitich, 103
social and emotional development, 2, 21–27
social interaction and learning, 78
social justice issues, 109
social studies
  C3 framework and Inquiry Arc, 96–97, 101, 109
  civics, 106–108
  country visit rubric, 102
  cultural understanding, 101, 103
  curriculum integration, 101
  economics, 105–6
  geography, 101, 103
  history, 104–5
  home-school connection, 108–9, 137
  integrated approach to, 97
  KWL chart use, 98, 100
  maps and globes use, 99–101
  meeting standards, 109
  national curriculum standards, 95–96
  problem-based learning, 97
  similarities and differences, 103
  social justice issues, 109
Social Studies for the Next Generation (NCSS), 96
Song, Dantong, 108
Sousa, David, 81
special needs children, 13–14
spelling, 58, 68
standard English conventions, 57–58
standards, meeting, and supporting best practices, 5–6
StoryBuddy app, 53
story maps use, 50
student perspective, 15

T

Tafolla, Carmen, 103
Tang, Greg, 78
tangrams, 88
Tate, M.L., 97
Taylor, Janye, 108
teacher productivity, 16
Teachers College Reading and Writing Project, 30–31, 33
teacher sensitivity, 15
teacher-student interactions, 15–17
TeacherTube, 59, 123
Teaching the Brain to Read (Willis), 60
technology investigations, 125–27
TED Talks, 132, 134, 138

ten frames use, 82
text complexity and reading literacy, 39–41
text selection and reading literacy, 30, 31
theater arts education, 135
think-pair-share strategy, 24, 75
time, study of, 86
timed testing, 74
timelines, 105
Todo Telling Time app, 86
Tolan, K., 109
Tomlinson, H. B., 5
Tompert, Ann, 88
Toontastic app, 133
Tux paint, 133
two-way conversations, importance of, 23
Two Way Interactive Connections in Education (TWICE), 7

U

Urban Programs Resource Network, 124

V

Vasinda, S., 44
Vehicles and Transportation theme, 106
Vennebush, G. Patrick, 78
visual arts, 132–33
vocabulary acquisition and use, 59–62
Vygotsky, L. S., 47

W

Wagner, T., 20
Walmsley, Katherine, 51, 105
weather conditions study, 124
welcoming room design, 8–10
Weulersse, Odile, 135
Willems, Mo, 50
Willis, Judy, 60–61
Winter, Jonah, 11
word analysis, 61
word and picture sorts, 42–43
word detectives, 61
word problems, 82
word recognition, 42–43
word study center, 67–68
Wright, T.S., 59
writers' workshop, 45–48
writing center, 65
writing conferences, 46–48
writing portfolio use, 46
writing skills
  adding details, 52
  anchor chart use, 56
  author's celebration, 48
  author's chair, 48
  graphic organizers use, 50
  history, 104
  idea organization, 52
  independent writing, 46–48
  informative/explanatory writing, 49–50
  Meet the Author studies, 49–50
  mentor texts use, 49
  mini lessons, 45
  narrative writing, 50–51
  opinion writing, 49
  partner talk, 46
  poetry writing, 51
  production and distribution of writing, 51–54
  range of writing, 55–56
  research, 54–55
  revising, 52–53
  story maps use, 50
  technology use, 53–54
  text type and purposes, 49–51
  topic focus, 51
  writers' workshop, 45–48
  writing conferences, 46–48
  writing portfolio use, 46
  zone of proximal development use, 47

Y

Yolen, Jane, 127
Young Explorer (National Geographic Society), 122
YouTube, 59, 123

Z

zone of proximal development (ZPD), 47